DECISION MAKING IN SMALL GROUPS
the search for alternatives

Albert C. Kowitz
California State University, Sacramento

Thomas J. Knutson
Communication Associates, Sacramento

ALLYN AND BACON, INC.
Boston   London   Sydney   Toronto

Library of Congress Cataloging in Publication Data

Kowitz, Albert C
    Decision making in small groups.

    Includes bibliographical references and index.
    1. Small groups.   2. Decision-making, Group.   I. Knutson, Thomas J., joint author.   II. Title. HM133.K68   301.18'5
79–12617   ISBN 0–205–06650–X

Printed in the United States of America

To the memory of
Professor John A. Oostendorp

Contents

PART II
INTERACTION STRUCTURE   41

PART III
GROUP STRUCTURE   75

Preface

This book, intended as an introductory text, grew out of our interest in the process of decision making in small groups. Material contained in this book is suitable for use in introductory small group courses in departments of Speech-Communication, Communication Studies, Psychology, Business, and in the many professional schools where group decision making plays a crucial role. The book reflects an interdisciplinary interest, which meets the diverse needs of many areas of study.

We believe that the search for alternatives to solve many of our commonplace as well as more complex societal problems can best be addressed by small groups of interested parties. We make this claim notwithstanding complaints frequently expressed by people engaged in small group decision making. We have heard descriptions of committee work as tedious at best and impossible at worst. *Decision Making in Small Groups* addresses these negative attitudes with realistic recommendations. Small group work can be not only productive, but even enjoyable if participants learn essential processes and skills.

The purpose of this book is to present a conceptual orientation to decision making in small groups and to describe skills and attitudes necessary for effective participation in these groups. The task of decision-making groups is to select the best alternative from a range of conceivable ones. Group members exchange comments, take on responsibilities within the group, and develop procedures for making decisions while selecting their alternative.

The practice of using small groups for decision making permeates nearly every segment of our society: the executive branch of the federal government, corporate board rooms, court rooms, churches, PTAs, and citizen action groups. When these groups arrive at sound and useful decisions, the practice of small group decision making pays off for their organization. Frequently, however, these groups do not use their resources very well. We believe that inadequate performance is not endemic to small groups, but rather to misconceptions about how to communicate and make decisions within these groups.

We assume that the primary function of decision-making groups is to process data in an effort to arrive at effective resolutions to difficulties or problems. This means that group members must search for information, process that information during group meetings, and use that information to arrive at effective decisions. Consequently, the group setting must be such that member resources are realized, coordinated, and used.

Decision Making in Small Groups is composed of five parts. Part I presents the conceptual framework for understanding and learning about participating in small groups. We present a model of decision making in task-oriented groups and discuss two approaches for describing group effectiveness. In addition, we describe the developmental sequence a decision-making group follows in mobilizing its resources and in arriving at a decision proposal.

In Parts II, III, and IV we develop our approach to the study and practice of decision making in small groups. We believe that three interdependent "structures" guide and influence the flow of decision making. These three interlocking structures form a comprehensive and logical system for both analysis and application.

The first of these structures, *interaction structure* is described in Part II. The basic elements affecting interaction in small groups may be thought of in three dimensions. The informational dimension encompasses the "content" of the task and includes the manner in which the group members think about their task, the search for information, and factors that affect the presentation and treatment of information within the group. The second dimension, the procedural dimension, affects the manner in which the group members coordinate and direct their efforts and activities. The information dimension refers to the "what" of discussion. The procedural dimension refers to the "how to" of discussion. The third part of interaction, the interpersonal dimension, refers to group member attitudes toward one another and perception of member traits. Behaviors related to all three of these dimensions affect the flow, content, and influence of messages in small groups.

The elements of *group structure,* discussed in Part III, include the roles and norms that emerge during the group's deliberations. Roles are the common expectations members hold regarding the behavior of one another within the group. Norms are rules about what members ought to do and should believe for the group's task and deliberations. Roles and norms affect the information search, interaction, and decision making in the group. The final element of group structure is member satisfaction with the group as a whole. The cohesiveness of the group affects both the manner in which people interact in groups and the decision-making structure of the group.

The third side of our triangle is the group's *decision structure,* which is developed in Part IV. We cover three main issues in this segment of the book. The first issue relates to the type of task and its requirements. Each type of task requires a somewhat different approach for successful resolution, and some tasks are inappropriate for group attention. The second issue relates to procedures a group uses to collect information and make decisions. The third issue relates to the manner in which the group approaches and manages conflict.

All three of these structures constrain and guide the group in selecting an alternative. The effectiveness of the group's decision making reflects the degree that these structures are understood and appropriately applied.

The final section of the book, Part V, was designed to help practitioners diagnose and resolve common problems of group process. This section gives assistance by focusing on small group problems, suggesting possible solutions, and referring to chapters in the book where the information designed to help solve these problems is presented in more detail.

At the end of each chapter we have compiled a list of conclusions and recommendations that were developed in the text of that chapter. This list of recommendations, not often found in textbooks, should prove useful in understanding and in applying the material.

Albert C. Kowitz
Thomas J. Knutson

Acknowledgements

We are especially grateful to those who reviewed the manuscript. We found their recommendations useful and feel their efforts helped us to improve the quality of the text. Since their efforts are reflected in the book we want to give them credit here: Dennis Gouran of Indiana University, Gary Cronkhite of the University of California at Davis, K. Phillip Taylor of Florida Technological University, Don Ellis of Purdue University, Joan E. Shields of Arapahoe Community College, John Kline of the Department of the Air Force, and John Wiemann of the University of California at Santa Barbara. In addition, Tom Young of West Virginia University provided valuable advice on the organization of the book's content.

We also want to express our appreciation to the staff of Allyn and Bacon for their patience and guidance.

1

INTRODUCTION

This book has two primary purposes: to present a conceptual orientation to decision making in small groups and to describe the essential skills necessary for effective participation in task-oriented groups. We assume that the primary function of task-oriented groups is to process data in an effort to arrive at effective resolutions to felt difficulties or problems. Chapter 1 presents an overview of the process of decision making in task-oriented groups. Chapter 2 deals specifically with our assumption that a group passes through a four-phase sequence in mobilizing its resources. Subsequent chapters develop in more detail the structure presented in Part 1.

CHAPTER 1

Perspectives on the Study of Decision-Making Groups

INTRODUCTION

We live in a complex and highly interdependent society. We often must work with others to achieve outcomes that are important and attractive to us. In fact, the achievement of a large percentage of our goals rests on enlisting the cooperation of others. As a consequence, we spend much of our time communicating with others in small groups.

The contexts of our small group experiences vary widely. Sometimes we participate in these groups at work; at other times we may be a member of a task-oriented group in our community. Study groups at school, juries, staff meetings, and task-force committees are all examples of settings where we rely on one another to achieve certain goals.

The aim of this book is to assist you in becoming a more effective participant in these groups. We cannot guarantee that your participation in small groups will always be to your liking. We are confident, however, that an understanding of the concepts, principles, and process presented in the following pages will increase your chances of finding these group experiences rewarding.

Our primary focus will be on task-oriented groups. However, many of the same concepts and processes apply to all types of groups. We define a task-oriented group as *a small group of interdependent persons who exchange and process information for the purpose of seeking means to control their environment.* We characterize this exchange as a complex process of symbolic transactions guided by a set of constraints. In the following sections we describe in more detail the key elements of this description of a task-oriented group.

INTERDEPENDENCE

A critical characteristic of task-oriented groups is the presence of interdependence. When group members are interdependent, they have expectations about one another's behavior, they influence each other, and members are dependent upon one another for attaining their goal (18). An aggregate of individuals, each pursuing a solution to a problem independently and then pooling their results, does not constitute a task-oriented group. Take, for example, two individuals studying why people do and do not wear seat belts in their cars. After they have finished their research, they give their information to a third person to prepare a final report. Contrast this situation with the three persons coordinating, collaborating, and interacting with one another as they work toward completion of their project. The first approach would not constitute a task-oriented group whereas the second situation would represent interdependence among group members.

Some of you may be asking why interdependence is an important element of a task-oriented group. Would it not be more efficient and effective to give assignments to members of the group and instruct them to work separately? For most cases (we will describe the exceptions in later chapters) the answer is no. There are a number of reasons why interdependence is preferable to individuals working separately.

Members working interdependently will generate more alternatives for the solution of tasks. One member will propose an alternative that in turn stimulates another member to generate another alternative. This interchange will spark other members to generate additional alternatives. You have probably experienced situations where some new idea occurred to you because of the comments of another person. In general, interdependent groups will generate more alternatives to a task than individuals working separately.

Another advantage of an interdependent group of persons is the greater likelihood that the group will identify hidden strengths and weaknesses of alternatives proposed by group members. An apparently effective solution to a problem may have detrimental side effects. Members of interdependent groups are more likely to discover these weaknesses (or strengths) than individuals working separately.

Members of interdependent groups are more likely to be committed to the group's decisions. Usually group members want their decisions to have some impact on their environment. Member commitment to decisions increases the likelihood that these decisions will be implemented. Finally, we are often stimulated to work harder on a task when we are members of interdependent groups. The rewards we receive through group interaction make our effort more enjoyable. A compliment from another member or a discovery that another member agrees with our point of view enhances our willingness to work on our task.

EXCHANGE AND PROCESSING OF INFORMATION

The process of decision making rests on the exchange and processing of information among group members. Understanding the exchange and processing of information gives us a better understanding of the manner in which decisions emerge in small groups. In Part 2 we devote two chapters to elements that influence interaction in small groups. This section presents the communication processes that are part and parcel of small group interaction. The material in this section was strongly influenced by several authors including Bormann (3), R. D. Laing and his colleagues (12), Littlejohn (13), and Miller and Steinberg (15).

The exchange and processing of information is more complicated than a one-way transfer of information. *This interchange is a complex process of symbolic transactions. The purpose of the exchange of information is to move toward shared meaning among group members.*

Process refers to changes in phenomena over time, and a complex process involves changes over time that are the result of many elements. Some of the elements that affect change in task-oriented groups are information that is available to the group, the traits, interests, and behavior patterns of group members, and the social and cultural context surrounding the group. One of our groups of students working on identification of hazardous toys for small children reflected these elements. Their exchange of information was influenced by FDA reports, laws, articles written on this topic, and their own investigation of local department and toy stores. The members of the group shared a common concern about these toys, partly because many of them had small children in their homes. Finally, their interest reflected a wider social concern about hazardous toys that supported their goal to produce and air a TV documentary on this issue.

The interchange among these group members was affected by all of these elements. The exchange was possible because members shared a common language and understood the rules for using this language. We refer to the use of language for the exchange and processing of information as symbolic transactions.

Symbols are words or signs that refer to events or experiences. Our excursion through Yellowstone National Park is a firsthand experience of that region. Our description of that experience to another person is a symbolic description of our experience. Our language system permits us to describe elements of our environment, to reason about them, and to make projections regarding future outcomes. Language also allows us to record past events and to transmit this information from one generation to another. Linguistic descriptions are often used as a substitute for experiencing events that are not a part of our immediate life space. Most American citizens know a good deal about events around the world, but few of us have traveled widely to experience these events firsthand. In short, language frees us from our immediate time and location.

Language allows us to communicate with one another. We can describe for others our observations and experiences that otherwise would only be our private domain. Sometimes we may not describe an event as clearly as we had hoped or we may find that others misinterpret what we say. Nonetheless, language is an extremely powerful vehicle for communication that we often take for granted. We have proposed that the exchange of information in small groups is a complex process of symbolic transactions. Symbols refer to our linguistic de-

Figure 1.1

scription of events. Transactions refer to the interchange between two or more persons.

Symbolic transaction refers to a reciprocating symbolic exchange of observations and experiences with another person or group of people. There is a considerable difference between transmitting information and a symbolic transaction between two or more parties. We are reminded of the department manager who drafted a memo and sent it to each member in the unit. Some days later he was upset because the employees were not incorporating the changes specified in the memo. The department manager claimed he had communicated with them when in fact all he had done was to transmit the information. Symbolic transaction involves a cyclical process of encoding and decoding thoughts and actions.

Encoding entails the process of converting our thoughts and experiences into written or spoken symbols we think are suitable for the person or persons with whom we are conversing. Decoding involves translating the "marks" on the page or the "sounds" in the air that we attend to into our language and manner of thinking. We are not empty containers when we attend to another. We selectively perceive the behavior of another (talking) and we interpret (decode) the behavior that we perceive.

A useful way of describing the decoding process is to say we "experience" the behavior of the other person. We first perceive various features of the other person's behavior and then we interpret, or give meaning to, our perceptions. Figure 1.1 diagrams the encoding-decoding cycle for two individuals.

Obviously, we have included only one-half of the picture for A and B. Person B also behaves and Person A then perceives and interprets that perception. *Symbolic transaction, then, involves the reciprocating process of encoding and decoding by two or more persons.* It is symbolic because we use language to describe the events of concern, and it is a transaction because one person's behavior is "experienced" by another. It is a little like one person throwing confetti into the air and another trying to grab the confetti and arrange it into a meaningful pattern.

The function of the complex process of symbolic transactions is to move toward shared meanings about information before the group. The notion of shared meaning implies that group members over time move toward similar interpretations of the information regarding their topic.

During the first meeting or two, members in the group working on hazardous toys had not read or studied the laws about these toys. They were not aware of features that made a toy hazardous for small children. Finally, they were not aware of toys on the market that were potentially hazardous. In time, they read, studied, and discussed the laws until there was a common understanding of them. They acquired the FDA list of hazardous toys and discussed this list. They also related their observations of toys they examined at local toy and department stores. Toward the end of their discussions, group members shared common interpretations of the laws and features of toys that made them potentially hazardous for small children. Their symbolic transactions enabled them to achieve shared meaning regarding information on hazardous toys.

We have frequently used the term information in the previous paragraphs. The following section describes in some detail what we mean by this term.

INFORMATION

For our purposes, information consists of statements of fact, opinion, and advice (3). Statements of fact refer to the descriptive realm of our reality and may be shown to be true or false. A statement about the number of policemen killed by handguns in New York City during any particular year can be verified as true or false by checking appropriate documents. A statement about the number of automobiles sold in California during September of a specific year also describes an event and can be shown to be true or false.

Statements of opinion express *value judgments, beliefs,* and *attitudes.* Statements of opinion cannot be shown to be true of false. Instead, they are evaluated by their desirability or appropriateness. Statements of value express the belief that a specific mode of conduct or end state of existence is personally or socially preferable (17). For example, one person may say that being broad-minded (mode of conduct) is very important in working with others. Another person may suggest that all individuals should have equal opportunity (end state) to attend a college or university.

A statement of belief asserts that an event can be described in a certain way or that one event is related to another event. For example, the statement, "The student council uses budget decisions as a political tool," asserts that the council is using the budget (event) as a political tool (description). The comment, "Reducing the speed limit to 55 will result in a reduction of traffic fatalities," is a belief statement that expresses a relationship between two events. Event one (reducing the speed limit) is said to be related to event two (reduction of traffic fatalities). Statements of this type cannot be shown to be true or false, but we do accept them as valid with some degree of probability (8).

Attitudinal statements are favorable or unfavorable comments about statements of belief or specific events. They usually represent a person's feelings regarding an issue or behavior. We like or dislike certain movies, teaching styles, or ways of doing things. Comments reflecting these likes and dislikes would be attitudinal statements.

The third type of information is statements of advice. Statements of advice propose courses of action. The comment that the automobile industry must manufacture small cars that get at least 25 miles per gallon to compete with foreign imports is a statement of advice. These statements cannot be shown to be true or false. Instead, they are considered to be useful or not useful and adequate or inadequate.

All three types of information are needed for effective group decision making. Statements of fact give your group an accurate and objective description of its task. Statements of opinion identify values, beliefs, and attitudes related to the task. Statements of advice specify the options open to the group. When a task-oriented group has an accurate description of its task and a clear picture of related values, beliefs, and attitudes, it is in a better position to evaluate proposed courses of action.

CONTROL

We meet with others in small groups to discover ways to control our environment. Environment refers to the numerous and different situations we encounter from day to day. Your home, family and friends, your educational setting, and your place of employment are all parts of your environment. Sometimes you may be content with your environment; at other times you may see the need to redefine, clarify, or change it.

The concept "environment" holds a central place in our treatment of decision making in small groups. We define decision making as the process of selecting the most acceptable alternative from a range of alternatives. The objective of decision making is to discover desirable ways to control our environment.

Often, however, we are not able to obtain those outcomes we find most desirable. On the other hand, we are not usually committed to undesirable outcomes. Fortunately for most of us, there is an opportunity to choose from various alternatives. Control begins with a set of alternatives, some of which are desirable. If our attempts at control are successful, then we have made a favorable (to us) impact on our environment. Control refers to implementation of the most desirable alternative selected from a range of alternatives.

Most people will agree that some outcomes are more desirable than others. We believe it would be better for ex-offenders to find useful employment than to continue a cycle of crime and punishment. Many of us prefer a challenging rather than a routine work environment. Many people are trying to discover alternative life-styles that conserve energy and natural resources.

A group in one of our classes was concerned about architectural barriers on campus for the physically handicapped. They surveyed the campus and discovered that some buildings did not have elevators. Other barriers included curbs and steps that prevented those in wheelchairs from easily entering buildings. The group's objective was to propose changes in the environment so that the physically handicapped would be able to access classrooms in these buildings. They had some ideas for controlling this environment and were partially successful in obtaining their objective.

The whole point of decision making in small groups is to search out alternatives regarding various issues in our environment. When we find an acceptable alternative, we hope that it will have a favorable impact on some part of our environment. Through this process we exert control over our environment.

CONSTRAINTS AND GROUP DECISION MAKING

Another concept central to our treatment of small groups is the notion of constraint. Whereas control implies implementation of a desirable alternative selected from a range of alternatives, constraint refers to the boundaries limiting the range of possibilities. In other words, constraint refers to what outcomes are possible given a specific situation and the people involved. Constraints are a direct consequence of the personal, social, and organizational environments that are a part of a small group. Suppose your group was discussing the pros and cons of abortion. A devout Catholic would be constrained by certain tenets of the Catholic Church regarding the sanctity of life. This personal constraint would limit the range of alternatives available for this group member. Another group member might sense constraints due to the feelings and opinions of his or her peers and friends. This social constraint would limit options available to this group member. In addition to one's personal beliefs and values, and the social pressures from friends and associates, there are the laws and community facilities with regard to abortion. The laws, birth control clinics, medical personnel, and medical facilities constitute organizational constraints that limit the range of alternatives open to the group.

You will find the notion of constraints appearing at several points in the following chapters. Your small group discussions will be constrained by the data members select for presentation. The social relations among members will shape the flow of discussion. The specific situation will likewise impose certain constraints on the group's deliberations. Sometimes we become upset about some constraints that surround our attempts to control our environment. At times we cannot find the material we need to evaluate various forms of mass transit, for example. At other times, we become upset because people fail to recognize and adopt needed changes such as alternative modes of transportation. To say that all constraints are bad, however, is to miss the implications of this notion in our small group activities.

At one end of the spectrum, we can think of a situation with no constraints. Suppose for example that group members would show up for meetings randomly during a 24-hour period; for example, John would be there at 8:00 A.M., Al at 12:00 noon, and Tom at 11:30 P.M. This situation would be one of almost random activity. At the opposite end of the constraint spectrum would be situations that are totally determined. Absolutely no choice would be available to us. These observations on the constraint spectrum suggest an important relationship between control and constraints. At both ends of the constraint spectrum, no opportunity for control is available to us. As a situation approaches a random state, there is less and less opportunity to select from a range of alternatives because the means for making a choice are not available. At the other end of the spectrum the outcome has been determined, so again the element of choice is missing. It is only as we depart from randomness or determinism that the opportunity for choice exists. The point here is simply that constraints are necessary for decision making, but on the other hand, they may become so complete that outcomes are known prior to group deliberations.

The purpose of much of our higher education is to bring out in the open ways of thinking that tend to overly structure our behavior and at the same time bring to our attention new patterns of thought. The study of literature, art, and philosophy as well as other subjects introduces us to new ways of thinking about various issues and alternative ways of controlling our environment. As with most activities, there is the possibility that study within a discipline will become too structured. One reason Jane Goodall was selected to observe chimpanzees in their natural habitat was because she did not have a university degree in the study of animal behavior. Leakey feared that her observations would have been too determined by such a course of study (10). On the other hand, she had gleaned on her own a great deal of information regarding primates that guided her observations. The point here is that constraints are the underlying structure on which we base our observations.

Some constraints may be inappropriate for the situation. The thrust of the O'Neills' book on open marriage is to describe several "inappropriate" constraints (16). The importance for us in terms of our participation in group deliberations is whether or not the constraints implicit in the present situation are appropriate. Does the set of constraints operative in our group permit the type of outcome we find desirable? Hence, it becomes critical that as group members we recognize the constraints that guide our discussions. We may not be able to alter the constraints, but at least we are aware of what impositions exist for our ability to control our environment. To ignore the presence of constraints is to be closed to the possibility of effective decision making.

IMPORTANCE OF THE DECISION-MAKING
GROUPS IN OUR SOCIETY

The centrality of the small group in our society has been emphasized by many commentators and scholars. The street corner gang, therapy groups, and problem-solving groups in various organizations have all received considerable attention. Recent trends in our society have created a new sense of importance for the small group. The philosopher Richard McKeon (14) has described three trends in contemporary society that support the need for effective small group communication. The first trend is an increased tolerance for cultural, group, and individual diversity. Within our society, we are observing a greater tolerance for alternative life-styles and new roles for both men and women.

The second trend in today's world is an increase in interdependence, both between and within cultures. A classic example of interdependence between cultures was the Arab oil embargo of 1973. A quick glance at the dependence of the United States on many countries for raw materials indicates as well the high level of interdependence among nations. Similarly, we have seen a growth of interdependence among people within our society. A recent mass transit strike in a western city has demonstrated the dependence of many citizens on this means of transportation. A union strike may result in the temporary shutdown of entire industries. The strict division of labor and specialization of many workers requires close coordination in the production of goods and services. Much of our social and recreational activity depends on our ability to enlist the cooperation of others.

A third trend in contemporary society is increased access to the means of communication. Television has made Americans aware of the customs and beliefs of the Vietnamese, the Arabs, and Africans. We also are more familiar with various cultural groups within our society such as blacks, Chicanos, and the American Indian. We have become a part of a "global village" where we are continuously exposed to different customs, religions, political philosophies, and standards of living.

These trends bear directly on decision making in task-oriented groups. Note that these trends imply that we will often form groups with people who frequently view the world differently from the way we do. Given the degree of specialization and greater need for cooperation, small group activity occupies a central position in our attempts to obtain the personal, social, and organizational rewards we desire. Attempts to discount those who are different from us may well lead to the withdrawal of their cooperation. This juxtaposition of diversity and the need for cooperation has implications for the function and importance of small group communication. The primary purpose for communication has shifted from a desire to persuade people to a common set of values and beliefs to understanding and negotiation (7). We recognize that group members will likely hold differing conceptions of problems. In such a case, recognition of the legitimacy of differing positions is critical. Our understanding of the diverse points of view toward an issue allows us to negotiate a solution that best reflects the dispositions of the total group. This process of negotiation, given the three trends, is an inevitable outcome in our society. An effective small group communication process is especially suited for negotiation. The presence of diversity and the recognition of our interdependence requires an effective communication system to resolve the issues that confront us daily.

FUNCTIONS OF DECISION-MAKING GROUPS

The purpose of task-oriented groups is to discover means of controlling our environment. This purpose implies three basic functions of task-oriented groups. These functions are discovery, decision making, and consensus. The first basic function is the discovery of alternatives. Individual group members think and deliberate under a set of constraints. These constraints differ somewhat from one member to another. The blind side of one member may be obvious to another member. The discovery process allows group members to overcome these constraints and articulate alternative means for environmental control.

Decision making involves selecting and integrating information to arrive at conclusions about various aspects of the group's task. A lot of information is brought before the group and group members need to put it together in a way that makes sense. For example, your group may be investigating the problem of juvenile gangs in large urban areas. You will need to arrive at an accurate description of the problem as well as create alternatives for solving this problem.

Consensus does not imply unanimous or complete agreement with the group's decision proposal. It does imply that all group members agree that given the task, the decision proposal is the most acceptable proposal possible. This acceptance implies commitment to the decision reached by the group. The function of consensus is important in task-oriented groups if a decision proposal is to be implemented. Remember that we live in a world and society marked by diversity. Some level of consensus must be reached if the task-oriented group is to be effective.

MODEL OF A DECISION-MAKING GROUP

In the previous sections we have defined task-oriented groups and their characteristic features. In the following sections we present a model of task-oriented groups.

A model of task-oriented groups provides us with a way of looking and abstracting from the total complexity of the decision-making process. Useful models provide a simplified version of the total process, but at the same time do not oversimplify. Our model emphasizes the essential components of the process, thereby permitting us to organize the process descriptively. Although the model helps to organize our thinking about the process, it does not allow us to make specific predictions regarding relationships among these components. These generalizations will appear in the chapters that follow.

We have emphasized that the group's contact with some part of the external environment distinguished task-oriented groups from other types of small groups. In one sense, the purpose of a group's existence rests on something in the environment that needs attention.

These "needs" are usually defined by some ongoing organization such as a university, the federal government, or a corporation. The organizational source of the issue provides the outer limits of the task and helps to define the range of issues. Often, the President of the United States commissions a group to resolve some issue such as campus unrest. Recently, university presidents have appointed affirmative action committees. Task groups were formed to study the issue of adequate protection for women and to study the quality of instruction on campuses. In summary, the focus of the task group is on some aspect of the environment, usually defined by the organizational setting.

The quality of the group's interaction will in large part determine the success or failure of the group (5). In general terms, we refer to this aspect of a task-oriented group as "group process." The components of group process include interaction structure, group structure, and decision-making structure. These components are explained in some detail in the next three parts of this book. We will only briefly describe these components here.

Interaction structure includes the manner in which group members exchange information. Group structure includes the roles and functions of group members, group norms, and cohesiveness. Finally, decision structure refers to the manner in which group members search for information, make decisions, and resolve conflict.

The final component of our model is the group's decision proposal. The decision proposal includes the group's findings, its recommendations, and its rationale for those recommendations. Some decision proposals are very elaborate and lengthy documents such as the report of the President's Commission on Campus Unrest. Others may simply be a verbal report to the corporation's vice-president. The quality of the decision proposal rests on three factors: group acceptance of the proposal, logical adequacy of the proposal, and empirical adequacy of the proposal. Group acceptance refers to the level of commitment group members hold toward the proposal. Logical adequacy relates to the "ideal" quality of the proposal. In other words, the logical adequacy of a decision proposal reflects those outcomes group members find to be highly desirable. Finally, empirical adequacy refers to the degree that the solution accurately reflects objective conditions in the environment and to the practical constraints of implementing the group's recommendations. Generally, a compromise arises between the logical adequacy and the empirical adequacy of the solution. For example, a massive new lighting system may be the ideal solution for adequate protection of women on campus; however, money may not be available to implement such a program.

Figure 1.2 pictures relationships between environment, group

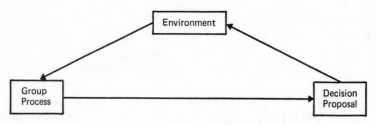

Fig. 1.2   Model of the Decision-Making Group

process, and decision proposal. Note that the environment holds a central position in our model. Some need in the environment provides the reason for the formation of a decision making group and eventually the decision proposal has some impact on the environment.

BASIC DIMENSIONS OF GROUP PROCESS

In the previous section we presented a model of a task-oriented group and briefly described the three "components" of group process. We have found it useful to divide each component into three dimensions.

When researchers began to investigate decision making in small groups, interaction was treated in terms of the task and socioemotional dimensions. The task dimension included such behaviors as introduction of new information, suggestion of solutions to the problem, and evaluation of (tests) information. The socioemotional dimension included behaviors such as complimenting the work of others, attempting to keep relationships cordial and friendly, and attempting to resolve conflicts between group members.

We have found that interaction in task-oriented groups can more usefully be described in terms of three dimensions. We have chosen to call these the informational, procedural, and interpersonal dimensions. In the two-dimension approach described above, the task dimension included both the processing of information and leadership functions. We believe that leadership functions can more appropriately be considered within the procedural dimension.

Information Dimension

The informational dimension refers to the content of the task. It includes the statements of fact, opinion, and advice regarding the task. This dimension also includes the way the group discusses, uses, and organizes its information.

Procedural Dimension

The procedural dimension relates most directly to what we commonly call leadership. We refer to this dimension in terms of "guidance" functions. Basically, procedural comments help to coordinate the activity of the group members and is analogous to the guidance system of a capsule headed for the moon. This guidance system keeps the capsule on course and makes adjustments as the capsule moves toward its destination. Note that the guidance system itself does not provide the energy or the mechanism for making adjustments, but instead provides instructions for the proper deployment of these mechanisms. The energy and related mechanical devices would be analogous to the informational dimension. The guidance system is similar in structure to the procedural dimension of task-oriented groups.

One of the most elaborate sets of procedural rules for group activity is found in Robert's Rules of Order. Sometimes task-oriented groups use selected parts of Robert's Rules of Order, but more frequently these procedural behaviors informally develop in the group. Common procedurally oriented behaviors include integrating and summarizing group activity, delegating and directing action, introducing and formulating goals, assisting in role and norm development, and in general keeping the group moving toward its goal.

Typically, leadership has been conceived in global terms, sometimes in terms of personal attributes of a leader, sometimes in terms of the style of the leader, and sometimes as anything that moves the group toward its goal. We believe that it is useful to consider leadership in terms of the required procedural functions needed for efficient group activity. We have seen groups with ample information before them fail because procedural functions were inadequately implemented in the group. This separation of the procedural dimension from the informational dimension permits us to more appropriately assess the success or failure of task-oriented groups.

Interpersonal Dimension

The interpersonal dimension reflects the attitudes members hold toward other members in the group (4) and the characteristics members attribute to other group members.

The attribution process in task-oriented groups involves three characteristics. One of the first impressions that develops is whether one perceives other members to be friendly or unfriendly. Typically in the research literature this impression has been described as the warm-cold variable (1, 11, 19). A second impression involves whether a

Dimension	Critical Behaviors
Informational	Giving Information
	Analyzing Information
	Integrating Information
Procedural	Giving Direction
	Coordinating Group Activity
	Maintaining Goal Direction
Interpersonal	Intermember Attraction
	Attributing Personal Characteristics

Fig. 1.3 Interaction Behaviors Related to the Three Basic Dimensions of Group Process

member is perceived as cooperative. A cooperative member considers the welfare of other group members as well as his or her welfare as important. The cooperative member shows a willingness to contribute to the achievement of the group's goal and displays loyalty to the group and its task (2).

A third interpersonal impression affecting interaction within the group is the attribution of member status. Attribution of status may be based on characteristics the member brings to the group such as a formal position a person holds (e.g., vice-president of the company), professional reputation, or social standing. Another aspect of status is the recognition that a member earns by superior performance in the group's deliberations. Hence, perceived status may be a function of external or internal factors or both. Whether or not status is derived from external characteristics or from task-oriented performance, high-status members exercise greater influence in the group (6, 9).

The flow of interaction in the group reflects these three dimensions. A pleasant interpersonal atmosphere assists the group in effectively discussing their task. If members are antagonistic toward each other, then energy and time normally used to work on the task are diverted toward affective conflicts. A basic level or procedural skill is necessary to efficiently mobilize and coordinate the group's energy. If the group is unable to achieve widespread participation, then some of the group's resources will be wasted. If the group is unable to resolve conflicts, then progress toward its goal will be blocked. Finally, comments relating to the content of the topic affect the quality of the group's decision proposal. If the group fails to develop an adequate information base, then the group's recommendations are likely to be inadequate.

Interaction Structure	Group Structure	Decision Structure
Informational Procedural Interpersonal	Informational Procedural Interpersonal	Informational Procedural Interpersonal

Fig. 1.4   Pattern among Components and Dimensions

We believe that these three dimensions help to describe and explain the process of small group decision making. These dimensions will appear repeatedly in subsequent chapters as we discuss various elements of the process. Figure 1.3 summarizes the essential characteristics of these dimensions.

The pattern between components and dimensions may be pictured in terms of a matrix. Each component may be described in terms of its informational, procedural, and interpersonal dimensions. Figure 1.4 shows this pattern.

Let us briefly summarize the conceptual overview presented in this chapter. A perceived need emerges in some aspect of our environment (e.g., hazards on the job, child abuse, or the energy crisis). A group of individuals volunteer or are assigned to work on this task. This interdependent group of people meet to achieve goals regarding the task. As they meet, information is discussed, group members' efforts are coordinated, and interpersonal impressions are formed. Through the exchange of messages during the group meetings, decisions are made and a decision proposal is developed. The quality of this proposal rests on its logical and empirical adequacy and the group members' commitment to the proposal. Finally, the implementation of the proposal has some impact on the environment. The purpose of this effort is to discover ways of controlling our environment. This discovery process is both abetted and curtailed by the personal, social, and organizational constraints associated with the group and its task.

SUMMARY

In this chapter, we have laid the foundation for consideration of the basic elements of small group decision making. We defined task-oriented groups as small groups of people in which members work interdependently through the exchange of messages to resolve some felt difficulty in the external environment. The purpose of such deliberations is to discover means for altering the environment and to select from those alternatives choices most acceptable to the group. The environment holds a central location in our analysis by both generating the reason for the existence of a task-oriented group and by providing the basis for evaluating the effectiveness of a decision proposal.

We have suggested that small group process is composed of three components: interaction structure, group structure, and decision structure. Each of these components may be described in terms of its informational, procedural, and interpersonal dimensions.

CONCLUSIONS AND RECOMMENDATIONS

1. A conceptual understanding of small group process and effective use of group skills are both prerequisites for effective decision making in small groups.
2. The purpose of small group deliberations is to discover means for control of our environment.
3. Both the range of alternatives and group deliberations are affected by a set of personal, social, and organizational constraints.
4. The general functions of small groups are discovery, decision making, and consensus.
5. Achievement of goals in small groups is a function of the quality of group process.
6. Interaction in small groups reflects interpersonal, procedural, and informational dimensions.
7. The focal point for task definition and for assessing solution effectiveness is the environment.

REFERENCES

1. Solomon E. Asch, "Forming Impressions of Personality," *Journal of Abnormal and Social Psychology* 41 (1946): 258–290.
2. Robert F. Bales, *Personality and Interpersonal Behavior* (New York: Holt, Rinehart and Winston, 1970).
3. Ernest G. Bormann, *Discussion and Group Methods: Theory and Practice,* 2nd ed. (New York: Harper and Row, 1975).
4. Donn Byrne and William Griffitt, "Interpersonal Attraction," *Annual Review of Psychology* 24 (1973): 317–336.
5. Dorwin Cartwright and Alvin Zander, *Group Dynamics: Research and Theory,* 3rd ed. (New York: Harper and Row, 1968).
6. Elizabeth G. Cohen and Susan S. Roper, "Modification of Interracial Interaction Disability: An Application of Status Characteristic Theory," *American Sociological Review* 37 (1972): 643–657.

7. Donald P. Cushman and Robert Craig, "Interpersonal Communication: A Paradigm for Inquiry," Michigan State University, unpublished manuscript.

8. Martin Fishbein, "A Consideration of Beliefs, Attitudes, and Their Relationships," in Ivan D. Steiner and Martin Fishbein (eds.), *Current Studies in Social Psychology* (New York: Holt, Rinehart and Winston, 1965), pp. 107–120.

9. Lee Freese and Bernard P. Cohen, "Elementary Status Generalization," *Sociometry* 36 (1973): 177–193.

10. Jane van Lawick Goodall, *In the Shadow of Man* (New York: Dell Publishing Co., 1971).

11. Harold H. Kelley, "The Warm-Cold Variable in First Impressions of Persons," *Journal of Personality* 18 (1950): 431–439.

12. R. D. Laing, H. Phillipson, and A. R. Lee, *Interpersonal Perception: A Theory and a Method of Research* (New York: Harper and Row, 1966).

13. Stephen W. Littlejohn, *Theories of Human Communication* (Columbus, Ohio: Charles E. Merrill Publishing Co., 1978).

14. Richard McKeon, "Communication, Truth and Society," *Ethics* 67 (1957): 89–99.

15. Gerald R. Miller and Mark Steinberg, *Between People* (Chicago: Science Research Associates, 1975).

16. Nena O'Neill and George O'Neill, *Open Marriage* (New York: M. Evans, 1972).

17. Milton Rokeach, *The Nature of Human Values* (New York: Free Press, 1974).

18. Marvin E. Shaw, *Group Dynamics: The Psychology of Small Group Behavior*, 2nd ed. (New York: McGraw-Hill, 1976).

19. Julius Wishner, "Reanalysis of 'Impressions of Personality'," *Psychological Review* 67 (1960): 96–112.

CHAPTER 2

Mobilizing Group Resources

INTRODUCTION

In the previous chapter we described the basic components of small group decision making and the three dimensions of group interaction. We now turn to productivity, the principal concern of task-oriented groups. For the most part, we hope that our group deliberations will lead to effective decision proposals. The general thrust of this chapter is a description of how a small group mobilizes and effectively uses its resources to arrive at an effective proposal.

PREDICTION OF GROUP PRODUCTIVITY

We will treat group productivity from two different points of view. The first focuses on the end product, whereas the second focuses on group process and assumes a direct relationship between effective process and effective decision proposals. We feel that both points of view are important in attempting to assess and improve group outcomes.

Maier (11) proposed that productivity or group effectiveness is equal to the quality of the decision proposal times group acceptance of the proposal. This relationship may be formulated as follows:

$$\text{Group effectiveness} = \text{quality} \times \text{acceptance.}$$

The multiplication sign is used to indicate that if either quality or acceptance is equal to zero, then the group has zero effectiveness.

Group acceptance of a decision proposal is largely a function of the level of commitment the members have regarding the decision. The members like or dislike the proposal to some degree. Quality of the proposal is somewhat more difficult to define. At one level, the quality of a decision proposal is related to the ability of group members to describe and analyze the nature of the problem before them. This analysis includes a careful factual description of the problem, a coherent analysis of the issues related to the problem, and an awareness of the value priorities associated with the problem. We refer to this analysis as the development of an adequate information base. Given an adequate information base, the quality of a decision proposal is determined by how effectively the proposal resolves the issues uncovered by the group's analysis of its task.

Given this analysis of quality, two related issues must be resolved. We refer to these considerations as the logical adequacy and the empirical adequacy of the decision proposal. The logical adequacy of the solution raises the following question: "What would be the ideal solution from the point-of-view of the group members?"

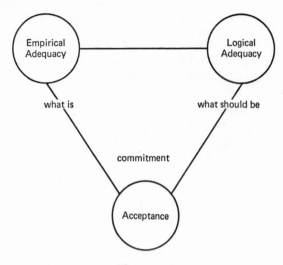

Figure 2.1

(9). The logical adequacy of the proposal obviously reflects the value priorities of group members. These value priorities relate to both how things should be done and what is a desirable end state of affairs.

The empirical adequacy of the proposal addresses two questions. First, "Does the decision proposal accurately reflect the environmental conditions?" We assume that an effective proposal must be based on an accurate and perceptive analysis of the current state of affairs. A decision proposal will be ineffective to the degree that critical environmental elements are ignored, overlooked, or misrepresented. Second, "What constraints exist in the environment that would prevent implementation of the ideal solution?" Obviously, if there are no constraints, then the ideal proposal could be implemented. However, in most cases the ideal proposal will need some modification for successful adaptation to the environment. The implicit criterion here is that the implementation of the decision proposal will result in some change in the environment. A decision proposal that has no effect on the environment will have no usefulness. Conversely, a decision proposal that has an undesirable effect on the environment is also of low quality. Hence, the consideration of both the logical adequacy and empirical adequacy of a decision proposal is crucial for the development of a quality decision (see Figure 2.1).

The Maier formulation emphasizes the qualities of the group's product. As we mentioned earlier, another point of view emphasizes group process. Steiner (13) suggested that the potential productivity

---

Group effectiveness = quality $\times$ acceptance
Quality = function (logical adequacy $\times$ empirical adequacy)
Logical and empirical adequacy = potential productivity — process loss

---

Fig. 2.2 Determinants of Group Effectiveness

of a task-oriented group is a function of task demands and member resources. This relationship may be formulated in the following manner:

Potential productivity = task demands $\times$ group resources.

Task demands refer to essential elements of the task that must be addressed by the group to achieve its goal. Group resources include the knowledge, abilities, and skills possessed by group members.

However, task-oriented groups seldom attain their level of potential productivity. The actual productivity of a decision-making group is equal to potential productivity minus process loss (13):

Actual productivity = potential productivity — process loss.

Process loss involves the degree to which the group is not able to mobilize and integrate its resources. Process loss implies that the necessary informational, procedural, and interpersonal functions of group interaction are inadequately performed. If these elements are not mobilized to their potential levels, then the group encounters loss in its potential productivity.

These two points of view can be merged into a single formulation. Starting with Maier, we propose that group productivity is equal to the quality of the proposal times group acceptance of that proposal. The quality of a solution proposal, we suggest, is a function of its logical and empirical adequacy. Finally, we suggest, logical and empirical adequacy is equal to potential productivity minus process loss. This formulation directs your group to think both about the information used to develop a decision proposal and the process your group uses to arrive at that proposal. Figure 2.2 lists the merger of the two perspectives. What follows is an explanation of how a group mobilizes its resources to arrive at an effective decision proposal.

GENERAL DESCRIPTION OF THE PHASE SEQUENCE

A task-oriented group develops its strategy and structure for achieving its goal by resolving informational, procedural, and interpersonal issues as the group passes through a series of distinct phases. We find that a clear understanding of these phases assists group members in adapting to the ebb and flow of events common to all decision-making groups. Knowing these phases also enables group members to appropriately assess problems that confront the group from time to time. The most critical notion, however, is to realize that resolution of critical issues during each phase provides the structure for mobilizing the group's resources. An understanding of the sequence of phases and the critical issues characteristic of each phase will help members of task-oriented groups to minimize many of the obstacles common to decision-making groups.

We are now faced with a central issue regarding the group process. How does a decision-making group effectively mobilize its resources? In one sense, the answer to this question is the focus of the remaining chapters of this book. In a more general sense, we are proposing here that a task-oriented group passes through a set of developmental phases. The resolution of issues as the group goes through these phases provides the environment for the emergence of effective group deliberations.

The normal life span of a decision-making group can be compared to the stages a child goes through in growing up. The child resolves issues at each stage that help to form his or her self-concept and ability to cope effectively with the environment. From one perspective, a child acquires a sense of identity in late adolescence or early adulthood.

The best thinking to date indicates that a decision-making group goes through four phases. Although each phase has specific characteristics, we should first note the following general characteristics of each phase:

1. Each phase has its own distinctive qualitative theme.
2. Each phase provides a unique contribution or set of tools for developing an effective decision proposal.
3. Each successive phase builds on decisions that were made at an earlier phase.

Briefly, the outcomes of phase one provide the necessary interpersonal atmosphere for communication and help the group delimit the task. During phase two the role structure of the group emerges, and the group decides what specific direction it will take to reach a decision proposal. Phase three, the major work phase, encompasses the development of the information base and emergence of alternative decision proposals. Finally, in phase four, a decision proposal is selected and acquires group support (acceptance). The manner in which the group resolves the issues at each phase is critical for the development of an effective decision proposal.

PHASE I: ORIENTATION

A small group has many decisions to make before a concerted effort toward solving its chosen task can be made. During the orientation phase, group members assess their respective group participation skills and the knowledge group members have regarding the task. The group begins to consider the parameters and requirements of the task, and they settle on acceptable styles of interpersonal behavior in the group (1).

Group participation skills will be described in detail in a later chapter. Generally, they include one's ability to communicate about the topic, to work cooperatively with other group members in making progress toward the group's goal, and to relate satisfactorily on an interpersonal level with other group members. For example, group members may observe that some persons in the group are willing to explore various points of view regarding the topic, whereas others are quite dogmatic in their approach when communicating about the task. An important element in moving the group along toward achievement of its goal is the appropriate release of tension. An awkward moment may arise in the group's discussion and one of the members will do something amusing to release this tension. The other members will notice that this person has a skill (tension release) that will be useful to the group in its deliberations.

Interpersonal impressions of group members will also emerge during this phase. One of the first interpersonal behaviors that members will notice is the level of friendliness of group members. Some members will be seen as outgoing and friendly. Others may be seen as quiet and reserved. Group members will be making judgments about the ascribed status of various members. Often a group member's job or profession will tend to create a status hierarchy in the group. Obviously, other impressions are being formed during this phase, but the above examples give a flavor of this aspect of interpersonal orientations in the group.

For the most part, members of task-oriented groups hope to successfully complete their task. The presence of an appropriate level of group skills and a pleasant interpersonal atmosphere provide a supportive base from which members can work. A well-developed information base, however, is necessary for successful completion of the task. During the orientation phase members assess the background each member has regarding the task. In some groups, they will note that members have specialties for various aspects of the task. Frequently, the members will learn that some members have important connections outside the group that will aid them in developing their information base. At the conclusion of this phase, they will have a fairly clear idea of how well informed group members are regarding the task.

The assessment of group member's participation skills and level of knowledge about the task is not approached directly during the first phase of the group although one may get that impression from the above description. During the initial meetings of the group these impressions of the members evolve as the group discusses its task. During this period of the group's life span, the members are in the process of redefining their chosen task in their own terms and ways of thinking (7). The group is trying to determine the basic issues and limits of the task. This exploration is not an issue of selecting a specific direction or strategy for approaching the topic, but rather a decision on the breadth of the task. This decision is an early critical choice the group must make in finally arriving at an adequate decision proposal. If the group chooses poorly at this point, the issue of what to include and what to exclude may plague them as they attempt to develop their information base. While the group members consider the parameters of their task, they implicitly assess the participation skills and knowledgeability of its members. Hence, the discussion of task parameters takes on a dual importance. From this discussion an adequate assessment of member group skills and level of knowledge emerges, and the limiting boundaries of the task are brought into focus.

Finally, during this phase group members implicitly decide on the manner in which they will relate to each other in the group. Member's judgment as to whether a specific type of behavior is appropriate is based on their perceptions of the reactions of other group members. For example, if informal jesting is met by frowns (negative reinforcement), the group is likely to adopt a more serious tone.

The general characteristic of participation during this period is uncertainty and cautious participation. There are a number of interaction patterns that seem to characterize member participation during the orientation phase (4). Group members tend to make tentative and ambiguous comments. Members tend to seek clarification of comments (seek information or seek opinions) and tend to agree more than in later phases. Agreement may function in phase one to facilitate the development of acceptable participation norms and to avoid the creation of an unpleasant atmosphere. Group members tend to reinforce ambiguous decision alternatives and to tentatively express their opinions. Member comments tend to move around the topic from several points of view and tend to jump from one idea to another in seemingly unrelated ways (12). Various decision alternatives may be proposed, but members are not willing at this point to strongly support any one position. The themes of this period, then, are ambiguity, seeking clarification, and tentative exploration. These observations support the notion that group members are attempting to learn the resources of the group, to establish an agreeable interpersonal atmosphere, and to define the parameters of the task.

PHASE II: FORMATION

By this time, group members have redefined the task in terms of their own way of thinking and they have formed their impressions of their fellow group members. During the formative phase, the group structure develops and stabilizes and the group agrees on the strategy they are going to use in achieving their goal.

The structure of the group relates to member's roles including the role of leader. During this period, group members begin to specialize in the functions they will perform for the group. In other words, expectations regarding the behavior of each member begin to stabilize. The most critical structural decision the group makes at this time is the selection of a group leader. Actually, during the orientation phase, the group members were taking the first step in the selection of a group leader by elimination of those members who were clearly seen as unsuitable for leadership. Those members who were quiet, perceived as uninformed or unskilled, or who took strong unequivocal stands were most likely eliminated as potential group leaders (5). After this first elimination phase, usually there is more than one member remaining in contention for leadership.

When two or more members are contending for the leadership role, the final selection of a leader hinges on how they treat the informational and procedural issues relating to the task. The contenders present their positions about how to proceed, hoping to obtain support from some or all of the other group members. The contenders generally believe in the validity of their approach and hope to convince the group to accept their respective points of view. In most cases, it would be misleading to think that the competitors seek leadership simply to be the group's leader, although occasionally this may happen. The leader emerges as the members discuss the positions presented by the contenders and choose the most acceptable approach. During the formation phase, the contender's proposals are the major issue and both the leader and goal direction emerge from this discussion.

One of the outcomes of the orientation phase was a determination of the range of the task. The group members attempted to discover what the task included and what was excluded. During the formation phase, however, the group builds on that outcome to identify the specific objectives it wishes to follow to achieve its goal. Specific objectives relate to the questions that must be answered to arrive at an adequate decision proposal (8). For example, take a task group that recently considered the issue of a student grievance procedure on a western campus. The general task was to determine if the student grievance procedure at their university was adequate to meet the needs of students. Their specific objectives were as follows:

1. To obtain a full description of the existing formal grievance procedure for students.
2. To determine the level of student awareness of the present grievance procedure.
3. To discover student opinions regarding the adequacy of the present grievance procedure.
4. To determine the level of student needs for a grievance procedure.
5. To determine the adequacy of the current procedure.
6. To make recommendations for an acceptable grievance procedure (if necessary).

This particular group did a thorough job of research and analysis and was able to obtain information to answer their objectives. Their decision proposal was well developed and given to student officials on campus for possible implementation. Another group may have prepared a different set of specific objectives. Obviously, any set of objectives must relate to the group's task. Note, however, that any task may be considered in terms of more than one set of objectives. These objectives give specific direction to the group's research and analysis. If a group does not agree on a set of objectives, it will have difficulty in preparing an adequate decision proposal.

During the formative stage, the group will also agree on the procedures it will follow to achieve its goal. Procedures include activities such as what official documents need to be reviewed, what publications and reports need to be examined, and what persons need to be interviewed. The group working on grievance procedures for students looked at the documents describing the present grievance system. They also surveyed a random sample of students on the campus to obtain student opinions regarding a grievance procedure. They interviewed officials on their campus and other area campuses to obtain information on the operation of other grievance procedures for students.

We refer to the agreement on a set of specific objectives and procedures for fulfilling those objectives as the *group's strategy* for achieving its goal. The development of this strategy is a critical time in the life of the group. If the group members fail to develop an adequate strategy, the problems of direction will confront them again, consuming time that more properly could be used for research and analysis.

In the development of its strategy, the group will experience conflict. The constructive management of this conflict assists the group in achieving an effective decision proposal. When informational conflict is properly channeled, it generally results in higher quality solutions (3). Avoidance of conflict, on the other hand, diverts the group's attention from the important issues surrounding its task. The group may choose an inappropriate leader and strategy in an effort to avoid or quickly resolve the conflict. This avoidance could later result in ineffective coordination of the group's work and reduce the quality of the group's effort. Intragroup conflict creates tension, frequently an unpleasant experience, and causes some members to withdraw from the discussion (2). An awareness that informational conflict is a useful and necessary part of small group deliberations helps group members to constructively develop their strategy.

The characteristics of member comments during this phase reflect the conflict usually present in resolving leadership and strategy issues. Positions are clearly stated, and the level of ambiguity dramatically falls. Unfavorable comments are frequently voiced, and assertions are often expressed in an argumentative manner. Assertions followed by unfavorable comments reflect the evolution of informational conflict (4).

The group at the formative phase settles the direction it will take in reaching a decision proposal. Conflict is one of the tools available to the group to carefully consider that direction. This refinement process creates the structure that allows the group to move toward an effective decision proposal. If group members blithely accept any direction that helps them come to agreement but avoid conflict, they have undermined one of the critical avenues available to them for effective group effort. An effective decision proposal, as explained earlier, is a function of quality and group acceptance. The first step toward quality develops during the formative phase. A further contribution to the quality of the group's decision proposal develops during the coordination stage.

PHASE III: COORDINATION

This phase encompasses the major "work period" of the group, and in most cases, it is the longest of the four phases. The development of the information base and a critical analysis of the assumptions the group uses to interpret the information compose the critical issues at this phase. The group's development has reached a point that facilitates or supports the behavior that is necessary to resolve these issues. The manner of relating interpersonally has been settled (orientation phase), and during the formative phase, the role structure, leadership, and the group's strategy for achieving its goal were settled. These implicit agreements or contracts among the members permit them to seek, analyze, and order their information base. Obviously, considerable information regarding the task has been brought before the group during the previous two phases. During this phase, the group begins to put this information into a coherent whole and to seek additional information as needed to fulfill its specific objectives.

The key words that seem to characterize this period of group life are accommodation and coordination. The group members make a concerted effort to collect information and mold it into a coherent whole. The specialized behavior of the group members compliments one another in their attempt to develop an acceptable information base. Information freely flows among members as they search out alternative interpretations of the issues and react to one another's comments (14).

Again, a sense of ambiguity tends to permeate the consideration of the task, but now the uncertainty relates to the alternative interpretations of data and the presence of several solutions. Conflict arises over alternative interpretations of the data, and its resolution grows out of the information the group has before it (6, 10). Favorable comments, substantiation of comments made by others, and interpretation followed by interpretation usually increase during this phase (4).

The effective analysis of the information base, assumptions regarding interpretation, and examination of alternative solutions determine the potential quality of the group's decision proposal. The last remaining task is to formalize the final decision proposal and acquire group acceptance of this proposal.

PHASE IV: FORMALIZATION

Eventually, the group must agree on the final form and content of its decision proposal. An effective decision proposal includes both the quality of the product (a function of the formative and coordination phases) and the group member's acceptance of that product. The key issues during this phase are agreement on the form and content of the proposal and acquiring member acceptance of the proposal.

The key words that describe this period are unity and consensus. Again, the level of conflict is generally low, but here it reflects unity of opinion among group members instead of a conscious avoidance of conflict as in the orientation phase. The preponderance of interaction tends to favor the decision proposal. Group members compliment or congratulate each other on their successes in developing their proposal (4).

Given our general definition of an effective solution, this reinforcement and camaraderie is especially critical in insuring that the group members show acceptance of the proposal. This commitment to the group's product gives impetus to the possibility of eventual implementation of the proposal. The implementation of the decision proposal, in most cases, is the ultimate goal and payoff, and the formalization phase provides the mechanism for achieving this commitment.

When the decision proposal is in written form, the group may face some new, unexpected difficulties toward the end of its life span. The skills required for preparing a written document are somewhat different from those needed for the group's effort to this point. We have seen many groups effectively resolve the issues at each phase of their development and then fail in their effort to prepare a written document presenting the group's work and decisions. We want to bring this potential obstacle to your attention and trust your group can accommodate this change.

The major issues associated with each phase and the characteristics of group interaction are presented in summary form in Figure 2.3. We have referred to this developmental sequence as the "normal" life span of a task-oriented group. We have argued that each phase involves a set of issues that must be resolved if the group is to develop the structural support it needs to achieve its goals. There will be times when these issues are arbitrarily resolved because of group membership or outside forces. For example, the leadership issue may be resolved by formal assignment by an external authority.

Theme	Issues	Key Descriptors
	Orientation	
Uncertainty and cautious participation	1. Assessment of members' group skills	Exploration Cautious
	2. Assessment of task parameters	
	3. Assessment of members' knowledgeability regarding the task	
	4. Establish acceptable interpersonal behavior	
	Formation	
Competitive participation	1. Resolve leadership role	Argumentative Conflictive
	2. Decide on specific task objectives	
	3. Decide on procedural directions	
	4. Member roles stabilize	
	Coordination	
Collection and interprepation of information	1. Develop information base	Accommodation Coordination
	2. Assess assumptions	
	3. Analyze decision proposals	
	Formalization	
Supportive and accepting participation	1. Selection of group's proposal	Unity Comradeship Reinforcement
	2. Group acceptance of the proposal	
	3. Formalizing content and form of the group's decision proposal	

Fig. 2.3   The Normal Life Span of a Task-Oriented Group

We have found, however, that group effort can be more effective if the group is permitted to resolve these issues through its own deliberations.

CHARACTERISTIC LENGTH OF TIME FOR EACH PHASE

The actual length of time the group takes at each phase is determined by the specific group and its task. The relative time spent during each period for the normal group is illustrated in Figure 2.4. The orientation phase is relatively short, and the formation phase is generally

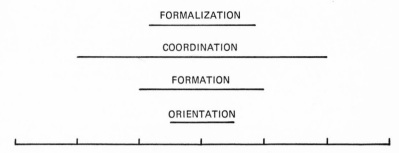

Fig. 2.4   Relative Length of Time Characteristic of the Four Phases

two or three times as long. The coordination phase encompasses the major length of time. The formalization phase is about as long as the formation phase, although the requirement to prepare a major written document may extend this phase.

ARRESTED DEVELOPMENTAL SEQUENCE

We have found that groups encountering major difficulties are usually arrested at the formative phase. These groups use their time quite differently. Whereas in the normal life span the major time span is during the coordination phase, these groups spend most of their time in the formative phase. Figure 2.5 shows this sequence. We make special note of this alternate use of time because most unsuccessful groups fail to resolve the issues that are associated with the formative phase. Generally, these groups go around in circles covering the same ground again and again without developing a sense of direction.

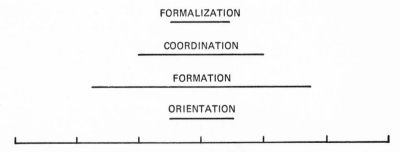

Fig. 2.5   Relative Length of Time Characteristic of the Four Phases: Arrested Development

ONGOING GROUPS

In the foregoing description of the normal life span of a task-oriented group, we assumed a newly formed group of people working on a single task. Frequently, however, an established group resolves an ongoing sequence of tasks. A management team at a state agency or corporate branch, for example, considers a sequence of problems that arise from the day-to-day operations of the organization. We find, with some exceptions, that the same developmental pattern characterizes these groups as well.

If the group membership remains constant, some of the issues associated with the orientation and formation phases remain settled from task to task. Generally, the group will not reconsider acceptable interpersonal behavior, and the group's role structure including leadership will likely continue unchanged. Nonetheless, issues related directly to the task will require resolution from task to task. As each new task comes before the group, the group will find it necessary to determine task parameters and member knowledgeability regarding the task. Usually, these issues will be resolved much more quickly in an established group than in a newly formed group. During the formation phase the group needs to agree on its strategy, including both specific task objectives and procedural directions. The issues associated with the coordination and formalization phases must be resolved for each task as the established group moves from task to task.

A somewhat different situation arises when the membership of an established group changes from time to time. Each time a new member is added to the group or a continuing member leaves the group, a new ambiguity confronts the group. When a new member joins the group, the group momentarily reverts back to the orientation phase in an attempt to accommodate the new member. Although the new period of orientation may be quite brief, the continuing members will assess the group skills and knowledge of the new member. Conversely, the new member will also assess the continuing members' skill and knowledge. Acceptable interpersonal behavior also may be altered. The new member will also need to discover how the group has defined its task and the progress the group has made towards a decision proposal.

This new period of adjustment may create difficulties for the continuing members. The new member may suggest different ways in defining task parameters or the new member may propose modifications in the group's strategy. The new member's presence may also require adjustment in the group's role structure including leadership. If the established group has spent time and effort in resolving these issues, considerable resistance to these changes may arise. Consequently, this period of accommodating a new member may result in an arrested developmental sequence. Normally, however, the ongoing group members are able to accommodate the new member, make new adjustments, and move toward the development of its decision proposal.

When a continuing member leaves the group, a somewhat different situation arises. The magnitude of change resulting from the member's departure rests on the member's centrality in the group's deliberations. If the member was vocal and influential in helping the group resolve issues associated with each phase, a major restructuring process will occur. The issue of leadership will likely need to be resolved again, and possible changes in the group's strategy may occur. Again, it is possible that the group will fall into an arrested developmental sequence. If the member's participation was somewhat peripheral to the group's discussions, then little adjustment will be required.

We have argued that the issues associated with the four phases of a task-oriented group's life span must be resolved to provide an adequate structure for small group decision making. This analysis applies to ongoing groups as well as newly formed groups. The developmental sequence also helps to explain what happens when a new member is added to an established group or when a continuing member leaves the group. In each situation, the group is creating structure necessary for developing an effective decision proposal. If a group fails to resolve these issues, it will likely fall into an arrested developmental sequence. In any case, inadequate resolution of these issues will result in an ineffective decision proposal.

SUMMARY

Environmental considerations and group process were merged as determinants of group effectiveness. Logical and empirical adequacy of the decision proposal as well as mobilization of group resources were proposed as causal factors in the development of an effective decision proposal.

The normal life span of a task-oriented group was described in some detail because it helps to clarify our thinking about the development of decision-making processes in small groups. We have suggested that task-oriented groups pass through a sequence of four phases. At each phase, a set of issues is resolved by the group. The resolution of these issues provides a structure for the group to effectively achieve its goal. Unsuccessful groups fail to adequately resolve these central issues.

CONCLUSIONS AND RECOMMENDATIONS

1. The focal point both for task definition and for assessing solution effectiveness is the environment.
2. Group effectiveness is a function of the quality of a decision proposal times group commitment to the proposal.
3. The quality of a decision proposal is a function of its logical and empirical adequacy.
4. The actual productivity of a group is a function of task demands and group resources minus process loss.
5. A group passes through four phases in the development of a decision proposal.
6. At each phase the group resolves informational, procedural, and interpersonal issues that provide the structure and support for achievement of the group's goal.
7. The degree of success the group attains in resolving the informational, procedural, and interpersonal issues is directly related to the group's decision proposal.
8. The major issues associated with the orientation phase are interpersonal atmosphere, assessment of member skills and knowledge, and boundaries of the task.
9. The major issues related to the formation phase are resolution of leadership and role structure and development of a strategy for achieving the group's goal.
10. The major issues during the coordination phase are development of the information base and consideration of alternative decision proposals.
11. The major issues associated with the formalization phase are preparation and justification of the group's decision proposal and group acceptance of the proposal.
12. Groups that are unsuccessful tend not to resolve issues associated with the formation phase.
13. Ongoing groups, such as a management team, must resolve informational and procedural issues associated with the phases whenever they encounter a new task.

REFERENCES

1. Robert F. Bales and Fred L. Strodtbeck, "Phases in Group Problem-Solving," *Journal of Abnormal and Social Psychology* 46 (1951): 485–495.

2. Ernest G. Bormann, *Discussion and Group Methods: Theory and Practice,* 2nd ed. (New York: Harper and Row, 1975).

3. Joseph L. Bower, "Group Decision Making: A Report of an Experimental Study," *Behavioral Science* 10 (1965): 277–289.

4. B. Aubrey Fisher, "Decision Emergence: Phases in Group Decision-Making," *Speech Monographs* 37 (1970): 53–66.

5. John G. Geier, "A Trait Approach to the Study of Leadership in Small Groups," *Journal of Communication* 17 (1967): 316–323.

6. Harold Guetzkow and John Gyr, "An Analysis of Conflict in Decision Making Groups," *Human Relations* 7 (1954): 367–382.

7. J. Richard Hackman, "Toward Understanding the Role of Tasks in Behavioral Research," *Acto Psychologica* 31 (1969): 97–128.

8. Theodore L. Harris and Wilson E. Schwahn (eds.), *Selected Readings on the Learning Process,* (New York: Oxford University Press, 1961).

9. Charles H. Kepner and Benjamin B. Tregoe, *The Rationale Manager: A Systematic Approach to Problem Solving and Decision Making* (New York: McGraw-Hill, 1965).

10. Thomas J. Knutson and Albert C. Kowitz, "Effects of Information Type and Level of Orientation on Consensus-Achievement in Substantive Small-Group Conflict," *The Central States Speech Journal* 28 (1977): 54–63.

11. Norman R. F. Maier, *Problem Solving and Creativity in Individuals and Groups* (Belmont, Calif.: Brooks-Cole Publishing Co., 1970).

12. Thomas Scheidel and Laura Crowell, "Idea Development in Small Discussion Groups," *Quarterly Journal of Speech* 50 (1964): 140–145.

13. Ivan D. Steiner, *Group Process and Productivity* (New York: Academic Press, 1972).

14. Bruce W. Tuckman, "Developmental Sequences in Small Groups," *Psychological Bulletin,* 63 (1965): 384–399.

2

INTERACTION STRUCTURE

Chapter 3: Elements Affecting Informational Exchange
Chapter 4: Elements Affecting Procedural and
Interpersonal Transactions

We emphasized in Part 1 that the exchange of messages was the vehicle for defining and achieving group goals. The development of roles and norms, the completion of a decision proposal, and the resolution of a multitude of issues during the life span of a task-oriented group all rest on symbolic transactions among group members. For the most part, we mastered our language at an early age. We are all technically able to carry on a reasonably intelligent conversation with others. Our emphasis in this section, then, is to present information that will help you effectively use these verbal skills for making decisions in task-oriented groups. We emphasize the need for objectivity in the search and presentation of information. Often our beliefs, values, and interests get in the way of objective information processing. We also stress the need for effective planning of member responsibilities and the need for effective guidance of group activity. Finally, we explain how interpersonal dynamics can both hinder and facilitate the effective exchange of messages. These chapters should help you to become a more effective participant in your group experiences.

CHAPTER 3

Elements Affecting
Informational Exchange

INTRODUCTION

Interaction is a word used to describe the message behaviors of people engaged in communication. Unless you are sitting alone in your room, singing in the shower, or engaging in some sort of communication by yourself, interaction characterizes your communication. Interaction refers to the process in which people exchange messages with one another. Jurgen Reusch, a prominent psychiatrist, sees interaction as a consequence of people's agreement to engage in communication involving mutual influence (13). That is, interaction involves at least two people who have agreed to exchange messages and to respond to them. Their communication behaviors are interdependent. They have agreed to be affected by each other. In a dyad, the number of messages sent by each person is usually similar. Both people act as sources and receivers on about a one-to-one ratio. In small group problem solving, however, the ratio changes somewhat. People tend to listen more and speak less in environments containing more people.

Gary Cronkhite (4) in his book on communication has suggested that we look at the process of communication in terms of why we produce one message instead of another and why we interpret a message one way instead of another. The "why" part of this view of communication, Cronkhite suggests, rests on our beliefs, values, and plans. Beliefs refer to probable relationships among events that comprise our view of ourselves, our view of others, and our image of the world at large. Values refer to desired ways of doing things or to desired outcomes or end states. Plans, as defined by Cronkhite, refer to our feelings about sequences of behavior that must be performed to achieve certain outcomes (4, p. 34). Our own constellation of beliefs, values, and plans guides what messages we produce and how we interpret the messages of others.

Assume for the moment that you are a member of a group working on the problem of child abuse. On the one hand, you harbor some beliefs regarding the fact of child abuse, how widespread it is, and the victims and culprits of child abuse. On the other hand, you hold some values regarding the undesirable effects of this practice on children. You probably believe that children should not be physically harmed. You also probably believe that child abuse results in undesirable psychological effects for both parents and children. Since you believe that children are being harmed and your value system tells you that child abuse is undesirable, you will likely be motivated to do something about it. You may believe an essential first step is to bring interested parties together in a task-oriented group. You may believe that remedial action should be taken through various service agencies. You might decide that doctors and nurses should be involved in a detection and treatment program.

We could continue to elaborate on the beliefs, values, and plans you might hold regarding child abuse. The point we wish to make here, however, is that the content and exchange of messages in a task-oriented group will be guided by the beliefs, values, and plans held by group members. We wish to emphasize the importance of this view of communication. We assume that most people in our society have adequate verbal skills. The secret of effective communication rests on our awareness of how beliefs, values, and plans affect our use of these skills.

We now turn to some general factors influencing interaction. Then we will turn to more specific message behaviors to assist you in communicating along informational, procedural, and interpersonal small group dimensions.

GENERAL FACTORS AFFECTING GROUP INTERACTION

Group Size

A large group is not necessarily a better group. In fact, as group size increases, interaction becomes more difficult. The number of potential channels of communication available for interaction increases much more rapidly than the simple arithmetic increase of people to the group. As a consequence, larger groups tend to break up into smaller clique groups, which in turn makes the management of interaction very difficult. Bales (1) has demonstrated that fewer people participate in larger group discussions, and Gibb (5) found that as group size increases, more aggressive people tend to dominate the conversation and stifle the comments of the other group members. This condition has an effect on the overall morale of the group. If members feel that their participation is limited, the satisfaction of the group decreases (2, 14). You need only think about groups where you "couldn't get a word in edgewise" to understand the frustration often associated with larger groups.

No single recommendation can be given with respect to group size because so much depends on the group's topic, the motivations and attitudes of the group members, the environment, and many other factors. Bormann indicates, however, that the optimal size for most problem-solving groups varies from five to seven and that five is an excellent number (3). Five people tend to insure a range of opinions and ideas while still allowing for each member to participate freely. When the group size increases beyond seven members, the participants tend to decrease their involvement with the group and become less personal with other members (20).

Group size has another impact on interaction that people often overlook. Even-numbered groups often are less effective than odd-numbered groups. In groups of four, six, or eight members, for example, an equally divided group can reach an impasse over a particular issue. In a four-person group, two people may favor one course of action and the other two an opposite position. The ensuing struggle for power under these circumstances can seriously hinder the group's progress. In an odd-numbered group, however, an impasse is highly unlikely, and the interaction tends to be more relaxed and satisfying. If you are responsible for forming a problem-solving group, you should consider not only the size of the group, but also whether the number of people should be odd or even.

Group History

Quite simply, group history refers to the length of time the members have been meeting as a group. For example, we would say that the U.S. Supreme Court would have a long group history since the members have had a chance to interact with one another on a relatively regular basis for several years. Because of this group history, the justices interact with one another in a fashion quite different from a group with a short group history or no group history at all. An example of a group without a history would be the U.S. Olympic basketball team at its first practice. Although the players have some commonalities in that they all share an ability to play basketball, the exact qualities of member relationships has not yet been determined.

The distinction between groups with a history and without a history has an implication for the manner in which members interact. Bormann has described the differential effects in terms of primary and secondary tension (3). Primary tension refers to anxieties and worries associated with getting acquainted with new people. Groups without a history tend to experience greater degrees of primary tension because group members lack the necessary information to predict how the other group members will behave. Consequently, interaction patterns in groups without a history during the early stages of discussion are characterized by tentative comments, long pauses, and short messages. Gradually, as the group members get to know one another, the primary tension decreases to a point where the group can work productively. If you join a group without a history, the interaction pattern during the first meeting should be characterized by considerable discussion on an interpersonal dimension. As your group gains more information about one another through this relatively nonthreatening conversation, you can gradually turn to discussion regarding the group's goal. Groups without a history should spend the initial phases of their discussion engaging in communication designed to reduce primary tension. Even groups with a history experience primary tension for a while each time they meet. The primary tension will probably not be as great as that for a group lacking a history, but nonetheless the members should devote the initial stages of the discussion to releasing primary tension. Think of a group to which you belong and which meets regularly. Even if you have been meeting for several weeks, you still experience primary tension. So do the other participants. The members wonder whether the others will behave as they did at past meetings. Will Jim be prepared? Will the group respond favorably to new ideas? Will we have an argument today? The anxiety surrounding these questions can be lessened considerably through interaction over nonthreatening topics. In simple words, primary tension refers to a "feeling out" period common to all groups in which the members seek information upon which to base predictions about future interactions. The only caution we would suggest to you is avoid an extended period of releasing primary tension. Unless your group eventually turns to goal-directed, functional matters, members will experience a frustration because the group is not making progress toward solving its problem.

Secondary tension occurs after the group has developed some history. This form of tension differs from primary tension in that it involves conflict or disagreement regarding informational or procedural issues before the group. The interaction pattern associated with secondary tension results in a high level of excitement. Members try to persuade one another to accept various positions, and a good deal of dynamic interaction occurs. We will discuss the interaction patterns designed to manage the conflict associated with secondary tension in Chapter 10. For now, remember that the interactions that occur during the initial phases of the group discussion differ from the interactions that occur later in the group's discussions.

Seating Arrangement

The manner in which a group arranges itself will influence the group's interaction patterns. Groups can deliberate while seated at a rectangular table, arranged in a circle, formed into a "V" or "U" pattern, or a variety of other distributions. Information about how groups arrange themselves enables us to make predictions about the interaction within the group. The seating arrangement of the group determines in part which relationships in the group will flourish and which interactions are likely to be discouraged.

Studies of small group communication have shown, for example, that people tend to interact more frequently with people seated opposite to them than adjacent to them (18). When researchers studied interaction patterns in seminar rooms, they found that the most participation came from those seated directly opposite the professor (17). In fact, even when the rest of the seats were occupied, students tended to avoid the two seats immediately adjacent to the professor. This observation is somewhat tempered, however, by the type of leadership operating within the group. When a group has a strong leader, group members interact more frequently with those in seats adjacent to them. With weak or minimal leadership, group members direct their comments to people sitting opposite them (8). In other words, considering the type of leadership in your group, you should probably select your seat carefully because to a large degree it will determine the person with whom you will interact most frequently.

When the group distributes itself around a rectangular table, another aspect of seating arrangement comes into play—the head of the table. People who sit at the head of the table generally have more influence over the group because they tend to interact with more people (19). We suggest that one of the reasons for this observation stems from the studies discussed in the previous paragraph. The person at the head of the table has a greater opportunity to interact with more people opposite than adjacent to him or her. Research studies seem to bear out this speculation. Most of the interaction in groups is directed toward high-status people, and the studies show that high-status people, given a choice, tend to select the head of the table as their seat. Unless you prefer to avoid interaction with group members, the only time you might intentionally avoid the head of the table would be in an exclusive restaurant. You see, the waiter will tend to interact more frequently with you too. That can be expensive.

The V- or U-shaped arrangement sometimes is used as a setting for group communication. Under these circumstances, people at the end of the V or U tend to interact more frequently than those occupying seats in the middle of the arrangement. The familiar principle of adjacent versus opposite explains this phenomenon. People in the middle of the arrangement have more people adjacent to them while

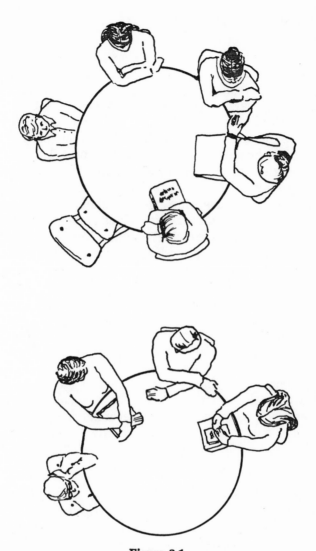

Figure 3.1

those on the ends have more people opposite them. As we have seen, we tend to communicate more with those seated opposite to us (see Figure 3.1).

Most people prefer discussion in a group arranged in a circle. In this fashion, each person starts with an equal chance to talk with anyone else in the group. The flow of interaction will change as a leader begins to emerge or as high-status people are identified, but at least everyone starts out with an equal chance. During a seminar for high school teachers one of the authors conducted, the group always sat in a circle. They expressed satisfaction with this arrangement and carried on vigorous discussions over a six-day period. At lunch, the group would visit a coffee shop near the school. Here the group changed their circle arrangement employed in the classroom to a rectangular table arrangement with one seat at the "head of the table." The same person occupied the head of the table every lunch period. We found out later that this person was the principal at the school where the seminar was conducted. The majority of the seminar participants taught at this school and viewed the principal's role as one of high status. The really interesting aspect about this story was that the restaurant had a circular table in the same room available for the seminar's use. However, the status variable became important when the environment was changed and the teachers elected to interact more with the principal at lunch. The point of all of this is that a circle arrangement provides the opportunity to interact with more people. This interaction contributes to the overall satisfaction of the group members.

The seating arrangement of a group contributes to the form of behavior of people in discussions and especially influences their communication interaction. If we know something about the environmental influences on groups, maybe we can create environments designed to maximize the effect of group deliberation. B. F. Skinner observes that behavioral change is a product of the environment (15). If we can control the environment, we can control behavior. To some extent, you can now affect the manner in which a group behaves simply by arranging the seats in certain positions.

Communication Apprehension

Communication apprehension operates as a significant influence in small group interaction. As opposed to stage fright, an anxious or tense condition normally associated with a particular public speech or performance, communication apprehension refers to a general worry about all forms of communication. Recent research indicates that as much as 20 percent of the population lives with communication apprehension (10). In and of itself, that figure means little until we realize the effect of the phenomenon on small group problem solving. The high communication apprehensive typically avoids interacting in groups. In fact, when the apprehensive individual joins a group, that person invariably selects a seat where the interaction is likely to be minimal. When this individual does interact, the content of the message ordinarily is irrelevant to the group's deliberation. The apprehensive person's communication tends to be of very short duration, and the anxious person seldom disagrees. Disagreement requires explanation, and explanation requires communication. Unlike most people who seek out communication with others, the communication apprehensive person is motivated to avoid interaction with others. Consequently, the apprehensive person tends to withdraw in group situations. This withdrawal affects the group's interaction and, additionally, the quality of the group's decision. An apprehensive person reveals little self-information, takes few risks, and displays little interest in the group's deliberation. These behaviors make the communication apprehensive person hard to get to know, and because of that, you will experience more trouble communicating.

You probably have been in groups where an apprehensive person has been a member. Because of the difficulties associated with the anxious person, the group is not likely to benefit from the information the apprehensive person has. (Research has demonstrated that no relationship exists between apprehension and intelligence.) In order to get the apprehensive person to participate, you must set up an environment that encourages communication. Remember, in any five-person group, you are likely to have one person who does not interact frequently because of communication apprehension. You must make your communication with this person as nonthreatening as possible. One strategy you might employ successfully would involve soliciting communication and then reinforcing the comments of the apprehensive person. You might also tactfully suggest that other group members engage in similar behaviors. In this fashion, you can make the apprehensive person feel more comfortable as well as reaping the benefits of that person's interaction.

Four general factors affect interaction in the problem-solving group: group size, group history, seating arrangement, and communication apprehension. Many other variables influence the patterns of interaction, but these four seem important enough to remember. We take the position that a high amount of interaction results in desirable consequences for the group in the decision's quality and the members' satisfaction. When forming or joining groups, you will want to consider these general factors as a method of increasing interaction. Now we will move to consideration of some more specific factors influencing interaction along the informational dimension.

SPECIFIC ELEMENTS AFFECTING
INFORMATIONAL EXCHANGE

We have defined the informational dimension of small group interaction as those interactions dealing with statements of fact, opinion, and advice. As such, communication referred to as informational deals directly with the content of the group's task. Any task-oriented group consists of members who vary widely in the amount of information they have about the group's task. In fact, the information about the topic that one member has is likely to be different from the information another member has. In other words, information exchange among the group members will be necessary in order to achieve their goals. This section examines some of the elements that influence this informational interaction.

Preparation for Discussion

Of course, the time people have to prepare for a discussion varies considerably. Only under highly peculiar circumstances, however, does an individual begin a task-oriented group discussion without an opportunity to engage in some preparation. Those who enter groups unprepared generally are quite unwilling to engage in interaction on the informational dimension in order to avoid demonstrating their ignorance. Consequently, these people feel much more comfortable in encouraging the group to discuss interpersonal matters or procedural issues. These activities are not completely without value; however, we are reminded of Tom Lehrer's line, "If you have nothing to say, the very least you can do is shut up." On the other hand, those people who are ready for the discussion through adequate preparation should volunteer their information to the group. When people with relevant information spontaneously share their ideas with the group, much time is saved and the group's efficiency increases (9). If people with information remain silent, for whatever reasons, the group runs the risk of wasting time on the interpersonal dimension or by engaging in time-consuming procedural efforts to solicit information.

Another important consequence of adequate preparation involves the manner in which other group members interact with the prepared person. Those who communicate information relevant to the group's task increase their status within the group (6). The cause of this increased perception of status is partly due to the other member's increased interaction with the prepared person. The high status resulting from the increased interaction also raises the satisfaction of the participant who has prepared. In order to appreciate the importance of adequate preparation, think of a group in which you were able to provide considerable information. You probably remember that group as an exciting, valuable experience. Now try to remember a group in which you were unprepared. Unless you have completely repressed the incident, you probably recall feeling anxious, nervous, and wishing the meeting would quickly end.

Tolerance for Ambiguity

Ambiguity refers to a situation characterized by uncertainty in the small group communication setting. People differ in their ability to handle ambiguous situations. Some group members simply cannot tolerate uncertainty. Consequently, this person is likely to interact with others in an attempt to get information with which to reduce the ambiguity. People with low tolerance for ambiguity try to find answers and evidence quickly. The problem with a low tolerance for ambiguity affects the quality of the information received. People who cannot tolerate ambiguity are often satisfied with low-quality information. This results in a premature closure and the interaction, at least on that topic, will cease. Group members who tolerate ambiguity, however, have less of a need for closure and can continue discussion over a period of time. Those with high tolerance for ambiguity are likely to avoid snap decisions and premature solutions because of their tendency to collect as much information on a topic as possible. A group composed of people with varying degrees of ambiguity often experiences problems. One group of people will insist that they have the answer to the group's task while the others will be reluctant to adopt their alternative. Those in the latter group will want to get more information in order to reach the best possible alternative. As we have seen, better decisions normally result from processing large amounts of information. Consequently, the best way to handle ambiguity involves the generation of information rather than the achievement of a quick decision.

Selectivity

The decisions we make about exposing ourselves to certain activities, attending to various stimuli, perceiving information, and recalling experiences are called selectivity. Of course, we cannot be in two places at once, so we selectively expose ourselves to certain environments. If you have a choice to make between attending a professional football game and going to the opera, you will select one of the events. People who voluntarily join groups (i.e., selectively expose themselves) behave differently from those who joined the group because they were required or forced to do so. Research demonstrates that people will seek out information consistent with their attitudes, beliefs, and values (11). People who join a group voluntarily probably see the group as a vehicle to reinforce their ideas. Therefore, these people tend to interact more frequently than those who were forced to join the group. Selective exposure also influences the content of the group's interaction. Members typically avoid discussion of topics contrary to their attitudes, beliefs, and values.

Once a person has decided to join a group, the person will experience variations in attention level. Some messages are not attended to as much as others. Assume for a moment that you are a Democrat. Another person in your group happens to be an avid Republican. How do you respond to the Republican's message? Often people simply dismiss contrary messages by thinking, "I am not going to pay attention." We tend to seek out messages consistent with our past decisions. We also attend to messages consistent with our past experiences (7).

Perception refers to the manner in which we give meaning to our experiences. Not only do we selectively expose ourselves to certain messages, but we also selectively attach meaning to the data we receive. Some years ago, the board of directors of a major airline decided to present passengers aboard their flights with what they thought to be helpful information. Since jet aircraft were allowing more and more people to fly, they reasoned that the novice air traveler should have information about the aircraft's performance in order to reduce their anxiety while on board. Consequently, they prepared a pamphlet to explain the various sounds the novice air traveler would hear during the flight. For example, the pamphlet explained that a slight thump would signify that the landing gear had operated properly. The board of directors predicted that this kind of information would alleviate the fears and doubts of the passenger. Their motives were obviously noble; however, they misperceived the reaction passengers would have to their message. It was somewhat disconcerting for the cabin attendants to explain to passengers that the thump they heard at 30,000 feet was not the landing gear operating. In other words, the pamphlet served to sensitize the passengers' perception to *any* noise rather than reduce their fears about flying. The board of directors perceived that passengers would use the information to reduce their anxiety. Passengers, however, worried about sounds throughout the entire flight. The selective perception of the board of directors, a problem-solving group, cost the airline considerable money and resulted in an increase, instead of a decrease, in the apprehension among their passengers. The pamphlets were removed from the airplanes after only one week.

Not only do groups often misperceive the consequences of their group's decision, but individual group members also frequently misperceive the comments made by their colleagues. We tend to perceive the messages of other people in terms of our own values, beliefs, attitudes, and wishes (16). Occasionally, we attach meaning to another's message in a fashion never intended by the other person. If we distort our perceptions so that another's viewpoint seems more similar to our own, we run the risk of an inaccurate, premature agreement. Interaction under these circumstances is limited and not very productive in terms of effective decision making.

Selective retention simply means that we tend to remember some things and forget others. As with exposure, attention, and perception, we tend to remember information consistent with our attitudes, beliefs, and values. We all prefer to remember the good things we experience but forget the unpleasant things that happen to us. The same principle applies to preparation for discussion on the informational dimension (12). Unless we exert a healthy amount of objectivity in our research, we are likely to report only that information supporting our viewpoint. In order to increase the quality of a decision, the group must have access to all information: good, bad, correct, incorrect, true, false, pleasant, unpleasant, and so on. Consequently, a conscious effort should be made to retain most of your research information so that you can share your work with the other group members.

Opinionatedness

Opinionatedness refers to a person's willingness to tolerate alternative positions and ideas. An opinionated person sees one answer and announces through interaction that that answer is correct. We all joke about the person who says, "My mind is made up. Don't confuse me with the facts." Unfortunately, the opinionated person behaves in the same fashion. He or she will try to get an early agreement, reinforcement for his or her ideas, and, following agreement and reinforcement, a change in the group's topic. In essence, an opinionated person is telling you that he or she has already decided to behave in a certain way and that your messages will have little effect. Under these conditions, we recognize quickly that our messages will probably have little effect. Consequently, the opinionated person creates a situation in which interaction on an informational dimension decreases.

We consider people who are unopinionated to have "open minds." The unopinionated person seems open to communication and willing to discuss a variety of alternatives. The ability to see more than one position on an issue contributes to more group interaction. Nobody likes to talk with people where their messages will not have an effect. On the other hand, we feel at ease communicating with an unopinionated person. Because of this, more information is generated, the information is analyzed on a higher level, and the quality of decision making is raised. In short, because the unopinionated person can tolerate relatively high degrees of ambiguity, discussion with these people tends to flourish.

Preparation for discussion, tolerance for ambiguity, selectivity, and opinionatedness all influence interaction on the informational dimension. The effective discussant will spend time preparing for a discussion, have a reasonable tolerance for ambiguity, recognize the influence of selectivity, and seek to maintain an unopinionated outlook. These characteristics increase the probability of informational interaction and, consequently, raise the quality of the decision and the level of member satisfaction. We are now ready to turn to the factors influencing the procedural and interpersonal dimensions of small group communication.

SUMMARY

The exchange of informational messages resulting in reciprocal influence and shared meaning provides the basis for making decisions in small groups. Several general factors such as group size, group history, seating arrangement, and communicator apprehension affect the exchange of messages in a small group. Awareness of the influence of these factors permits members to more effectively control the flow of interaction in a small group.

We defined the informational dimension of small group interaction as messages dealing with statements or facts, opinions, and advice; that is, the substance of the task. Group members' preparation for discussion, tolerance for ambiguity, selectivity in attending to, perceiving, and recalling information, and opinionatedness influence the exchange of messages related to the informational dimension. Awareness of the impact of these factors enables group members to more effectively control the substantive quality of the group's discussions.

CONCLUSIONS AND RECOMMENDATIONS

1. The exchange of messages in a small group results in mutual influence and interdependence among its members.
2. As group size increases, the flow of interaction is dominated by smaller subsets of group members.
3. As a member's opportunity for participation becomes restricted, his or her satisfaction with the group will tend to fall.
4. For most tasks the group should be composed of either five or seven members.
5. The initial moments of a group's meeting will be characterized by primary tension.
6. Group members tend to interact more frequently with people seated opposite to them than seated adjacent to them.

7. Group members that sit at the head of a rectangular table tend to have greater influence over the group's flow of interaction than those seated at the sides of the table.
8. A circle seating arrangement tends to provide maximum opportunity for all members to participate in the group's discussion.
9. The communication apprehensive group member should be given frequent positive reinforcement for participation in the group's discussions.
10. The exchange of informational messages forms the basis for selecting effective solutions to the group's task.
11. Proper preparation for discussion tends to increase exchange of informational messages.
12. Those who communicate relevant information tend to increase their status within the group.
13. Group members with low tolerance for ambiguity tend to seek quick resolution of issues.
14. High tolerance for ambiguity tends to increase the exchange of informational messages.
15. Group members selectively expose themselves to informational sources.
16. Group members tend to perceive messages in terms of their beliefs, attitudes, and values.
17. A conscious effort toward objectivity in our informational search is necessary to prevent the reporting of information that only supports our personal point of view.
18. An opinionated group member tends to ignore messages that do not agree with his or her point of view.
19. The exchange of messages characterized by low opinionatedness tends to result in higher levels of information processing.

REFERENCES

1. Robert F. Bales, et al., "Channels of Communication in Small Groups," *American Psychologist* 6 (1951): 324 (abstract).
2. Alex Bavelas, "Communication Patterns in Task-Oriented Groups," *Journal of the Acoustical Society of America* 22 (1950): 725–730.
3. Ernest G. Bormann, *Discussion and Group Methods: Theory and Practice,* 2nd ed. (New York: Harper and Row, 1975).
4. Gary Cronkhite, *Communication and Awareness* (Menlo Park, Ca.: Cummings Publishing Company, 1976).
5. Cecil A. Gibb, "The Effects of Group Size and of Threat Reduction upon Creativity in a Problem-Solving Situation," *American Psychologist* 6 (1951): 324 (abstract).

6. J. C. Gilchrist, Marvin E. Shaw, and L. C. Walker, "Some Effects of Unequal Distribution of Information in Wheel Group Structure," *Journal of Abnormal and Social Psychology* 49 (1954): 554–556.

7. Howard Gilkinson, Stanley F. Paulson, and Donald E. Sikkink, "Conditions Affecting the Communication of Controversial Statements in Connected Discourse: Forms of Presentation and the Political Frame of Reference of the Listener," *Speech Monographs* 20 (1955): 253–260.

8. Gordon Hearn, "Leadership and the Spatial Factor in Small Groups," *Journal of Abnormal and Social Psychology* 54 (1957): 269–272.

9. John T. Lanzetta and Thornton B. Roby, "The Relationship Between Certain Process Variables and Group Problem-Solving Efficiency," *Journal of Social Psychology* 52 (1960): 135–148.

10. James C. McCroskey and Lawrence R. Wheeless, *Introduction to Human Communication* (Boston: Allyn and Bacon, 1976).

11. Judson Mills, Elliot Aronson, and Hal Robinson, "Selectivity in Exposure to Information," *Journal of Abnormal and Social Psychology* 59 (1959): 250–253.

12. Donald A. Norman, "Toward Theory of Memory and Retention," *Psychological Review* 75 (1968): 522–536.

13. Jurgen Reusch and Gregory Bateson, *Communication: The Social Matrix of Psychiatry* (New York: W. W. Norton and Co., 1951).

14. Marvin E. Shaw, "Communication Networks," in Leonard Berkowitz (ed.), *Advances in Experimental Social Psychology*, vol. 1. (New York: Academic Press, 1964).

15. Burrhus F. Skinner, *Beyond Freedom and Dignity* (New York: Alfred A. Knopf, 1971).

16. George H. Smith, "Size-Distance Judgments of Human Faces," *Journal of Genetic Psychology* 49 (1953): 45–64.

17. Robert Sommer, *Personal Space* (Englewood Cliffs, N.J.: Prentice-Hall, 1969).

18. Bernard Steinzor, "The Spatial Factor in Face to Face Discussion Groups," *Journal of Abnormal and Social Psychology* 45 (1950): 552–555.

19. Fred L. Strodtbeck and L. Harmon Hook, "The Social Dimensions of a Twelve Man Jury Table," *Sociometry* 24 (1961): 397–415.

20. John E. Tsouderous, "Organizational Change in Terms of a Series of Selected Variables," *American Sociological Review* 20 (1955): 206–210.

CHAPTER 4

Elements Affecting Procedural and Interpersonal Transactions

INTRODUCTION

In the previous chapter on small group interaction, we presented information about general factors that affect the flow of interaction among group members. We also explained how various behaviors affect the exchange of messages for the substance of the task. In this chapter, we will present material describing behaviors relating to the procedural and interpersonal dimensions of small group interaction. The procedural dimension relates to the coordination of member activities. Agenda setting, goal formation, and directing a group toward its goal are examples of behaviors related to the procedural dimension. The informational dimension refers to the "what" of discussion. The procedural dimension refers to the "how to" dimension. Any problem-solving group must have a method for organizing the information it collects into some meaningful pattern. Interpersonal behavior reflects our attitudes toward group members and our perception of their traits. Interpersonal behavior does not provide the substance for achievement of the group's goals. It does, however, provide a base that sets the pattern and tone of the group's deliberations.

ELEMENTS AFFECTING EXCHANGE ON PROCEDURAL MATTERS

Agenda Setting

Groups composed of members who engage in communication about the organization of the discussion and the steps in solving a problem work more efficiently tend to have more positive attitudes for and higher levels of satisfaction with their product (5). The preparation of specific agenda items serves a useful purpose in that members can determine the progress that they are making toward solving a problem. As the group proceeds through the various agenda items, members begin to develop success experiences. The group can sense the progress it is making, and membership in the group becomes more important. Groups without a clear agenda tend to muddle along not knowing whether or not they are succeeding. On the other hand, a series of successful completion of steps on the way to solving a problem allows a group identity. Achievement of the steps necessary in reaching a goal acts as a reinforcement to the group. Members ought to be able to explain what they accomplished at any given meeting. Those who respond, "I don't know," in response to the question, "What did your group accomplish today?" typically have a negative attitude toward the group's work in general. Agenda setting is important, then, because it defines the goal and enables members to experience success as each step is made toward solving the problem. The situation is analogous to taking a long trip in your car. You use a map to guide you toward your destination. As you chart your progress toward your destination, you can readily see the increasing probability of your arrival. The agenda serves the same purpose as a map. We can determine what we have done, where we are going, and where we are at any given moment. This function serves to increase our security and build a positive attitude toward the group.

Planning Communication Responsibilities

As we noted above, group members have varying amounts of information on any given topic. This characteristic often results in several advantages for group communication, but some planning must be done to facilitate the exchange of information. One of the primary causes of frustration with committee work stems directly from a failure to anticipate and control procedural interaction. Often people assume that the advantages of small group communication will occur simply because people are meeting. This naive assumption overlooks the procedural dimension. Not only should we prepare what we have to say, but some set of responsibilities should be prepared as well. Groups who spend time determining how they will deliberate before actually exchanging information typically succeed in developing an efficient style of discussion (31). If the group tries to organize and discuss informational responsibilities simultaneously, the pressure of the task may interfere with the organization of information. On the other hand, groups who have planned procedures for exchanging and analyzing information avoid unnecessary interaction, duplication of effort, and frustrating discussions about responsibility. You can probably recall being in a group where the phrase, "I thought you were going to be responsible for that," was heard too frequently. The frustration implicit within that statement could have been avoided through planning the interaction on the procedural dimension. In other words, the group should not only prepare *what* they will discuss, but also *who* and *how*.

Orientation Behavior

Orientation statements are messages designed to facilitate the achievement of a group's goal. These messages really do not have an informational or interpersonal component, but they are very useful nonetheless. Orientation statements allow a group to examine its progress along the procedures it has developed. In a way, orientation statements serve as a road map of the group's discussions. As such, orientation statements keep the group progressing toward its goal. Here are some examples of orientation statements:

"Well, let's stop for a second and summarize where we are."

"That's a good point. Do we have any more information on that?"

"Can we go on to point C on our agenda?"

Researchers have found that orientation statements affect the consensus of the group (12, 19). In groups containing members who engage in high levels of orientation, the people are significantly closer to consensus than groups in which the orientation level is low. If consensus is a desirable goal, and we think it is in most instances, members should engage in orientation statements on the procedural dimension.

Orientation statements also influence the way others perceive you. In separate studies, researchers found that people who engage in orientation statements are viewed as credible participants by the other group members (19). People who make orientation statements are perceived by other group members as competent, trustworthy, dynamic, and objective. It is not surprising, therefore, that investigators found a relationship between leadership and orientation. Those who are perceived as leaders in groups engage in significantly more orientation behavior than nonleaders (20). In other words, the ability to keep a group headed toward its goal seems just as important to other group members as the ability to provide information in terms of facts, figures, opinions, and evidence.

Orientation statements are also useful in managing group conflict, a topic we will cover more extensively in Chapter 10. The procedural dimension serves as a vehicle to defuse the emotional friction normally associated with conflict. Groups containing people providing orientation reach higher levels of consensus and conflict management than groups whose members engage in low amounts of orientation.

ELEMENTS AFFECTING INTERPERSONAL TRANSACTIONS

In our day-to-day conversations, we permit others to exert influence over our decision-making practices. However, we are selective in choosing people with whom we associate. Those we permit to exert influence possess special characteristics. Sometimes we accept another's advice because we know they are especially informed or knowledgeable. We may conform to their opinions because they are members of the same club or political group. Other times we may accept their advice or opinions because of friendship ties. Certainly there are other reasons as well that we use to guide our acceptance of influence from others, but in each case our conformity depends on our attitudes toward the other person and our perception of the personal characteristics of that person.

Conformity to the comments and directives of others in task-oriented group deliberations reflects a similar pattern. Our responses to other members in the group reflect our attitudes toward the members and our perception of their traits (23). These attitudes and perceptions of other members reflect three basic dimensions of interpersonal behavior (4). We suggest that all interpersonal reactions incorporate the three issues of control, emotional tone, and task orientation.

Control Behavior

Control refers to the regularity with which some members initiate communication and the degree with which other members reinforce this initiative. The locus of control may be widely shared among group members or may reside in one or two members. The locus of control may also be a function of the specific activity of the group at that time period. When a group is discussing statistical matters, for example, Tom may be especially active, whereas when the discussion moves to the logical consideration of alternatives, Al may take the initiative. The two variables that relate to control behavior by some group members are perceptions of status and competence of the members.

Our perception of a group member's status relates to the characteristics and reputation the member brings to the group. Many persons hold physicians in high esteem for the reason that they are medical doctors. Positions within organizations are associated with different attributions of status. The president of a company is generally held in higher regard than a first-line supervisor. Status is also sometimes associated with arbitrary characteristics such as sex, age, or kinship (28). Regardless of the basis of our perception of status of group members, higher status members perform more control behavior than lower status members. In general, high-status group members initiate and receive more messages than low-status members (3, 11, 25). Hence, high-status members tend to exert greater influence over group deliberations than do low-status members. Berger and his colleagues have shown the centrality of the status variable in small group interaction. They concluded that when task-oriented group members are seen as differing in status because of some external characteristic (title, profession, etc.), this status difference determines the influence within the group whether or not the characteristic is related to the group's task (7). You may have witnessed this halo effect at one time or another. We have seen a well-known admiral exert considerable influence over educational policy in the United States. The basis of his influence over educational policy was his reputation as a naval officer. Physicians many times have considerable influence over decision making unrelated to medicine because they are medical doctors.

Obviously, the amount of influence exerted over group deliberations will not be the same for all members. Some members will have considerably more influence than others. We want to express a note of caution, however. One's reputation in one field does not necessarily qualify him or her as an expert in another field. This word of caution is not to say that a medical doctor cannot become an expert on urban transportation, for example. Our concern is that group members use an appropriate basis for permitting group members to exert greater amounts of influence over the group's deliberations. We believe that the appropriate basis for accepting influence is the group member's competence.

Member competence refers to the expertise one has in the content area related to the task. The competence of group members is central to the deliberations of task-oriented groups. The quality of contributions influences the effectiveness of the decision proposal and the pattern of interaction within the group. The behavior of a competent person includes presentation of relevant information before the group, providing direction, clarifying explicit and implicit assumptions in the material before the group, and summarizing and integrating the material before the group. In short, verbal facility reflecting relevant content and effective use of group process skills characterize the competent group member.

In one sense, the objective competence of group members determines the level of quality the group will achieve in reaching a decision proposal. Objective competence would include items such as level of general intelligence, training and experience related to the task, and assessment of peers regarding that person's ability. In forming task-oriented groups, these characteristics are generally considered. Nonetheless, the pattern of interaction within the group forms the basis for the subjective impression members come to make about each other. The determining factor is how one perceives the ability of other group members.

There are a number of potential pitfalls we can make when forming an impression of competence. The two most common are assuming that those who talk a lot are well informed and that those who agree with our own point of view are more competent than those who disagree with us.

The perception of a person's competence is often associated with how much he or she talks. In other words, those who talk a lot are thought to be knowledgeable. Certainly we need some information on which to go. Very quiet persons tell us very little about themselves, and we frequently assume that such persons may have limited ability. The relationship between frequency of talking and attribution of ability is well documented in the research literature (14, 26, 27). Perhaps in our day-to-day experience we come to associate ability with talkativeness. From a logical point of view this association may be one-sided. We simply are unaware of a quiet person's ability because we have so little information on which to go. As group members we cannot assume that quantity of talk is necessarily an indication of superior ability.

Perhaps it's only natural that we see those who agree with us as more intelligent or competent. In fact, those who take an extreme position on an issue that is in the same direction as our own belief are often seen as significantly more competent than those who take a moderate position. A person who takes an extreme position in the direction opposite to our own is many times seen as least competent (10, 17). Basing our assessment of competence on whether a person agrees or disagrees with us may indeed subvert the small group decision-making process. In practice, this method of assessing competence means that we will not be attentive to those who present views contrary to our own. Fortunately, there are a number of other more reliable cues we can use to determine level of member competence (21). Comments that are both concrete and abstract, comments that articulate assumptions group members are making when discussing the material, and asking intelligent and probing questions are indicators of competence. A member who shows a willingness to admit mistakes and who communicates a willingness to search (as opposed to having all the answers) is often seen as more competent. Finally, an expressed interest in working with others to achieve the group's goal, a desire to receive feedback from others, and a task orientation (as opposed to socializing) indicate competence.

A competent person wants to achieve, but mainly through democratic methods that value their motives and needs. This person is not very oriented to "human relations" and not very concerned with the social and prestige aspects of the group environment. Task performance is what interests the competent person, concrete tasks that can be achieved through nonauthoritarian interaction with others. This person is able to deal with concrete as well as abstract ideas as opposed to abstract ideas only.

Emotional Tone Behavior

We have suggested that behavior related to the control dimension of interaction determines the level of influence one will have during group deliberations. A second dimension that moderates the group's pattern of interaction is the emotional tone that emerges among group members. Emotional tone may be simply defined as the level of friendship that exists among group members. These feelings of friendliness (or lack of friendliness) may reflect warm-cold, harmonious-strained, or relaxed-tense feelings.

In our day-to-day encounters, one of the first qualities we notice about others is whether they appear friendly or cold. For the most part, we are attracted toward friendly persons and tend to avoid those that are unfriendly. This warm-cold impression constitutes one of the basic dimensions that determines our responses to others in social situations (1). An early study on person perception revealed that warm and cold constitute central traits that influence our impressions of others (2). Persons perceived as warm are also likely to be seen as generous, happy, good-natured, considerate of others, and imaginative (2, 18, 32). Persons perceived as cold are not so favorably described.

Our impression of another's friendliness influences the way we interact with others. Students were found in a study by Kelley (18) to participate more frequently in classroom discussions when the instructor appeared to be warm or friendly. Our level of participation with others tends to be strained and restricted when we sense hostile or unfriendly behavior. A pleasant interpersonal atmosphere creates a climate conducive to effective group interaction. When the atmosphere becomes unpleasant, we tend to withdraw from the discussion, doodle, lose interest in the task, or in other ways restrict our participation (13). Since one condition for effective group actions is an open exchange of information, interpersonal impressions that restrict participation inhibit effective movement of the group toward its goal. Some behaviors that reflect friendliness include comments showing enthusiasm, giving credit, and applauding the work of others. Unfriendly acts include showing indifference, displaying an impersonal demeanor, appearing secretive, blocking others participation, arbitrary commands, and appearing isolated or detached from the group (4).

If we consider friendly and unfriendly reactions as rewards and punishments in small group interaction, then the case for the value of a pleasant interpersonal atmosphere becomes even stronger. In one sense, friendliness engenders friendliness, and hostility generates hostility (6). A higher presence of rewards by one person results in more attempts by others to be rewarding (24). On the other hand, a higher presence of punishments given by one person encourages more attempts by others to be punishing. Hence to blame or admonish another group member may result in further unfriendliness, possibly diverting the group from making progress toward its goal.

A supportive atmosphere tends to be more productive than one in which persons are attacked or blamed. When a member is blamed or held responsible for a negative outcome, interaction patterns change that may in turn lower the quality of the group's decision proposal. Accused members are stigmatized and given less opportunity to participate. This unfriendly behavior diverts the group from task-relevant activities and may also lead to suppression of some opinions (29, 30).

Although a congenial atmosphere provides a base for effective group participation, like so many desirable conditions, the sword cuts both ways. The complaint that group members spend their time socializing is frequently voiced. When group members associate success with pleasant social relations instead of defining success by effective task effort, the group's potential productivity may not be realized (22). Aside from this diversion, desire by group members to maintain a pleasant atmosphere as an end in and of itself interferes with effective group interaction. Frequently, group members characterized by emotional supportiveness and warmth are correspondingly low on more task-oriented behaviors (4).

The pressures to maintain friendly social relations may also suppress the expression of minority opinions and disagreements. Concurrence seeking becomes so dominant in some groups that it overrides a realistic appraisal of information and alternatives before the group. In reference to this type of group, Janis (16) noted that "At their meetings, all the members are amiable and seek complete concurrence on every important issue, with no bickering or conflict to spoil the cozy 'we-feeling' atmosphere." One of the major barriers to effective group problem solving is behaviors that prevent the open expression of ideas. Diversity of viewpoints and ideational conflict promote more effective problem solving (15). A member's overriding interest in not rocking the boat for fear of creating interpersonal strain among group members often results in a lower quality outcome.

We trust that the issue is clear. Warm interpersonal communication within the group provides a foundation for open and free expression of ideas. A pleasant interpersonal climate, however, should not be confused with concurrence seeking at any price. The appropriate atmosphere supports the give and take associated with ideational conflicts and scrutiny of information. The ideal situation is where group members come to expect freedom from personal harrassment as well as freedom to critically analyze alternatives before the group.

Cooperative Behavior

The assessment of member competence and the creation of an appropriate interpersonal atmosphere are two of the three factors affecting interpersonal behavior in small groups. The third factor affecting interaction relates to the sense of cooperativeness that is engendered among group members. Each group member potentially has a unique contribution to make toward the achievement of the group's goal. As the group discusses issues related to the task, group members specialize in activities required to complete the task. Ideally, group members work toward fulfilling their responsibilities as well as possible. Under these circumstances, each member would place the welfare of the group on the same plane as his or her own welfare. If this orientation reflects the sense of the group members, then a cooperative atmosphere is obtained (9).

A cooperative atmosphere as opposed to a competitive climate best facilitates movement toward the group's goal (8). Some group members may, however, choose to take a competitive posture. A competitive orientation implies a member wants to do as well as he or she can for himself or herself and also wants to better other group members. In one sense, this member wants the credit for goal achievement and simultaneously wants it to appear that other group members failed to make worthwhile contributions to the group's task. The competitively oriented member is likely to take on responsibilities that legitimately belong to other group members. Between group competition may enhance the work of a group, but within group competition disrupts the group's activities and slows progress toward the group's goal.

Consent to become a member of a task-oriented group involves considerable risk. A member does not have full control over the group's discussion and eventual decision proposal. An effective decision proposal depends on the willingness of all members to make a conscientious effort toward fulfillment of the group's goal. If some members are not committed to a quality effort, then the final product will likely be inferior. An inferior product may adversely reflect on a member's reputation. Each member will invest considerable time in group discussions as the group moves toward its goal. Group members expect their investment of time to be wisely used, but in the end their effort may prove to be wasted.

The experience of interaction with the group may prove to be unpleasant. A part of this unpleasant exchange may result from challenges to one's beliefs and values. Perhaps some members of the group will simply be unfriendly toward others. Finally, there is always the possibility that the group will disintegrate and end in chaos. A member's acceptance of the potential risks involving task-oriented groups suggests a willingness to trust other members to do their part. The development of trust rests on the assurance that other members are committed to the task. Mutual trust not only depends on the belief that the others intend to fulfill their responsibilities, but also that they have the ability to perform their tasks.

The establishment of mutual trust is the first condition necessary for the development of a cooperative atmosphere (9). Given a base of mutual trust, characteristics of the task and anticipated interaction further the level of cooperation. The task characteristics include whether the task is significant, interesting, clear, and challenging. Elements of group interaction that are related to the development and maintenance of a cooperative atmosphere include the likelihood that the desired goal can be achieved only through member cooperation. Rewarding group meetings and the attractiveness of working with other members also influence one's level of cooperation.

The central focus of a highly cooperative group member is on commitment to task achievement. This member expects others to refrain from expressing negative feelings that would momentarily divert the group from attention to the task. He or she expects other members to check their individualistic tendencies and concentrate on requirements of the task. For this member, group unity is preserved through loyalty to the task rather than positive affectionate ties (4).

The comments of the highly cooperative member tend to be directed toward the group as a whole rather than to specific individuals. This member is rated high on giving opinions, giving direction, and analyzing the task, but is rated low on giving factual information. This member is also rated high on initiating comments and receiving comments and consequently has a central position in the interaction network. He or she is a serious figure in the group who seems neither friendly nor unfriendly and seldom shows tension or laughs. The comments of the highly cooperative member reflect his or her concern with achievement of the group's task.

Members who are rated high on expressing warmth and emotional supportiveness may have some difficulty in accepting the cooperative member's exclusive concern with the task. Members who are highly individualistic are also likely to encounter difficulty in working with the task-oriented cooperative member. These members are the most probable sources of interpersonal conflict with the cooperative member (4).

The uncooperative member is the mirror image of the cooperative member. This member is ambivalent toward the task and is rated low on initiating and receiving comments. He or she does not seek to influence the group, and his or her participation is seldom encouraged by other members. This member is rated high on showing tension and laughing and tends to "goof off" in the group. He or she is rated low on giving suggestions or opinions, although he or she may be high on giving factual information. The uncooperative member exercises a more or less silent restraining influence on the group and may be the recipient of hostile forces (4). It is apparent that the uncooperative member would irritate the cooperative member, potentially leading to interpersonal conflict. The contribution of the uncooperative member may be to create a less serious atmosphere and to force the group to examine assumptions made by the group members as they move toward a decision proposal.

We have suggested that the interpersonal dimension of small group interaction reflects the perceptions and attitudes members form of one another. These perceptions and attitudes relate to the pattern of influence exerted by group members, the expression of friendliness, and the manifestation of a cooperative attitude. The interpersonal dimension of small group interaction does not dictate the content of the group's interaction, but much like the procedural dimension, determines the pattern and tone of the group's deliberations.

SUMMARY

The procedural dimension of small group interaction relates to co-ordination and organization of group members' efforts toward goal achievement. This type of behavior includes such activities as agenda setting, planning communication responsibilities, and division of labor. Orientation statements help the group to be aware of its progress as well as what activities should be undertaken at that point in the group's life span. Orientation statements also help the group to manage conflict. The procedural dimension can be thought of as the group's guidance system.

The interpersonal dimension relates to the attitudes group members hold toward one another and to the perception of member traits. Control behavior refers to the regularity with which some members initiate communication, that is, control the flow of interaction. Our willingness to reinforce this behavior rests on our perception of the status and competence of our fellow members. Emotional tone of our group's deliberations relates to the level of friendliness that exists among group members. A pleasant interpersonal atmosphere creates a supportive base for effective group interaction. A sense of cooperativeness reflects the third factor of interpersonal behavior. Cooperative behavior reflects the attitude that the welfare of the group is placed on the same level as the welfare of individual members. The central focus of the cooperative person is on commitment to achievement of the group's goals. The interpersonal dimension of small group interaction does not provide the substance for completion of the task nor guidance for achieving the group's goals. The primary importance of the interpersonal dimension is to provide a supportive base for the effective exchange of messages about information and procedural matters.

CONCLUSIONS AND RECOMMENDATIONS

1. The creation of an agenda permits the members to assess progress toward their goal.
2. A sense of progress toward goal achievement results in higher levels of member satisfaction.
3. Planning communication responsibilities results in a more efficient use of group resources.
4. Groups containing members who engage in high levels of orientation behavior have a greater probability of achieving consensus.
5. Group members who make orientation statements are perceived by other members as credible participants.
6. Higher status members perform more control behavior than lower status members.
7. Attribution of high levels of status is often based on member characteristics unrelated to the group's task.
8. An appropriate basis for permitting group members to exert greater levels of influence is a member's competence.
9. A possible pitfall in assessing member competence is to assume that those who talk a lot are competent.
10. Sometimes our perception of member competence is based on whether or not he or she agrees with us.
11. A reliable means of assessing member competence is to consider that person's informational and procedural comments.
12. One of the first impressions we make about others is whether they are friendly or unfriendly.
13. A friendly interpersonal atmosphere tends to facilitate the exchange of messages among group members.

14. Blaming members for undesirable group outcomes tends to restrict the exchange of messages.
15. A cooperative atmosphere as opposed to a competitive climate best facilitates movement toward the group's goals.
16. The establishment of mutual trust is necessary for the development of a cooperative climate.
17. The cooperative person focuses on the group's task rather than the individualistic tendencies of group members.
18. The overriding concern of the cooperative member with the group's task may result in interpersonal conflicts.

REFERENCES

1. Michael Argyle, *Social Interaction* (New York: Atherton Press, 1969).
2. Solomon Asch, "Forming Impressions of Personality," *Journal of Abnormal and Social Psychology* 41 (1946): 258–290.
3. Kurt Back, "Influence Through Social Communication," *Journal of Abnormal and Social Psychology* 46 (1951): 9–24.
4. Robert F. Bales, *Personality and Interpersonal Behavior* (New York: Holt, Rinehart and Winston, 1970).
5. Bernard M. Bass and Harold J. Leavitt, "Some Experiments in Planning and Operating," *Management Science* 9 (1963): 574–585.
6. Mae Bell, "The Effects of Substantive and Affective Conflict in Problem-Solving Groups," *Speech Monographs* 41 (1974): 12–23.
7. Joseph Berger, Bernard P. Cohen, and Morris Zelditch, Jr., "Status Characteristics and Social Interaction," *American Sociological Review* 37 (1972): 241–255.
8. Morton Deutsch, "An Experimental Study of the Effects of Cooperation and Competition Upon Group Process," *Human Relations* 2 (1949): 199–232.
9. Morton Deutsch, "Cooperation and Trust: Some Theoretical Notes," *Nebraska Symposium on Motivation* 10 (1962): 275–320.
10. Richard Eisinger and Judson Mills, "Perception of Sincerity and Competence of a Communicator as a Function of the Extremity of His Position," *Journal of Experimental Social Psychology* 4 (1968): 224–232.
11. Harold Gerard, "Some Effects of Status, Role Clarity and Group Goal Clarity upon the Individual's Relations to Group Process," *Journal of Personality* 25 (1957): 475–488.
12. Dennis S. Gouran, "Variables Related to Consensus in Group Discussions of Questions of Policy," *Speech Monographs* 39 (1972): 16–22.
13. Harold Guetzbow and John Gyr, "An Analysis of Conflict in Decision-Making Groups," *Human Relations* 7 (1954): 367–382.

14. Donald P. Hayes and Leo Meltzer, "Interpersonal Judgments Based on Talkativeness: I. Factor Artifact?" *Sociometry* 35 (1972): 538–561.

15. Richard L. Hoffman, "Group Problem Solving," in Leonard Berkowitz (ed.), *Advances in Experimental Social Psychology*, vol. 2 (New York: Academic Press, 1965), pp. 99–132.

16. Irving Janis, "Groupthink," *Psychology Today* 5 (1971): 43–46 and 74–76.

17. Jerald M. Jellison and Deborah Davis, "Relationships Between Perceived Ability and Attitude Extremity," *Journal of Personality and Social Psychology* 27 (1973): 430–436.

18. Harold H. Kelley, "The Warm-Cold Variable in First Impressions of Persons," *Journal of Personality* 18 (1950): 431–439.

19. Thomas J. Knutson, "An Experimental Study of the Effects of Orientation Behavior on Small Group Consensus," *Speech Monographs* 39 (1972): 159–165.

20. Thomas J. Knutson and William E. Holdridge, "Orientation Behavior, Leadership and Consensus: A Possible Functional Relationship," *Speech Monographs* 42 (1975): 107–114.

21. Abraham K. Korman et. al., "Perceived Characteristics of 'Competent' People," *Journal of Vocational Behavior* 3 (1973): 145–152.

22. Joseph E. McGrath, "The Influence of Positive Interpersonal Relations on Adjustment and Effectiveness in Rifle Teams," *Journal of Abnormal and Social Psychology* 65 (1962): 365–375.

23. Joseph E. McGrath, "A Descriptive Model for the Study of Interpersonal Relations in Small Groups," *Journal of Psychological Studies* 14 (1964): 89–116.

24. Norman Miller, Donald C. Butler, and James A. McMartin, "The Ineffectiveness of Punishment Power in Group Interaction," *Sociometry* 32 (1969): 24–42.

25. S. Frank Miyamoto, Laura Crowell, and Allan Katcher, "Communication Behavior in Small Discussion Groups," *Journal of Communication* 7 (1957): 151–160.

26. C. Robert Regula and James W. Julian, "The Impact of Quality and Frequency of Task Contributions on Perceived Ability," *Journal of Social Psychology* 89 (1973): 115–122.

27. Henry W. Riecken, "The Effects of Talkativeness on Ability to Influence Group Solutions of Problems," *Sociometry* 21 (1958): 309–321.

28. Marvin E. Shaw, *Group Dynamics: The Psychology of Small Group Behavior*, 2nd ed. (New York: McGraw-Hill, 1976.)

29. Marvin E. Shaw and G. R. Breed, "Effects of Attribution of Responsibility for Negative Events on Behavior in Small Groups," *Sociometry* 33 (1970): 382–393.

30. Marvin E. Shaw and Trueman R. Tremble, Jr., "Effects of Attribution of Responsibility for a Negative Event to a Group Member upon Group

Process as a Function of the Structure of the Event," *Sociometry* 34 (1971): 504–514.

31. Gerald H. Shure, Miles S. Rogers, Ida M. Larson, and Jack Tassone, "Group Planning and Task Effectiveness," *Sociometry* 25 (1962): 263–282.

32. Julius Wishner, "Reanalysis of 'Impressions of Personality'," *Psychological Review* 67 (1960): 96–112.

3

GROUP STRUCTURE

As groups continue to meet over time, members come to anticipate the reactions and behaviors of other group members. Members work out their roles with their group. Roles are the common expectations we hold about the behavior of ourselves and others in our group. Over time, we tend to consistently perform our role in our group. As members work out their roles in the group, norms develop as well. Norms are expectations about what members ought to do and believe. We refer to group structure as the roles and norms that emerge in a group. When stable roles fail to develop, groups tend to have difficulties in completing their task. Norms also guide and regulate member behavior. Appropriate norms facilitate the group in successfully completing its task. Inappropriate norms tend to interfere with successful task completion. It is the responsibility of each group member to see that appropriate norms emerge in her or his group. Another part of group structure is the members' attraction to the group. Group cohesiveness often facilitates the exchange and processing of information, but it also may inhibit effective information processing. Sometimes members are fearful of "rocking the boat" and consequently do not intelligently discuss their task.

An understanding of this section should enable you to help your group effectively mobilize its member resources and to assist your group in developing effective work norms.

CHAPTER 5

Process of Role Emergence

INTRODUCTION

As a group continues to meet, each person in the group develops a pattern of interaction that others come to rely on and expect. Your group may look to Joe or Marsha to crack a joke during a tense period. You learn to depend on Jerry and Mary to thoroughly research your topic and report their findings to the group. You look to Ray and Diane to guide your group, give direction, and encourage quiet members to speak up. Most clubs and other social organizations have elected positions. You expect the president to take charge of meetings. The treasurer is in charge of the group's finances. The minutes of the group's meetings are taken by the secretary. These expected behaviors have emerged over time and are accepted by the group members. In fact, if members behave unexpectedly confusion will likely occur. If the secretary decided to run the meeting instead of the president, group members would be upset and disoriented. We have been describing roles that group members take on in groups. Roles refer to the common set of expectations group members have about behavior of its members.

FUNCTIONS NECESSARY FOR EFFECTIVE GROUP PROCESS

Every group structures itself into various roles. A role is a composite of functions important to the group for achieving goals. Functions refer to specific behaviors, such as tension release or information giving, that are necessary for completion of the group's task. A person may take on more than one function in a group providing the group reinforces those behaviors. A group with too few functions tends to develop problems in completing its task. The group may not have the necessary member abilities to complete their task. Steiner (23) indicates that the potential productivity of a group is a function of task demands and group resources. When the member roles do not encompass the necessary functions, the group may have developed its roles too narrowly. Knutson and Holdridge (13) found that when too many people perform the same function (in this case trying to perform leadership functions), the group had trouble reaching agreement on their task. Perhaps a reason for this finding involved too few functions related to the informational and interpersonal dimensions of group interaction. A group whose roles encompass a diversity of behaviors on all three dimensions of group interaction will be more effective in reaching a successful conclusion to its task.

An exhaustive list of all potential functions would be difficult to compile. Some functions, however, are quite common to groups (2).

One useful means for listing common functions is to look at the informational, procedural, and interpersonal needs of a group.

Informational Functions

1. Creative analysis of task. Comments that suggest ways to define the task, different ways of thinking about the task, or suggestions regarding the most important dimensions of the task.
2. Information giving. Comments that relate statements of fact, or statements of opinion and advice based on authoritative sources.
3. Opinion giving. Comments that clarify the values pertinent to the group's task or propose what values the group should adopt in reaching a decision proposal.
4. Evaluation and criticism. Comments that evaluate the adequacy of the information before the group and the adequacy of the group's analysis of the task.
5. Elaboration. Comments that clarify, extend, or support statements of fact, opinion, or advice made by group members.
6. Integration. Comments that show relationships among the statements of fact, opinion, or advice made by group members.

Procedural Functions

1. Eliciting communication. Comments that encourage group members to relate their research and opinions to the group.
2. Delegating and directing action. Comments that organize the group's activity including assigning responsibilities to group members.
3. Summarizing group activity. Comments that summarize what has occurred, indicate level of progress of the group toward its goal, or show deviation from group goals.
4. Conflict management. Comments that help to resolve informational disagreements or resolve differences about procedures and goals.
5. Process evaluation. Comments that assess the effectiveness of the group's discussion pattern, work habits, and decision-making rules.
6. Tension release. Comments that reduce primary tension or comments that reduce tension associated with conflicts.

Interpersonal Functions

1. Positive reinforcement. Comments that praise, offer commendation, or in other ways reinforce the work and behavior of other group members.

2. Solidarity. Comments that express interpersonal warmth, friendliness, and group comradeship among members.
3. Cooperativeness. Comments that indicate commitment to the group goal and significance of the group's activity.
4. Respect toward others. Comments that reinforce the self-esteem of group members.

The role structure of your group should contain functions that reflect each of the three dimensions of group interaction. Most successful groups will have members who have acquired multifaceted roles. Several studies support the notion that roles should include functions drawn from the informational and interpersonal dimensions (1, 5, 6). These researchers combined informational and procedural functions into a general task dimension. Taken as a whole, the studies suggest the desirability of a role structure that encompasses functions from all three dimensions of small group interaction. You are no doubt familiar with the phrase, "Too many cooks spoil the broth." Another way of looking at this proverb from a small group communication perspective involves the recognition that if too many members try to behave in the same way, then group productivity will fall. In order to increase group effectiveness, members should recognize the advantage of diversifying the group members' responsibilities.

One word of caution about essential functions in the small group: beware of what kinds of behaviors you reinforce. We have noted the need for diversity of roles and we have suggested that roles emerge through a process of reinforcement. Frequently, when a group begins to work on a specific task, some members may engage in behaviors potentially harmful to the group's successful completion of its task. If these behaviors are reinforced, negative functions may emerge. One function dangerous to group success involves dismissal. If a group member says, "This is a stupid question and we will never solve this problem" and another member of the group reinforces that observation either by agreement or silence, the dismissal function may emerge. The group has the time and ability to solve the problem, but because of the negative behavior of one member, the group will have trouble reaching its goal. The goal of the group can be dismissed unless the members are cautious in reinforcing behaviors that will assist the group rather than harm the group.

We cannot specifically describe the roles you must have in order to experience successful group communication. You should remember, however, that a diversity of roles typically benefits a group. Roles should incorporate functions from the informational, procedural, and interpersonal dimensions of the group. You should also be cautious in reinforcing behavior that may eventually harm the group.

PROCESS OF ROLE EMERGENCE

When you first meet as a group, much of the initial tension surrounding the meeting is caused by an inability to make effective predictions about the behavior of others in the group. Roles have not emerged. Members try out certain behaviors to determine if they will be acceptable to the other group members. This process of "trial and error," necessary for the emergence of roles, frequently makes for a rather uneasy initial encounter. This condition, called primary tension (3), continues until people in the group develop some minimal abilities to make predictions about how other group members will behave. Hare (12) views the early stages of a group discussion as a period in which the discussants try to find out what each person brings to the situation and how each person plans to use what he or she brings. This initial process is characterized by a degree of tension as the group members **try** to get to know each other. The communication during the early stages reflects caution and reservation. In a way, this whole set of uneasiness results whenever we are becoming acquainted with new people. Primary tension may also occur when we meet people we already know, but under new and different circumstances. One of the reasons few people enjoy being the first guests to arrive at a party involves a desire to enter a group in which roles have already begun to emerge. Obviously, if you happen to be the first person to show up at a party, roles will not yet have emerged. The emergence of roles enables the prediction of the behavior of others. To the extent these predictions are reasonably accurate, the tension and uneasiness we feel dissipates. We know of no magic formula to handle this tension except to recognize that this initial uneasiness marks the beginning of the process of role emergence.

Group structure begins to emerge in a small group as the members tentatively discuss issues related to their task. These initial comments about the task and the emergence of roles go hand in hand. Members may complain or think that the group is wasting time. "No one knows what to do" captures the feeling during this time of role emergence. In fact, a great deal of progress is being made toward successful completion of your group's task. You are learning how to behave in this group and what you can expect from others in the group. There is a danger, however, that faces groups during this time of orientation and formation. (See Chapter 2 for discussion of these two phases.) The group may try to proceed too quickly. One of the authors recalls a sad experience while in elementary school. The teacher would occasionally form study groups under the assumption that groups would automatically benefit the individual students. Shortly after the groups began their discussion, it was not unusual to hear the teacher inquire, "What's the matter with you people? Stop horsing around and work on your job!" This sort of comment not only caused the students needless anxiety and tension, but it also seriously interfered with the development of the various group role structures. What appeared to the teacher as irresponsible behavior was in fact an attempt by the group members to become acquainted with the skills of each other needed to solve the problem. The teacher really forced the children to begin working before they knew what they could do. This condition, lack of roles, produces considerable frustration in groups.

Groups are usually formed to achieve some goal. People do not randomly organize themselves into groups for no apparent purpose. The task influences the manner in which the group role structure emerges; successful completion of the group's task requires a group structure. Shaw and Gilchrist (22) report a study of group problem solving in which the members very quickly recognized their need to organize in a way that would enable effective group performance. For a group to achieve serious task achievement, therefore, some kind of organization must be apparent.

As we note in Chapter 7, groups provide a means for individuals to achieve satisfaction. In order to attain this satisfaction, members of groups need to decide what kind of behavior is suitable for each specific group member. These distinctions about the roles in the group characterize all groups (9). The group begins to structure the various roles of its members as it begins to work toward completion of the group task. The process of role emergence begins as the members perceive each other's attributes during the discussion. The group, through reinforcement of individual behaviors, actually determines or teaches the roles that emerge. Certain members begin to specialize and work out their roles with the other group members. The process of working out the various member's specialties is referred to as the process of role emergence.

A member of a group engages in certain behaviors. The other group members react to these behaviors. If the reaction tends to be positive, the likelihood that the person will repeat the behavior becomes fairly high. As the person continues the behavior, her or his role begins to emerge. Remember, we defined a role as a pattern of expected behavior. From experience you know that the best predictor of future behavior is past behavior. As a person tries out a role behavior, is reinforced by the other group members, and repeats the role behavior because of reinforcement, the remaining group members begin to expect this person to behave in a similar fashion in the future. As the group begins to expect certain behaviors from each member, roles emerge and the group structure develops. For example, imagine yourself in a group for the first time. As we have already seen, tension operates on a fairly high level during the process of acquaintance. One of the ways of dealing with this preacquaintance tension involves humor. You might tell a joke or make a humorous remark and find that the other members of your group laugh and generally encourage your behavior. Because of the reaction to your remark, you decide to make another humorous remark that is also reinforced by the laughter of your colleagues. You can feel the tension lifting, an inherently reinforcing event, and the other group members begin to see you as playing the role of tension-reliever. To the extent you want this role and to the extent others want you to have this role, the role of tension-reliever will be one of your group responsibilities. When the group experiences tension on future occasions, you will be expected by virtue of your past reinforced behavior to assist the group in reducing tension.

The roles in which we engage in small groups vary as the nature of the group varies. You cannot expect, for example, to behave as the tension-reliever in every group you join. Someone else may be better at fulfilling that role. You should, however, seek to behave in a role that is perceived by the other group members as beneficial to the group's ultimate success. In short, you need to find through discussion with the other participants the kinds of abilities you have that can best serve the group. Your role in groups, therefore, will vary as a function of the group to which you belong. You can see how your roles vary from group to group by thinking about the groups to which you already belong. In one group you may be very serious and provide considerable information. In another group you may joke around more. In short, we behave differently depending on the group with which we happen to be. The reason for this variance in role behavior involves the notion of learning and reinforcement. Different groups need your different skills for different reasons in different ways.

As we see them, roles are not formal positions to which group members are elected or appointed. Roles emerge in the group as a function of individual behavior and subsequent group reinforcement. When the group first meets, members try out various behaviors and the group encourages or discourages these actions. As a behavior is reinforced, the group member learns that he or she is expected to act in a certain rewarding fashion. The group typically rewards behavior perceived as helpful or beneficial to the group.

EMERGENCE OF LEADERSHIP

Of all the roles available in a small group, the leader occupies a special position. Probably because of the importance of this role, researchers have devoted considerable effort to understanding leaders and leadership. First of all, let us draw a distinction between leaders and leadership. The term "leader" refers to a person behaving in a specific role and is often limited to one person per group. "Leadership" refers to a general study of how leaders lead. We think that this distinction is important because it reflects a common misconception: one leader per group. We take the position that leadership in a small group can be best visualized as a potential role for any group member. Each group member should be made to feel that he or she can provide leadership for the group. In fact, each group member should be prepared to take the role of leader whenever the group may require that role behavior.

A person behaving as leader is engaging in role behavior. As such, the emergence of a leader follows the same guidelines of role emergence that we discussed above. The leader possesses necessary skills and abilities that are reinforced by the group. In order to become a leader, a person must want to lead, must have certain needed skills, and must be reinforced by the group. This section of the chapter examines the skills needed by leaders and the degree to which each group member engages in leadership.

In order to operate as a leader in the small group, a person must engage in some observable, identifiable behaviors that the other group members identify and reinforce. The identification and reinforcement of these leadership behaviors causes the emergence of a leader (7). Probably the most frequent identification of leadership involves participation (16). That is, the person identified as the emergent group leader also communicates most frequently with most of the other group members (13). Morris and Hackman (18) suggest that the emergent leader may not necessarily be the person who talks most in a group, but he or she is always among the high participatory members. In order to be identified as a leader, then, the group member must communicate. Based on the research, one conclusion appears certain. You cannot expect to emerge as a leader if you remain silent.

It would be rather naive for us to assume that the person who talks a lot will always become leader. Remember our basic notion of role emergence. The leader must say something which benefits the group. Let us now turn to some specific behaviors you can employ to identify and reinforce an emergent leader. If you want to be a group leader, you can engage in these behaviors; if you would rather not be a group leader, you can reinforce the behavior of others that falls into the leader role.

On the informational dimension of small group communication, the leader initiates themes (14, 19). During the initial stages of group deliberation, several people will initiate themes for the group to pursue.

The person who analyzes the situation in a way that makes sense to the group will emerge as a group leader. That is, the group reinforces the behavior that best helps it achieve its goal. This observation points to the necessity for preparation prior to the group discussion, a topic we discussed in Chapter 3. If you wish to emerge as a leader by using the informational dimension, you must have sufficient information to initiate group themes.

The leader who emerges in the group most frequently operates primarily on the procedural dimension of small group communication. In fact, most of the behaviors associated with leader emergence are found on the procedural dimension (19). Knutson and Holdridge (13) found that the people who emerge as leaders engage in significantly more orientation communication than do those who do not emerge as leaders. The leader has a rather strong concern for the manner in which the group discusses issues. The emergent leader encourages participation, keeps track of group progress, and generally assists the group to reach its goal. You may have been in groups in which the leader did not know very much about the specific content or substance of a problem but did know quite a bit about organizing the information presented by other group members. In a way, the President of the United States performs this type of leadership. One person could not possibly possess sufficient information about all governmental agencies. Consequently, the president forms a cabinet of people responsible for specific aspects of the government. The president's job, as leader of the government, involves organizing the contributions of the other members into an effective political program. The point here is not that the president lacks information, but that the primary presidential job requires a person capable of organizing the facts into a clear set of procedures. In a small group discussion, the group often sees the person capable of operating effectively on the procedural dimension as the emergent leader.

On the interpersonal dimension, the emergent leader tends to place the group goal beyond her or his personal goals. Stogdill (24) found that leaders tend to be more sociable than nonleaders. The leaders were more cooperative, dependable, popular, and engaged in considerable social behavior. This behavior is very helpful during the initial stages of a group's meeting. Other research suggests that leaders tend to be more agreeable than nonleaders (17, 21). To the extent agreement acts as a reinforcer, leaders should agree with the behaviors deemed valuable to the group's purpose.

In addition to the actual behaviors engaged in by group members who emerge as leaders, recent research has investigated why members interact so frequently with the emergent leader. Lashbrook (15) using

Gibb's (10) interaction theory of leadership as a base for her idea, suggested that "... an individual will interact most with the member whom he perceives to have the most positive attributes for the group task situation" (p. 310). Consequently, she sought to identify the characteristics perceived by group members that distinguish leaders from those who did not emerge as the group's leader. In order to identify these characteristics, she observed several groups who interacted for three-week periods. After these discussion periods, members of the groups evaluated one another on a variety of instruments designed to measure each group member's perceptions or attitudes toward other group members. She found three perceptual characteristics that discriminated leaders from those who did not emerge as leaders: task attraction, character, and extroversion. In task attraction, leaders were perceived as dependable and members were confident that the leader would get things done without "goofing-off" on the job. These behaviors correspond roughly to our informational and procedural dimensions. The group members distinguished leaders from other members in terms of character by their perception that leaders were just, good, and unselfish; perceptions related to the interpersonal dimension. Not surprisingly, in light of our previous comment that leaders interact more than other members, Lashbrook found that group members perceived leaders to be more verbal, bold, and talkative. In other words, leaders are perceived by other group members to be people the members would like to work with on a task. Leaders are also perceived as extroverted and possessing high character. If you are able to influence the perceptions of other group members along these dimensions, you will more likely emerge as the group's leader. By the same token, if someone else in your group is perceived by you in this fashion, you will probably support that individual as your group's leader.

In summary, people who emerge as group leaders tend to initiate group themes, provide procedural guidelines, and contribute to a pleasant interpersonal environment. They are also perceived by other members as having high task commitment, extroversion, and character. Geier (11) has proposed that the emergence of leaders entails two phases. The selection of a leader during these phases seems to follow a "principle of residues." That is, those who are not qualified to lead the group are gradually eliminated. During phase one, those who are obviously unqualified for the group's leader are eliminated. These include members who appear uninformed about the group's task and those who do not participate in the group's discussion. Members who tend to be rigid in their comments, overly directive, and offensive in their verbalization are also typically eliminated during phase one. During phase two, typically two members are still in contention for the leader's role. These contenders acquire a supporter. The supporting member reinforces the suggestions and comments of the contender. The group then selects the individual that initiates the most attractive group themes, seems most skillful at guiding the group, and expresses greater concern for the group. If the group members have been sensitive to the comments of the contenders, the best available person should emerge as the group leader.

The leader, therefore, is a group member who arrives at this role through her or his interacting with the other group members. The leader performs several functions for the group: considerable interaction, theme initiation, procedural guidance, and social reinforcement. People in the group are attracted to work with the leader by virtue of her or his task ability, extroversion, and character. The leader of a group emerges just as other group roles emerge, that is, through a process of reinforcement. You should probably recognize that anyone in the group can perform these functions. The person eventually agreed upon by the group as its leader is the member who performs a majority of these behaviors over a period of time.

We have identified the types of behaviors and perceptions that tend to result in leadership emergence. The success of a specific leader, however, depends on a variety of other factors: the nature of the task, the relationship between the group members, and the style with which the leader directs the group (8). The nature of the task requires that group members be capable of analyzing information peculiar to the task. For example, if a group were concerned about the regulations for the preservation and sale of fresh meat and one of the participants happened to be a butcher, the butcher would have considerable insight regarding the task. That is, the nature of the task makes some group members more suitable as leaders than other group members. In the same fashion, the relationship between the group members influences who will be leader. If you belong to a group in which several members happen to be friends, you will probably not emerge as the group leader until you are able to demonstrate your friendship to the other group members. In addition to the nature of the task and the member selections, the style used will influence the success of the leader. If a person employs a directive approach in a group in which nondirective leadership is most appropriate, the group will probably not arrive at a successful solution to their task.

The point we are making is that leadership is a highly complex subject dependent on many factors. You should recognize that certain situations may occur in which you would like to emerge as leader, but for the good of the group you probably should avoid leadership. In addition, remember that you cannot expect the same person to perform as leader in every group. The precise nature of the leader depends on the group's reinforcement of some behaviors as opposed to others. The butcher who may emerge as a leader in the group discussing the regulation of fresh meat sales would probably not emerge as a leader of a group discussing U.S. foreign policy. Remember, too, that everyone in the group should have a chance to exercise leadership at some point during the group deliberations. Shared leadership is not only desirable from a member satisfaction point of view, but also possible because of the vast array of complex interactions that produce the group leader.

RELATIONSHIP OF ROLE STABILIZATION AND GROUP EFFECTIVENESS

You now have some idea about the emergence of roles in a group and the roles necessary for effective group process. You also know something about leadership, an important role in any group. Remember that all groups working on tasks structure themselves into roles [9]. We have defined a role as a set of behaviors expected from a person in a group. Bormann [3] found that after a varying period of time, group members began to specialize in performing certain roles. This section of the chapter discusses the manner in which roles stabilize for the most effective group performance.

As a group develops a history, we have seen that certain roles emerge to enable the group to complete its task. Individual group members begin to learn what other participants expect of her or his ability to engage in specific role behaviors. As these roles begin to stabilize for a certain task, the group is better able to perform and function effectively. In fact, Gibb [10] defines a group as "... a system of interactions within which a structure emerges by the development of relatively stable expectations for the behavior of each member" (p. 270). If the roles do not stabilize, conflict may occur and the group may spend valuable time attempting to figure out what is expected of the participants. Steiner [23] refers to this condition as "process loss." That is, when members of a group do not clearly differentiate among their roles, the unique qualifications of each respective member do not become apparent. Much of the group's time is spent deciding who will do what instead of clearly analyzing the informational content of its task. When process loss occurs, members have difficulty assessing their progress toward the group goal, and consequently, member satisfaction decreases [20]. Role stabilization, therefore, increases a group's progress toward its goal as well as the members' satisfaction.

Stabilization of roles in a group is a good indicator that the individual member's needs are being met (4). Remember that people frequently join groups to fill certain needs. If the roles stabilize, one can be virtually certain that those needs are being fulfilled through rewarding roles. Not only do stabilized roles demonstrate need fulfillment, but also stabilization of roles itself is a reward. People fit in. Members know what to do. Individual abilities are recognized, expected, and appreciated. In the Minnesota Studies, Bormann (3) found that role stabilization increased the group's attraction for its members. Think of one of the groups to which you belong and toward which you feel attracted. Probably your attraction stems from a fair knowledge of what you are expected to do and how the other group members will react. An important consequence of role stabilization involves the decrease in tension associated with trying to make reasonably accurate predictions about the behavior of others in the group.

Two factors produce role stabilization: (1) the individual members perceive their respective roles as satisfying their needs, and (2) the group makes progress toward its goal and, hence, individual roles are reinforced. If the members' roles satisfy members' needs but the group fails to solve its problem or make progress toward its goal, roles will change. In addition, if the group makes progress toward its goal but members are dissatisfied with their roles, group members will change their expected behaviors. In other words, for role stabilization to occur, the members must behave in roles that satisfy their needs. These roles must also be clearly linked to a group task achievement. We know of a medical group consisting of physicians, nurses, and social workers that clearly demonstrated the problems of a failure to achieve role stabilization. The social workers were consistently reminded of their "low status" by the physicians and never really perceived themselves as behaving in ways essential to the group's success. After a couple of consulting sessions, each of the group members began to see her or his responsibility as necessary for group task completion. Only after this realization did the roles stabilize and the group start to operate as a team.

SUMMARY

Roles are the set of behaviors our fellow group members come to expect us to perform in a small group. Group members acquire their roles through a process of positive and negative reinforcement during the group's early discussions. If a member receives a positive reaction to his or her behavior, then he or she is likely to incorporate that behavior into his or her group role.

Certain behaviors must be performed to enable the group to achieve its goal. Information must be introduced, discussed, and integrated. The activity of the group must be coordinated and directed. Conflicts need to be resolved. Members need to find the interaction interpersonally rewarding. Hence, for a group to operate effectively, informational, procedural, and interpersonal functions must be represented in member roles. This specialization enables the group to effectively use its resources.

The leadership role occupies a central position in the group's role structure. Leaders tend to rate high on introducing task themes, participation, and guiding and directing the group. The emergence of a leader in a small group generally follows a two-phase pattern. During the first phase members who show no interest in becoming the group's leader or who are otherwise unqualified to be the group's leader are eliminated from contention. During the second phase, the contender who seems best suited for the leader role emerges as the group leader. The emergence of a member as the group leader is dependent upon the skills and knowledge of the member, the nature of the task, and individuals in the group. A person suited for the leadership role in one group may not be the best choice in a second group.

Stabilization of the role structure in a small group enables the group to function more effectively. Members know what is expected of them and what to expect of others. Stabilization of the role structure suggests that members find their role fulfilling and that the role structure facilitates achievement of the group's goal.

CONCLUSIONS AND RECOMMENDATIONS

1. Roles refer to the common set of expectations group members hold about the behavior of its members.
2. Primary tension refers to the uneasy feelings members experience when members are unsure about how to react to other members or when they are unsure of how other members will react to them.
3. Roles emerge in a small group through a process of interaction and reinforcement.
4. The role one acquires in a group is dependent on his or her abilities, group membership, and the nature of the task.
5. A member's role encompasses one or more functions.
6. Groups whose roles encompass informational, procedural, and interpersonal functions will be more effective in achieving goals than groups whose roles do not encompass functions from all three dimensions.

7. Group leaders tend to be rated high in participation, introduction of task themes, delegating and directing action, and commitment to group goals.
8. A group leader acquires his or her role through a process of elimination.
9. The emergence of a group leader is a function of his or her skills and knowledge, group membership, and the nature of the task.
10. Stabilization of member roles is a good indicator that member needs and group goals are being met.

REFERENCES

1. Robert F. Bales, "Task Roles and Social Roles in Problem-Solving Groups," in Eleanor E. Maccoby (ed.), *Readings in Social Psychology,* 3rd ed. (New York: Henry Holt, 1958), pp. 437–447.
2. Kenneth D. Benne and Paul Sheats, "Functional Roles of Group Members," *Journal of Social Issues* 4 (1948): 41–49.
3. Ernest G. Bormann, *Discussion and Group Methods: Theory and Practice,* 2nd ed. (New York: Harper and Row, 1975).
4. Norman M. Bradburn, "The Cultural Context of Personality Theory," in Joseph M. Wepman and Ralph W. Heine (eds.), *Concepts of Personality* (Chicago: Aldine, 1963), pp. 333–360.
5. Peter J. Burke, "The Development of Task and Social-Emotional Role Differentiation," *Sociometry* 30 (1967): 379–392.
6. Peter J. Burke, "Role Differentiation and the Legitimation of Task Activity," *Sociometry* 31 (1968): 404–411.
7. Launor F. Carter, "On Defining Leadership," in Muzafer Sherif and M. O. Wilson (eds.), *Group Relations at the Crossroads* (New York: Harper and Row, 1953), pp. 262–265.
8. Fred E. Fiedler, "A Contingency Model of Leadership Effectiveness," in Leonard Berkowitz, ed., *Advances in Experimental Social Psychology,* vol. 1 (New York: Academic Press, 1964), pp. 150–191.
9. Cecil A. Gibb, "An Interactional View of the Emergence of Leadership," *Australian Journal of Psychology* 10 (1958): 101–110.
10. Cecil A. Gibb, "Leadership," in Gardner Lindzey and Elliot Aronson, eds., *Handbook of Social Psychology,* vol. 4 (Reading, Mass.: Addison-Wesley, 1969), pp. 205–282.
11. John Geier, "A Trait Approach to the Study of Leadership," *Journal of Communication* 17 (1967): 316–323.
12. A. Paul Hare, "Editor's Forward," *Sociological Inquiry* 41 (1971): 133–139.
13. Thomas J. Knutson and William E. Holdridge, "Orientation Behavior, Leadership, and Consensus: A Possible Functional Relationship," *Speech Monographs* 42 (1975): 107–114.

14. Carl U. Larson, "The Verbal Response of Groups to the Absence or Presence of Leadership," *Speech Monographs* 38 (1971): 117–181.

15. Velma J. Lashbrook, "Leadership Emergence and Source Valence: Concepts in Support of Interaction Theory and Measurement," *Human Communication Research* 1 (1975): 308–315.

16. William B. Lashbrook and Velma J. Lashbrook, *PROANA 5: A Computerized Technique for the Analysis of Small Group Interaction* (Minneapolis: Burgess, 1974).

17. Gayle Lumsden, "An Experimental Study of the Effects of Verbal Agreement on Leadership Maintenance in Problem-Solving Discussion," unpublished Ph.D. dissertation, Indiana University, 1972.

18. Charles G. Morris and J. Richard Hackman, "Behavioral Correlates of Perceived Leadership," *Journal of Personality and Social Psychology* 13 (1969): 350–361.

19. C. David Mortensen, "Should the Group Have an Assigned Leader?" *Speech Teacher* 15 (1966): 34–41.

20. Bertram H. Raven and Jan Rietsema, "The Effects of Varied Clarity of Group Goal and Group Path upon the Individual and His Relation to the Group," *Human Relations* 10 (1957): 29–44.

21. Hugh C. Russell, "An Investigation of Leadership Maintenance Behavior," unpublished Ph.D. dissertation, Indiana University, 1970.

22. Marvin E. Shaw and J. C. Gilchrist, "Intra-Group Communication and Leader Choice," *Journal of Social Psychology* 43 (1956): 133–138.

23. Ivan D. Steiner, *Group Process and Productivity* (New York: Academic Press, 1972).

24. Ralph M. Stogdill, "Personal Factors Associated with Leadership: A Survey of the Literature," *Journal of Psychology* 25 (1948): 35–71.

CHAPTER 6

Development of Group Norms

INTRODUCTION

You probably belong to certain groups in which specific demands are placed on the members' behavior. Your family may have a rule about being present and on time for meals. If a family member shows up late for dinner, he or she had best have an explanation. If the same family member continuously appears late for meals, the family will begin to exert pressure on the tardy person to be more punctual and considerate. By the same token, other groups to which you belong influence your behavior. You probably would not think of attending a church meeting while under the influence of alcohol. If you showed up for a meeting of your chemistry club without having prepared your section of the program, your fellow members would probably react negatively. Members of the National Football League who gamble on professional sports are disciplined, and overweight professional dancers find it difficult to get jobs. Members of college Greek letter associations religiously avoid criticizing their sisters and brothers in the presence of the uninitiated, and students are expected by teachers to attend class regularly. In short, depending on the group to which you belong, your behavior will be influenced, changed, and regulated by the norms of the group. These regulations are called norms, or ". . . rules of conduct established by the members of the group to maintain behavioral consistency" (15:250). This chapter examines norms as well as their emergence and function. We will also investigate the pressures a group exerts upon its members to abide by the rules established by the group.

DEFINITION AND FUNCTION OF GROUP NORMS

As suggested above, norms are really rules that govern the behavior of every person in the group. If a group failed to develop norms, each individual in the group would have a frustrating time trying to figure out how to behave. Group norms are like roles in that they let the individual members know the forms of acceptable behavior expected of them. Homans provides a definition that best describes our notion of norms: ". . . an idea in the minds of the members of a group, an idea that can be put in the form of a statement specifying what the members . . . should do, ought to do, are expected to do under given circumstances" (8:123). Homans goes on to note that these kinds of statements can be considered norms only if failure of the members to follow the group regulations results in some sort of punishment. In one of the groups the authors observed in class, for example, the members developed norms of both punctuality and responsibility. On the day of one of the group's more important meetings, one of its members neglected to prepare adequately for the discussion. In fact, the other group members were relying on this person to report information crucial for the development of an efficient group decision. When the group recognized that one of its participants failed to abide by the norms of responsibility and punctuality, it was interesting to observe the group reaction. Initially the group maintained a period of silence, itself a form of punishment, that indicated the group's dis appointment with one of its members. This period of discomfort w sr followed by the members' verbal description of their disappointment that the group would probably not have as good a decision or product because they lacked the essential information that the "abnormal" participant was to have provided. The person who was responsible for this information reacted apologetically and made it clear that the information would be forthcoming quickly. Without explicitly stating it, the member was reacting to the group's unfavorable reaction by attempting to demonstrate that the norm of punctuality and responsibility was important and that the deviate member would endeavor to conform to this group norm. This behavior was suitable to the group, but additional punishment was also forthcoming. Because the lack of this specific information inconvenienced the group, the group decided that the person who failed to abide by the norm would be responsible for additional work in preparation for the group's next meeting. Because the person was concerned about the behavior contrary to the norm, the additional work was cheerfully accepted. At the next meeting, the group functioned well and everyone behaved in accordance with the norm of responsibility and punctuality. One final note about our story. If the person who behaved contrary to the group norms had not been prepared for subsequent meetings, the group probably would have excluded that member from future group discussions.

Lest we view norms in a completely negative fashion, you should probably also realize that enforcement of norms is not always associated with punishment. Scholars have begun to recognize the problems associated with punishment as a means of changing behavior and suggest that other methods can be applied to reestablish normative behavior. Punishment may result in the deviant person withdrawing from the group. If the deviant person has valuable contributions that he or she would make to the group, those contributions may be lost if the group relies solely on punishment to secure adherence to group norms. In some instances, punishment can contribute to interpersonal conflict; members may engage in emotional bickering. This form of conflict can interfere with group task progress (11).

You should consider at least two other devices designed to secure behavior compatible with group norms: positive reinforcement and lack of reinforcement. Reinforcement involves praise, agreement, and compliments that are given to people in the group who behave according to the norms. If you have a person in your group who fails to abide by an important group norm, you should examine the reasons for the abnormal behavior. If it appears that the group member prefers to do "something else," make that something else contingent on normative behavior. Premack (13, 14) showed that behaviors that have a high probability of occurring can be used to reinforce a behavior that does not occur as frequently, in this case normative behavior. For example, for some group members, idle social conversation can be more important than normative discussion about the group's task. If the highly probable behavior (social conversation) is made contingent upon the lower probability behavior (task discussion), task discussion will increase. In other words, to increase normative behavior (task discussion) a member may say, "This social talk really interests me, but let's hold off until we get some of our work done." This approach may cause the deviant member to engage in more normative behavior because he or she can anticipate more social interaction later. In any case, the use of this strategy is not likely to cause the problems associated with an exclusive reliance on punishment as a means of controlling normative behavior. When the person who has not been following the group's norms engages in normative behavior, the other group members should reinforce this activity by reinforcement. The deviate must be made to realize that normative behavior provides him or her with rewards.

Extinction, a decrease in responses, results when reinforcements are removed. Some group members engage in certain behaviors contrary to group norms because these behaviors draw attention to them. In turn, this attention acts as a reinforcement that prolongs the deviate behavior. In order to change the abnormal behavior under these circumstances, the group members should ignore the previously reinforced behavior. For example, if a group has developed a norm of careful analysis of problems and one member continually insists on hurrying ahead without much concern for analyzing, the initial attention received by the less cautious member may reinforce his or her behavior. Under these conditions, the group would be wise to ignore the deviate's behavior because absence of reinforcement typically reduces behavior. If extinction is to occur, however, the deviate's subsequent normative behavior must be reinforced.

A norm, therefore, is a behavioral rule developed and accepted by members of the group. All members of a group may not accept the norm, but a significant number of the participants must view the norm as a rule regulating behavior. Failure to comply with a group norm usually results in attempts to secure compliance through some kind of group influence. Frequently, the attempts to influence group members to behave in agreement with group norms involves the use of punishment. At times, punishment is needed. Often, however, the application of punishment results in negative group consequences. Therefore, group members should be aware of reinforcement and withholding reinforcement as devices to secure normative behavior.

EMERGENCE OF GROUP NORMS

Numerous studies show that "... interaction among persons tends to decrease the variance in their behavior and, in the extreme, can produce highly standardized behavior patterns" (16:223). This emergence of standardized behavior patterns is the reason for our ability to make reasonably accurate predictions about the success of certain groups. If you watch a classroom group over a period of several weeks, you begin to see the norms emerge and develop. If one group seems to require a serious analysis of information reported by the members, you can probably predict that their group product will be of high quality. On the other hand, if a similar group of people tend to meet late, leave early, and spend most of their time socializing when they ought to be problem solving, you can usually anticipate that this group's decision will be of lesser quality than the group that developed the serious, analytic norm. As you can see, norms do influence group behavior as well as our evaluations of group behavior. This section of the chapter analyzes how roles emerge and what you as a member can do to influence the development of norms useful and suitable for the context in which your group finds itself.

The norms developed by a group to regulate its behavior emerge in much the same fashion as the norms of the individual participants. As we have seen, a group of people as they interact across time creates relatively common expectations of behavior. Norms and roles develop through the same process that we described in Chapter 5. As the group begins to familiarize itself with its goals, personnel, environment, and procedures, members engage in considerable communication. Bormann (3) draws the analogy between the early stages of a discussion and the shakedown cruise of a new ship or aircraft. He points out that the officers and crew of a new craft need to become acquainted with their vehicle just as the members of a small group must become familiar with the various aspects of the discussion situation. As the members of a group figure out the manner in which to engage in communication, they either explicitly or implicitly agree on certain group regulations or standards. They begin to make value judgments about what *should* be done. These judgments, when reinforced through the agreement of a majority of the participants, result in the group's norms. One of the authors recently participated in the formation of a group designed to evaluate graduate students. The group spent considerable time during its early meetings deliberating over such factors as criteria for evaluation, meeting times, place of meeting, rights of nonsmokers, and the development of an agenda. Gradually, as the interaction continued, the faculty members were able to establish certain norms. They agreed that the meetings would be held during lunch hour, that members would bring their own lunches, that nonsmokers would sit apart from smokers, and that only two graduate students would be evaluated at one meeting. The members also agreed that each faculty member would take responsibility for introducing and explaining how his or her graduate advisee met or failed to meet the committee's criteria for assessing graduate student progress. These norms emerged through discussion and developed to guide the members during their meetings. Considerable disagreement took place over the specific norms, but once a majority decided on appropriate behavior, most of the members behaved accordingly.

Norms develop through interaction and reinforcement just as roles emerge. Norms indicate what behavior the group expects of its members while roles refer to the patterns of behavior expected from an individual member. When roles differ from group norms, you can usually expect the role to change. The stereotypical college student bookworm who is invited to join a social organization had best change his or her role if he or she wishes to be accepted as a group member. Conflicts between roles and norms can be humorous, if painful, experiences. You have probably heard the story about the marine home on his first leave from boot camp. His parents invited several relatives for dinner during which the young recruit asked his mother to pass the "... (expletive deleted) butter." Mortified by his abnormal behavior, the marine became embarrassed and excused himself to another room. His father, a very understanding man, followed his son, empathized with him, and told him that he understood why the boy said what he had. He invited the marine back to the dinner table and his son responded, "Aw Dad, I can't; I'd just screw it up again." The role learned at the boot camp was not compatible with family norms.

Groups do not form norms randomly. Nor do they create norms for every possible situation. Groups form norms about behaviors that have a special significance for the group. If the group happened to be primarily a social group, one would expect norms to emerge primarily on the interpersonal dimension. The group working to solve a particular problem establishes norms emphasizing the information and procedural dimensions of small group communication. As with role emergence, norms tend to be those rules of conduct that the group members agree as being important and rewarding. The group perceives norms as regulations designed to facilitate goal achievement.

You may have been in groups in which everyone did not obey the norms, and yet the group functioned well. It is not necessary for all members of a group to adhere strictly to the emergent norms. As we have seen with roles, some members operate in a task-oriented, problem-solving group as tension-relievers. Even though the group norm emphasizes information and the analysis of evidence, certain people may behave on the social dimension with group awareness of their value. Certain people in a group may contribute to goal achievement. As these contributions increase, the person builds up credits that allow for deviancy (7). The important thing to remember is that norms emerge if a majority of the people in the group reinforce the norm.

Why do norms emerge? Festinger (5) suggests two reasons. First, people need some source of validation for their beliefs, attitudes, and values. If one cannot depend on physical reality for support, he or she will look for others to provide social support. People often join or form groups because the members have similar attitudes, beliefs, and values that in turn emerge into a comfortable group norm. For example, you would probably not join an antiabortion committee if you were in favor of abortion. Norms emerge, then, as a form of support for the members of a group. Festinger also points out that people need some kind of coordination in their groups. This need for coordination acts as the second reason for norm emergence. The coordination and regulation of member behavior is necessary for the group to arrive at a goal.

In summary, norms emerge in a group through the same process of reinforcement that results in role emergence. Roles refer to the patterns of behavior expected from specific group members while norms refer to the general ways of behaving the group demands of its members. Norms emerge because people need support for their behaviors and coordination of their efforts in order to achieve their goals.

TYPES OF NORMS

There are two general types of norms: explicit and implicit. Explicit norms consist of formal regulations clearly spelled out for the group members either in writing or specific oral commands. Many groups have a set of written bylaws or codes of ethics. Upon leaving graduate school, for example, many people take jobs as faculty members at various institutions. In order to qualify for promotion, retention, and tenure, many academic departments require a norm of publication. You have heard the phrase, "publish or perish." This norm has emerged in many departments over the years, and new faculty members are often given a faculty handbook in which the precise criteria for publication are explained. If the faculty member does not comply with the norm of publication, he or she can never hope to achieve promotion and tenure. Promotion and tenure act as group rewards designed to insure adherence to this norm. In some departments, failure to publish results in the application of punishment. People who fail to publish are not retained by the department. Other explicit norms require the faculty member to teach a certain number of courses, maintain a certain number of office hours per week, and engage in various departmental service activities. Other explicit norms may not be written down, but nevertheless group members have little doubt about their importance. These explicit norms are distributed through conversation. Group members may be told that the group expects the participants to be on time for meetings or that wearing informal clothing contributes to a desired group informality. In some faculty groups, members are often told to inform the department chairperson about how frequently you visit your office and how much time you spend there. These norms are seldom written down, but they are just as important to the group members as the more formal written regulations. In some cases, nonretained faculty members often explain their dismissal by saying, "I never knew what to do." This explanation rests, at least in part, on the department's failure to set forth explicit norms describing exactly what is expected of the individual faculty members.

Some group norms are never explicitly stated either in writing or speech. These norms are called implicit norms. Have you noticed, for example, that members of groups tend to occupy the same position at the table every time the group meets? No one assigned seats, but the members maintain their seating position at each group meeting. In fact, violation of the implicit norm frequently results in considerable confusion. If someone takes a seat that another group member has been occupying, the participants are likely to respond by saying, "Hey, that's not your seat." Try taking someone else's seat at your family dinner table and you will quickly see the operation of the implicit norm: "That's where Mom is supposed to sit." Other implicit norms involve the use of language. Some groups implicitly suggest that profane language is unacceptable, while other groups tolerate a wider range of language behavior. You would probably not say "bullshit" at a Bible study group meeting even though this norm is seldom explicitly stated. Both types of norms are learned, and both types of norms have rewards and punishments associated with them. Explicit norms are formally stated, and implicit norms emerge without a formal written or spoken word.

Let us turn now to more specific types of norms, both explicit and implicit, that characterize the informational, procedural, and interpersonal dimensions of small group communication. Parsons (12) developed a system to classify norms that is roughly equivalent to our small group dimensions. On the informational dimension, Parsons talks about achievement and success as consequences of the norms valuing certain types of member behavior related to information processing. Informational norms reflect a common set of beliefs, values, and plans about the substance of the group's task. Some informational norms we have observed in small groups include:

"Prisons should be structured to rehabilitate prisoners."
"Changes in departmental curriculum should reflect student opinions."
"Learning should be a pleasurable experience."

Although it is sometimes difficult for a group member to identify informational norms, an outside observer can easily identify the norms that underly your group's information processing. These norms guide and direct the group's consideration of issues related to your task. Information will be considered important or unimportant given these norms. Other items of information will simply be ignored. For example, if your group accepts the position that learning should be a pleasurable experience, then your group will look for teaching methods and classroom environments that students find pleasurable. Small groups cannot avoid the development of informational norms, nor would they want to. If your group members could not agree on what values, beliefs, and attitudes were important, then it would be impossible to reach agreement on an acceptable decision proposal. The critical issue for your group is to make these norms, which are usually implicit norms, explicit in your group's discussion. At least you should take some time during your discussions to examine the usefulness of these norms. This examination will help your group to avoid acceptance of norms that would result in a weak or ineffective decision proposal. When your group finds the informational norms useful, you will be able to obtain a higher level of commitment to your group's decision proposal.

Kiesler and Kiesler (10) report the results of a study investigating norms in problem-solving groups. Two problem-solving conditions were studied: formal and informal. In the formal condition, the group members received careful instructions from the experimenter who was very concerned with the group's success. In the informal condition, other groups were presented with a problem by an experimenter who was sloppily dressed and very casual in his explanation of the problem. A confederate was engaged by the experimenter to behave impolitely and disrespectfully during the discussions. After completing their discussions, group members in both conditions were asked to rate the confederate. In both the formal and informal conditions, the confederate was disliked, but he was disliked much more by the participants receiving the formal instructions. Apparently, the dress and serious behavior of the experimenter in the formal condition gave rise to a norm of serious consideration of the issue. Because of the experimenter's casual behavior in the informal condition, the seriousness norm did not emerge. Consequently, where the group norm required serious consideration of the issue, the group expected members to behave responsibly. To the extent the confederate deviated from this norm, one would expect the other group members to view the confederate with disfavor. On the informational dimension, then, groups should develop a norm of careful analysis of all information presented by the group members. Failure to develop this norm will probably result in failure to question evidence, and as a result the quality of the group's solution suffers. The group should impose standards that not only insure the maximum amount of information, but also enable the careful analysis of the information presented. A group that continually accepts information uncritically from only a few of the members invariably winds up dissatisfied or, even worse, embarrassed at the effectiveness of the group's output.

On the procedural dimension, Parsons (12) refers to norms dealing with control and decision making. Some groups rely on one or two persons to make all of their decisions, whereas other groups prefer a more democratic input by urging each member to take responsibility for group decisions. Procedural norms also regulate the manner in which a group structures its task. You have seen groups such as congressional committees in which each member has a certain amount of time allotted for him or her to speak. Another member would not think of interrupting without asking, "Will the gentleman/lady yield?" Less formal procedural norms characterize other groups in which free, open, and spontaneous conversation is encouraged. Some groups agree to stay on the same subject until the group agrees to discuss another topic. In capital cases, juries must reach consensus or unanimous agreement if they wish to convict a person accused of a serious crime. If this norm cannot be adhered to, the accused cannot be convicted. In short, group norms operate not only on the informational level regulating *what* the group discusses, but also on the procedural dimension regulating *how* the group discusses. Procedural norms are the shared set of expectations about methods for achieving your group's goals. Groups should have some agenda guidelines, engage in summaries, and know the responsibilities of each group member for solving the problem.

Norms also emerge and play an important role on the interpersonal dimension. Parsons (12) refers to these norms as rules regulating the affective, personal relationships among group members. As we mentioned earlier, emotional or social tension usually characterizes the beginning of every small group. Bormann (3) found that the manner in which groups handled this tension in his Minnesota studies resulted in the emergence of interpersonal norms. When a group successfully reduces social tension, the members tend to rely on the methods used to reduce tension and an interpersonal norm emerges. If the group finds that joking helps to reduce the early tension, humor may emerge as a norm to be employed in future situations characterized by tension. When groups successfully reduce the social tension, the manner employed to manage the tension often emerges as the norm. You may have observed groups in which difficulties occur on the informational or procedural dimensions that threaten the group's progress. Frequently, the group members handle these difficulties by turning to the interpersonal dimension in which norms have been more firmly established. It is almost as if group members are thinking, "This problem bothers me; let's go back and discuss something I feel comfortable with." Consequently, since interpersonal norms tend to be established early in the group's history, the group discusses social matters in an effort to develop a means for reassuring the members that the group can get through informational and procedural problems. One word of caution. The group that relies too heavily on interpersonal norms may find itself making very slow progress on the informational or procedural dimensions of the discussion. Other interpersonal norms involve the use of language. Some groups use profanity; other groups frown on that type of language. Some groups develop a pattern of extreme formality in dealing with one another; other groups urge members to be informal. Some groups contain members who meet socially outside the group; other groups maintain a norm that precludes members from dating or meeting outside the group. Sometimes, especially if a group plans to continue meetings over a period of time, members deal with one another with extreme politeness. Kiesler and Kiesler (10) report a series of experiments where people planned to interact over a period of time and other people did not plan future interaction. When people did not plan future interaction, they tolerated a good deal of insulting behavior. In the situation in which people planned to interact in the future, however, a different social norm emerged. In these conditions, people insisted that behavior be polite, and norms requiring more moderate conversation emerged. When people find themselves in situations requiring that the members work together over a period of time, the interpersonal norms tend to emphasize regulations that insure smooth and pleasant interaction. One critical interpersonal norm relates to authority relationships in small groups. This norm is especially evident in organizations in which supervisors and sub-ordinates are asked to meet and solve work-related problems. Some members will defer to the supervisor simply because of the super-visor's position. This interpersonal norm would inhibit the careful analysis of information that is basic to effective problem solving.

Interpersonal norms will emerge, but the group should be cautious in adopting these rules. Just as with the other types of norms, members should create interpersonal norms that assist the group in reaching its goal. An effective group participant will monitor the development of interpersonal norms carefully in order to be certain that the most helpful social regulations emerge.

In summary, we have noted that norms emerge in all groups through a process of reward and reinforcement. Some norms are ex plicitly set forth, whereas others are more implicit. Each dimension of small group interaction has norms. Informational norms guide the group's analysis of substance and content. Procedural norms regulate the manner in which groups go about their deliberations. The interpersonal norms control the interpersonal reactions among members. We want to emphasize again that norms are key determinants of the manner in which your group will process information. Norms are an inevitable and necessary component of small group discussions. The issue is not whether conformity to norms is good or bad. Absence of conformity to these norms creates an impossible situation for productive interaction. The critical issue is whether the norms that emerge in your group are useful. To the degree that these norms serve the purpose of your group, the more productive and satisfying you will find your group experience.

CONSEQUENCES OF DEVIATING FROM GROUP NORMS

As we have seen, there is some latitude to which members are required to conform to group norms. This section of the chapter examines the pressures placed on members to conform to group norms, the consequences of those pressures, and the manner in which a group maintains its standards. Let us begin by examining an often misinterpreted notion: conformity. You know some people who always go along with the crowd and others who you may refer to as nonconformists. Probably you have different feelings toward each type of person. The conformist is not too exciting and the nonconformist may be so "wierd" that you feel uncomfortable in his or her presence. The term conformity, however, should be relatively free of value judgments. Conformity by itself is not as important as the norms to which people conform. Conformity can be a good thing, but it can also refer to the tendency to allow others to do our thinking for us. The uncritical acceptance of norms frequently causes problems because members blindly adhere to unquestioned standards of behavior. On the other hand, when the emergent stages of group norms are carefully monitored and useful rules are established, deviation from these norms probably will hinder the group and conformity to the norms will probably help the group. For example, if you drive a car, you must realize the importance of other motorists' conformity to traffic regulations. The nonconforming motorist may receive a ticket, have an accident, wind up in jail, or, worse yet, end up as a traffic fatality. In some situations, then, conformity to certain norms is valuable if not essential to the effective functioning of a group. The important thing to remember is that conformity is not necessarily bad; if the norms are thoughtfully and critically developed, conformity operates as a desirable behavior. The problems occur when group members conform to bad norms.

When we use the term conformity, we are referring to behavioral change a group member undergoes as a function of pressure from other group members (10). We are using the term conformity to refer to the instances in which a group member behaves according to group norms. Some group members may comply with the group's wishes without ever really believing in what he or she is doing. Even though the person may privately reject what the group expects of him or her, the person's public conformity to the group's norms reflects the operation of group pressure. This conforming behavior results in considerable reinforcement to the other group members. That is, the group gives the appearance of a united front and the members find strength in the similar behavior of others. For example, John Dean in his book *Blind Ambition* (4) writes that he engaged in a variety of illegal cover-up activities when he served as counsel to President Nixon during the Watergate scandal. He behaved illegally even though he understood that his actions involved criminal liability punishable by fine and imprisonment. The Senate Watergate Committee found Dean's criminal behavior particularly confusing. After all, Dean was an attorney and knew that his actions were wrong. Why would someone engage in illegal behavior when aware that the behavior could result in considerable punishment? Dean does not attempt to justify his action, but he does explain it. Dean was a member of a select group of presidential advisors. In a very real sense, the people responsible for advising the president can be viewed as a small group. Dean describes one of the norms shared by this group as one of loyalty to the president. No advisor should ever do anything that could even remotely jeopardize the people's faith in their president. To the extent Dean conformed to this norm, he was reinforced with larger office facilities, use of the White House limousines, access to more and more important information, and a variety of other privileges. For a time, as the advisors conformed to the loyalty norm, they actually believed that they would succeed in protecting the president through their illegal activities. When Dean violated the loyalty norm and attempted to point out the illegal nature of various Watergate activities to the advisory group, he was urged to "stonewall it" and protect the president. Initially, this group pressure was very effective and Dean conformed to the loyalty norm. Even though Dean recognized his behavior as illegal, he conformed to Haldeman and Erlichman's expectations. It was only when Dean rejected the group norm of loyalty to the president that the real Watergate story emerged. The point here is that pressure exerted by a group can influence individual behavior even though the group member may be aware that the behavior is wrong, unethical, or illegal. Moreover, adherence to the group norm by one member increases the conformity of the other group members. Operating as a unified front reinforces individual behavior.

The emergence of norms described earlier now takes on a new importance. Not only are norms necessary for effective group functioning, but emergent norms also regulate members' behavior. Consequently, during the early stages of group development, participants should exercise caution in the manner in which norms emerge. By the same token, when you decide to join a new group, you should look very carefully at the norms of the group. If you see certain norms as improper or useless, make your position known before the group firmly accepts this prescription for regulating individual behavior. People who do not abide by the group norms are exposed to considerable pressure to conform. If you are comfortable with the group norms and you believe in them, you are less likely to become involved in problems similar to those experienced by John Dean. Remember, the norms that emerge can come back to cause you considerable distress later.

The major consequence of deviating from group norms, then, is pressure exerted upon the individual to abide by the group norm. As a group develops a history, the members begin to divide labor, create systems for solving problems, and social relationships emerge. The group begins to develop norms that contribute to the effective and efficient completion of the task. Members become interdependent and rely on each other for successful group work. Consequently, to the extent an individual member fails to abide by the emergent norms, that person is likely to be perceived by the other group members as a deviate interfering with the group's progress and in addition blocking whatever rewards are available to the group. Under these conditions, the nonconformist tends to be rejected by the group (2). The group perceives its norms as contributing to the group's success. Abnormal behavior, therefore, results in the perception that the failure to abide by the norm can contribute to the group's failure on its project. In other words, make sure that you see the group's norms as compatible with your attitudes, beliefs, and values or be prepared to risk rejection by your fellow group members.

The pressures to conform to group norms typically intensify as group cohesion increases (9). Cohesive groups, discussed in Chapter 7, involve a strong attraction for its members and the participants desire to remain in the group because of the rewards associated with membership. A deviate in a cohesive group usually poses a threat to the other group members. If continued over a period of time, deviant behavior can reduce the group's cohesiveness and result in member dissatisfaction. Consequently, the cohesive group tends to deal with the deviant member quickly and harshly. We know of a professor who was a member of a highly cohesive and prestigious research team. The professor was expected to conform to a norm of scholarly responsibility and integrity, but his colleagues discovered that he had plagiarized substantial portions of his published research. Not only was the professor fired, but also his colleagues contacted the editor of the journal in which the plagiarized material appeared. The editor wrote an editorial condemning the offending professor and withdrew all of his material from publication. After other professors around the country read the editorial, no one was willing to hire the professor who had failed to conform to the norm of academic integrity. To the best of our knowledge, this professor still cannot find scholarly employment. You can probably think of your own examples of the consequences associated with deviance in cohesive groups. We can all recall instances in high school, for example, where an athlete was forced off a team because he or she neglected training norms. We expect that this dismissal probably occurs much faster on cohesive teams. The deviant who clearly refuses to adopt the team norms poses a threat to the winning record. In situations in which the group has not developed cohesiveness, members tolerate a wider range of behaviors. Since the group is not important to the members, deviant members pose relatively little threat. On the other hand, cohesive groups typically demand a greater adherence to norms because of the threat deviance presents.

Some research evidence suggests that group pressure to conform to norms does not have as much impact on more prestigious group members (6, 7). People who have gained status in the group usually acquire their position by adhering to group norms. If a person has clearly demonstrated a willingness to contribute to group goals and a capability to successfully move the group to a decision, other group members may allow this person more flexibility. It is almost as if the high-status person has "paid dues" and can have more freedom. Even with this freedom, however, the high-status person generally conforms more to group norms than members with lower status (1). If you wish to change norms, the research suggests that you will have greater impact by demonstrating to your fellow discussants that you do conform to most norms and value membership in the group. Working with the group allows you the flexibility to work for change providing you have emerged as a valued and needed group member.

In summary, conformity to group norms is usually rewarded. The consequences of deviating from norms involve application of group pressures. Since conformity introduces organization and order into the group, most people conform to group norms. Conformity to the group norms usually improves the group's ability to solve its problem and accomplish its task. Undesirable consequences of conformity occur when group pressure is exerted to secure compliance with norms of questionable value. Since pressure will be exerted on group members to comply with norms, you should exercise care to see that your group develops beneficial regulations during the period of norm emergence.

SUMMARY

Norms refer to regulations developed by a group that govern conduct and establish consistent group behavior. Groups exert pressure on individual members to behave according to the norms. The process by which norms emerge resembles the process of role emergence. Members begin to point out what the group *should* do in a variety of important situations. When these recommendations are reinforced by group agreement, the norm emerges. Groups do not develop norms randomly; norms concern behaviors having a special significance for the group. Norms emerge to support the attitudes, beliefs, and values of group members and to coordinate and regulate member behavior in order to arrive at a goal. Norms can be stated explicitly or implicitly. Explicit norms occur in the form of written regulations or spoken statements of expectations; implicit norms occur without a formal written or spoken record. Norms govern members' behavior on the informational, procedural, and interpersonal dimensions of the group. When members fail to behave according to the norms, pressure by other members is exerted on the deviant member to conform. Conformity, an often misunderstood concept, usually improves the group's ability to function. The undesirable consequences of conformity occur when members comply with norms of questionable value. Since pressures for conformity occur after norms have emerged, members should carefully develop the norms that will ultimately govern their behavior.

CONCLUSIONS AND RECOMMENDATIONS

1. Group norms inform individual members of acceptable behaviors expected of them.
2. Group members frequently react unfavorably toward individual members who violate group norms.
3. Norms emerge through interaction and reinforcement during the early stages of a group's life span.
4. Norms emerge in small groups to coordinate and regulate member behavior.
5. Norms provide support for group member's beliefs, attitudes, and values.
6. Norms may be either explicit or implicit.
7. Informational norms reflect common beliefs, attitudes, and values held by group members about their topic.
8. Often it is useful for the group to make informational norms explicit.
9. Procedural norms reflect expectations about information search, information processing, and decision making.
10. Interpersonal norms regulate personal relationships among group members.
11. Interpersonal norms related to the status hierarchy in the group may inhibit careful analysis of information during group discussions.
12. Conformity by itself is not as important as the *norms* to which people conform.
13. Individuals who deviate from group norms can expect pressure from other members to abide by the group norms.

14. Pressures to conform to group norms increase as group cohesiveness increases.
15. Members who have demonstrated that they value group membership and goals will have greater success in their attempts to change group norms.

REFERENCES

1. Irwin A. Berg and Bernard M. Bass (eds.), *Conformity and Deviation*, (New York: Harper and Row, 1961).
2. Leonard Berkowitz and Robert C. Howard, "Reaction to Opinion Deviates as Affected by Affiliation Need (n) and Group Member Interdependence," *Sociometry* 22 (1959): 81–91.
3. Ernest G. Bormann, *Discussion and Group Methods: Theory and Practice*, 2nd ed. (New York: Harper and Row, 1975).
4. John Dean, *Blind Ambition* (New York: Simon and Schuster, 1976).
5. Leon Festinger, "Informal Social Communication," *Psychological Review* 57 (1950): 271–282.
6. Edwin P. Hollander, "Competence and Conformity in the Acceptance of Influence," *Journal of Abnormal and Social Psychology* 61 (1960): 365–370.
7. Edwin P. Hollander, "Conformity, Status, and Idiosyncratic Credit," *Psychological Review* 65 (1958): 117–127.
8. George C. Homans, *The Human Group* (New York: Harcourt, Brace and World, 1950).
9. Irving L. Janis, "Groupthink," *Psychology Today* 5 (1971): 43–46, 74–76.
10. Charles A. Kiesler and Sara B. Kiesler, *Conformity* (Reading, Mass.: Addison-Wesley, 1970).
11. Thomas J. Knutson and Albert C. Kowitz, "Effects of Information Type and Orientation on Consensus Achievement in Substantive and Affective Small Group Conflict," *Central States Speech Journal* 28 (1977): 54–63.
12. Talcott Parsons and Edward A. Shils (eds.), *Toward a General Theory of Action*, (Cambridge, Mass.: Harvard University Press, 1951).
13. David Premack, "Toward Empirical Behavior Laws: I. Positive Reinforcement," *Psychological Review* 66 (1959): 219–233.
14. David Premack, "Reinforcement Theory," in David Levine (ed.), *Nebraska Symposium on Motivation, 1965* (Lincoln: University of Nebraska Press, 1965, pp. 123–180.
15. Marvin E. Shaw, *Group Dynamics: The Psychology of Small Group Behavior*, 2nd ed. (New York: McGraw-Hill, 1976).
16. Victor H. Vroom, "Industrial Social Psychology," in Gardner Lindzey and Elliott Aronson (eds.), *The Handbook of Social Psychology*, vol. 5 (Reading, Mass.: Addison-Wesley, 1969), pp. 196–268.

CHAPTER 7

Elements of Member Satisfaction and Group Cohesiveness

INTRODUCTION

As we have indicated, one of the problems frequently associated with small group communication involves member satisfaction. People often find little good in groups and occasionally state their dissatisfaction publicly. You may recall a morale problem associated with groups to which you have belonged. People may have left the group dissatisfied and complaining. Perhaps they felt that your group could have accomplished more or that the interpersonal relations lacked depth or content. Members may have lacked enthusiasm about joining the group in the first place and, following their experience, certainly did not look forward to meeting with the group again. In short, many people tend to hold negative attitudes about group work because their group experiences fail to satisfy their needs. They tend not to look forward to their group meetings and sometimes take steps to avoid group work. We take the position that much of the dissatisfaction and lack of cohesiveness that people experience in groups can be overcome with some knowledge about small group communication. We do best that which we know how to do. In general, we tend to like those things at which we are successful and dislike those things at which we are not. We hope much of the dissatisfaction you have felt in past groups will be overcome as a function of reading this book and becoming proficient in small group communication. Unfortunately, however, many of your future small group colleagues will not have had an opportunity to have read a book like this one. Since your attraction to a group depends in part on the satisfaction of your colleagues, this chapter examines the sources and consequences of member satisfaction and small group cohesiveness. You can build your own satisfaction with the group by assisting your colleagues' development of a positive attitude toward the group. The more satisfied the members of a group, the greater the degree of small group cohesion. Conversely, the greater the cohesion, the greater the individual member satisfaction. Most importantly, however, as both member satisfaction and group cohesion increase, the probability that the group will be productive in reaching its goals also increases. This chapter examines both member satisfaction and group cohesion with an eye toward increasing group productivity.

DEFINITION OF MEMBER SATISFACTION AND COHESIVENESS

Member satisfaction refers to a condition in which the members enjoy their group experiences and feel that certain needs have been met. Individual member satisfaction depends upon the member's subjective judgment about the affective or emotional aspects of her or his experience in the group. If the person feels that the group provided her or him with rewards or reinforcement, that person will likely be satisfied with the group. Specifically, member satisfaction depends on the individual's perception of goals (12). If a member performs in a fashion enabling her or him to achieve an established goal, he or she will probably be satisfied. On the other hand, if the group or individual goals are impossible or extremely difficult to reach, member dissatisfaction and frustration will probably develop. Satisfaction, therefore, refers to the respective group member's positive attitude toward the group and a general feeling of liking the group (4, p. 189).

Group cohesiveness, a concept similar to member satisfaction, refers to the extent to which the individual members of the group actually behave as a group. A cohesive group consists of members attracted to one another and who desire to remain in the group. Group cohesiveness is "the resultant of all forces acting on the members to remain in the group" (8, p. 274). The chief distinction between member satisfaction and group cohesiveness is that the former refers primarily to an individual's attraction to the group while the latter considers the totality of the members' attraction to the group. A highly cohesive group tends to be more active, experiences fewer absences at its meetings, and generally consists of members directly concerned about the success of the group. A low cohesive group contains members who simply do not care to belong to the group. Thus, cohesiveness refers to the degree to which group members are attracted to the group.

RELATIONSHIP BETWEEN MEMBER SATISFACTION AND COHESIVENESS

As you have undoubtedly observed, member satisfaction and group cohesiveness are closely related concepts. Satisfaction refers to the fulfillment of individual needs and cohesiveness refers to the kind, degree, and number of satisfactions the group can provide the members. Given this distinction, you are probably not surprised to learn that members of cohesive groups tend to be more satisfied than members of noncohesive groups. People typically do not remain in groups with which they are dissatisfied. Therefore, one of the ways to increase the overall effectiveness of any group involves the meeting of individual needs. The more satisfied the group members are, the greater the degree of group cohesiveness. We view satisfaction and cohesiveness as desirable goals that affect each other. Members of cohesive groups tend to be satisfied, and conversely, satisfied members contribute to the establishment of group cohesiveness. You have probably been a member of a newly formed group and have experienced this phenomenon. One of the authors recently joined a bowling team. At first, no individual member of the team bowled very well, and consequently, member satisfaction was not very high. As the season progressed, however, individuals began to improve and some members were reasonably satisfied with their performance. When the team began to increase its standing in the league, members became more satisfied with their efforts. By the end of the season, it was not unusual for the entire team to continue their relationship outside of the bowling alley at a local tavern. As the individual members of the team became more satisfied, the group as a whole became more attractive. Without the individual satisfaction, however, group cohesiveness probably would not have occurred.

CONSEQUENCES OF MEMBER SATISFACTION AND COHESIVENESS

Many authors incorrectly assume that a highly cohesive group consisting of satisfied members will automatically be a productive group. Sometimes cohesiveness and satisfaction develop even when a group has developed a norm of low productivity. Schacter and others [20] and Berkowitz [1] found that cohesive groups that agree on low productivity may still be attractive to the members. Shaw and Shaw [23] found a similar negative relationship between productivity and group cohesion. By definition, members of cohesive groups are attracted to and receive rewards from each other. Under these circumstances, in the absence of a real group commitment to productivity, the group may engage in social activities to such an extent that they spend too little time on task-related issues. You may have experienced this phenomenon in groups. If your group successfully completed an important task, the members became satisfied and cohesiveness developed. Under these circumstances, it was unusually difficult to begin work on a new task. We saw this phenomenon clearly demonstrated recently in the National Football League when the world champion Super Bowl winners lost the first four games in the season following their tremendous success. Group cohesiveness and member satisfaction *alone* are insufficient to insure group productivity.

In spite of the above evidence, however, you should still continue to work for member satisfaction and group cohesiveness because of their potential for increasing group productivity. Productivity depends upon the degree to which the group's norms, goals, and member responsibilities contribute to the solution of the group's problem. Cohesive groups consisting of satisfied members invariably achieve their goals more efficiently and effectively than noncohesive groups; as you have seen, however, goal achievement is not necessarily the same as productivity. In order for member satisfaction and group cohesiveness to contribute to a group's productivity, the group's norms, goals, and member responsibilities must be suitable for solving the group's problem. Specifically, review the material on planning communication responsibilities in Chapter 4 and the development of group norms in Chapter 6. When the group has developed following the guidelines in these chapters, then member satisfaction and group cohesiveness will contribute to high group productivity. In short, for member satisfaction and group cohesiveness to result in high group productivity, you must remember to monitor carefully the group's production goals.

Satisfied members in cohesive groups communicate with each other more frequently than dissatisfied members in noncohesive groups (19). The members tend to be more friendly and try to cooperate with one another in the cohesive groups, but the members of noncohesive groups tend to behave more as individuals rather than as members of the group. Members of noncohesive groups tend to be dissatisfied and uncooperative (23). A cohesive group contributes to member satisfaction by allowing more opportunity for participation. Members of these groups are not afraid to talk, and the lively communication contributes to increased satisfaction and cohesiveness. People in cohesive groups also disagree more because the group climate allows for different opinions without causing severe strains on member satisfaction. The management of this disagreement probably contributes to the increasing amounts of communication found among satisfied members in cohesive groups.

One of the sources of member satisfaction involves communication with people we like. By definition, we tend to like people in cohesive groups. Consequently, members of cohesive groups exert more influence over each other than members of noncohesive groups. When group members are satisfied with the group, the members are motivated to behave in ways consistent with the other group members. You may belong to groups in which you adopt the behavior of others. Fraternities, sororities, and various other social clubs often have certain formal or informal dress codes. You have probably heard people say, "I know he's a Sig Ep because he was wearing their blazer." We are influenced by the people we like and we tend to go along with judgments of the cohesive groups to which we belong (26). Recognition of this tendency should enable you to resist group influence when you wish and to develop strategies for avoiding an early rush to reach agreement. Satisfaction and cohesiveness are desirable as long as we resist the influence of the majority simply because they are a majority.

Satisfied members of cohesive groups behave in a responsible fashion within the group. The more attracted you happen to be to a group, the greater the likelihood that you will accept various tasks and jobs within the group (17). Think for a moment about the groups that you find satisfying as a member. We have already seen that you find that membership rewarding and, consequently, you will probably do more for that group than for others to which you belong. We have all heard of the "team player," the participant who holds group goals more highly than individual goals. People who occasionally exclaim, "There's nothing I wouldn't do for that group," demonstrate the effects of cohesion and satisfaction on individual behavior. This participation, as we have seen, also produced increasing amounts of satisfaction and cohesiveness. If a member's participation results in success, he or she will develop more attraction to the group. These task-oriented activities also produce stronger friendships, and the active person is likely to turn to the group for assistance in solving future problems (5). In other words, the satisfied member of a cohesive group will take on jobs within the group that result in increased levels of satisfaction and cohesiveness.

While the development of member satisfaction and group cohesiveness creates a more harmonious atmosphere in which to work, you should remember that this condition is only helpful to the group insofar as the group continues to meet appropriate goals and make suitable decisions. Some groups find satisfaction and cohesiveness by communicating only on the interpersonal dimension and tend to ignore informational and procedural issues. When these groups are called upon to report their decisions, frequently they experience considerable embarrassment. They have nothing to report. They spent their time happily talking about social matters, drinking coffee, and generally avoiding their task functions. They developed member satisfaction and group cohesiveness as ends rather than using the satisfaction and cohesiveness to facilitate the group's activity in the informational and procedural dimensions. Member satisfaction and group cohesiveness are useful tools to assist a group in developing a decision proposal only if they are used to that end. In other words, do not let your group become too cohesive or your members too satisfied *without working on your task.*

Thus, the consequences of member satisfaction and group cohesiveness depend on whether they facilitate discussion on the informational and procedural group communication dimensions. When they do, the consequences involve a potential for higher productivity when group goals are appropriate to the task, increased amounts of communication among group members, considerable group influence over the behavior of participants, and greater responsibility among members in performing work for the group.

SOURCES OF MEMBER SATISFACTION

As we have noted, member satisfaction leads to cohesiveness, which in turn results in a more effective group climate. We are now ready to pursue the causes of member satisfaction in order that you can, at least to some degree, influence your fellow discussants' perceptions of their degree of satisfaction. If you can help others become satisfied with your group, you should begin to establish group cohesiveness.

When people voluntarily join groups, the research indicates that they do so because they perceive the group as a means of satisfying certain needs (25). In other words, people join groups in search of satisfaction. Rewards or reinforcements operate to increase member satisfaction (4, p. 188ff; 7). If you are aware of the kinds of rewards used to meet members' needs, you can begin to use those rewards to develop others' satisfaction. Furthermore, if you are aware of rewards that cause satisfaction, you may be in a better position to decide whether or not to join a certain group.

Stop and think for a moment about the sources of your satisfaction in a given small group setting. Some groups of which you have been a member have probably provided you with considerable satisfaction, whereas others probably failed completely to give you any satisfaction. A summary of hundreds of studies dealing with satisfaction in small groups may help us to locate the sources of satisfactory group experience. Heslin and Dunphy (13) found that three factors most often affect member satisfaction in small groups: status congruence, perception of progress toward group goals, and perceived freedom to participate. Status congruence describes the degree of agreement among group members on the identity of high-status members. If the members of a group agree on the identity of people occupying high-status positions within the group, member satisfaction is generally quite high. If the group fails to agree on a reasonably stable status or role structure, member satisfaction decreases. When you perceive your status as fairly high, but the other group members do not perceive you in the same way, you can begin to feel the frustration that lessens your satisfaction. Perhaps the best way to handle status congruence is to realize that your status and the degree to which others perceive it depends largely on the situation, the group task, and your ability to facilitate the group toward its goal. Remember that one cannot possess consistently high status in all situations. A clear recognition of status differences can contribute to member satisfaction as long as the group meets satisfaction on the other two dimensions: perception of progress toward group goals and perceived freedom to participate.

If you are like countless other people who take long automobile trips, you can begin to understand the satisfaction associated with progress toward your destination. As the miles pass, you experience a sense of completion and accomplishment. When you arrive at your destination, you are typically satisfied with the trip providing that you did not experience extraordinary difficulties. A similar situation applies to small group communication. The procedural dimension of small group communication discussed in Chapter 4 helps the group members to see the progress they are making. If members fail to perform functions related to the procedural dimension, chances are the members of the group will experience dissatisfaction. Comments such as, "I don't see that we're accomplishing anything," and "Nobody knows what we're supposed to do," indicate member dissatisfaction because group members fail to perceive any progress toward a goal. This dissatisfaction frequently gives rise to a common negative observation about groups: "They just spin their wheels and get nowhere fast." In order to develop member satisfaction, the members must see themselves as accomplishing something. The key point here is perception. The group may not be accomplishing anything, but if the participants perceive progress, member satisfaction will increase.

The third variable affecting member satisfaction is the individual's perception that he or she has freedom to participate. Of course, each person in a group cannot participate equally; the world does not structure itself in such a fashion. As in perceived progress toward a group goal, again the important concept here is perception. Group members must feel that they have the freedom to participate on a regular basis. Even if members elect to remain silent, the knowledge that others will listen if they do speak will contribute to member satisfaction.

Status congruence, perception of progress toward group goals, and perceived freedom to participate influence member satisfaction because of the inherent rewards associated with the variables. Satisfaction with task-oriented groups is a result of the rewards one receives in the group. A reward, as we define the term, involves the achievement of a need. For example, if you happen to be hungry, you need food. Eating a sandwich under that condition is an inherently rewarding behavior because the food satisfied your need. By the same token, group communication provides for the achievement of certain needs. The achievement of those needs acts as a reward that produces member satisfaction in turn.

Let us now turn to specific sources of satisfaction in groups by analyzing the rewards available on the informational, procedural, and interpersonal dimensions. We will begin with the informational dimension by noting that the successful completion of a group task produces member satisfaction. Hoffman (14) reported that group members who believed that they had successfully completed a task also tended to be highly satisfied. In other studies, when group members were informed that they had succeeded or that people outside the group had positively evaluated the group, satisfaction also increased (2, 6). Obviously, one of the major components for successful completion of a task involves knowledge about the task. Shaw (22) found that members who have information about a problem experience higher levels of satisfaction than those who do not have as much information. In order to receive the rewards available on the informational dimension, adequate preparation for discussion is essential.

In addition to the specific substantive preparation, one should also know about group communication. The studies cited above provide us with justification for our earlier comment that knowledge about small group communication will increase your satisfaction. As you begin to develop proficient small group communication skills, the number of success experiences you have in group communication should also increase. As your success increases, so will your satisfaction with group communication. Some time ago several people formed a group to increase their potential for success in show business. Their success led to a great satisfaction previously unavailable to the individuals. The group? Ringling Brothers, Barnum, and Bailey. In order to increase member satisfaction on the informational dimension, therefore, it is important for someone to make the group realize that it has successfully solved certain problems. In addition, your satisfaction will increase if you have information about the topic under discussion. Effective preparation for discussion will contribute to your satisfaction by providing you with information about your topic.

Several rewards are also available on the procedural dimension of small group communication. The Heslin and Dunphy (13) finding that perceived freedom to communicate contributes to member satisfaction falls on the procedural dimension. The greater the chance we have to communicate, the higher our level of satisfaction. Leavitt (18) found that people who were able to interact with everyone in a group experienced high levels of satisfaction. This satisfaction could be attributed to another related phenomenon, leadership. Those who interact most frequently with other group members often become group leaders (16). Leaders typically have high amounts of procedural communication and have high status in the group. Additional studies show that people with high group status also have high degrees of member satisfaction (10, 11). On the procedural dimension, therefore, a group member must be made to feel that he or she can communicate whenever he or she wishes. That realization, in and of itself, will contribute to member satisfaction. In addition, remember that people who communicate with the other group members most frequently in the procedural dimension are often perceived as leaders, a role with status attached to it. Before we leave the rewards associated with the procedural dimension, one other observation must be made. In groups where one or two members remain silent, the satisfaction of every group member decreases (24). Consequently, in order to secure the rewards needed for procedural satisfaction, every effort should be made to secure participation from each member.

The interpersonal dimension of small group communication also provides rewards associated with member satisfaction. One of the rewards to be derived from group communication involves meeting the need for interpersonal communication. These rewards can be made even stronger and more satisfying by recognizing the important interpersonal dimension. Remember, the interpersonal dimension refers to the attitudes the members have toward group members. On the interpersonal dimension, satisfaction is produced by interaction with people we like and people who like us. If we have an idea that people in our group like us, we typically experience satisfaction. In an early study, Exline (7) told some groups that they were congenial and that the members would probably get along well with one another. He told other groups that the members were probably not congenial. Even though there were no real differences between the two groups, members who perceived high compatibility with their group members experienced significantly higher levels of satisfaction than the members who thought, wrongly, their groups incompatible. On the interpersonal dimension, then, you ought to try to develop an atmosphere of compatibility. One of the ways this condition can be achieved involves an avoidance of self-oriented needs (9). Members typically experience higher levels of satisfaction in groups in which the individuals are more concerned with the group's success than they are with their own ego. You have probably experienced the frustration and dissatisfaction associated with the person who wants to leave the group early because he or she has a date or something else to do. By the same token, we are not usually satisfied with people who talk only about themselves. The interpersonal dimension of group communication allows for member satisfaction through the development of compatibility. Compatibility can be created by referring to group goals and needs rather than personal needs.

We mentioned earlier that for most people interaction with others is an inherently rewarding activity. Few of us can genuinely be called hermits or lone woives. We need other people to give us information about ourselves. A poet once observed: "If only God would gift us, to see ourselves as others see us." Group communication can meet this need by providing us with validation for our beliefs and attitudes (24). If you make a particular point in a discussion group and one of your colleagues responds, "That's a good idea, I really like that a lot," you can begin to feel the reward that results in your satisfaction. Thus, one of the ways to increase member satisfaction involves rewarding the comments others make. Obviously, we do not suggest that you reward everything anybody says. However, when you hear a viewpoint you believe to be valuable, you ought to say so. The problem here is simple. Too many of us fail to reward or reinforce the comments of others, even those we love most dearly. Interpersonal reward contributes directly to member satisfaction, and we ought to be sensitive to providing rewards to others by our behavior.

In summary, member satisfaction involves the positive attituae a member holds for her or his group. We have suggested that this positive attitude can be developed by virtue of the rewards available to the members on the three dimensions of small group communication. On the informational dimension, goals should be set so as to allow the group to succeed. Early task success leads to member satisfaction. Members also should prepare for discussion in order to achieve the rewards on the informational dimension. On the procedural dimension, satisfaction is developed through participation. People who have the chance to communicate usually experience satisfaction. On the interpersonal dimension, satisfaction results from the members' perceptions of compatibility. Members ought to indicate clearly and frequently through their behavior the degree to which he or she likes the other group members.

SOURCES OF GROUP COHESIVENESS

If each member of a group experiences satisfaction with the group, the level of group cohesiveness should be quite high. One of the basic causes of cohesiveness requires an awareness of the procedures to increase member satisfaction. A highly cohesive group consists of satisfied members; they have a group loyalty and the individual members seek to work for the good of the group. From our perspective, group cohesiveness requires constant sensitivity to the satisfaction of others in your group. Remember our definition states that cohesiveness results from the total impact of all the forces acting on the members to remain in the group. As such, member satisfaction constitutes an important cause of cohesiveness.

Researchers have investigated cohesiveness extensively, and this section of the chapter reviews some of those studies. Many research efforts have merely pointed out the differences between cohesive and noncohesive groups. It is important to remember that observed differences do not necessarily mean that the differences cause varying levels of cohesiveness. We have interpreted this research in a fashion designed to enable you to increase the cohesiveness of any group of which you are a member.

Members of cohesive groups have been found to appeal to the group as a whole more frequently than members of noncohesive groups. The use of plural pronouns ("we," "us," etc.) contributes to the perception of individual members to see the group as a whole (21, p. 200). Remember that one of the causes of member satisfaction involved the avoidance of communicating self-oriented needs. Likewise, the development of group cohesiveness involves appealing to the other members' needs rather than relying exclusively on personal needs, wants, and desires. Rather than saying, "I want to move to the next point on the agenda," the group member concerned with building group cohesiveness would say, "We probably ought to move on to our next agenda item. What do the rest of you think?" In this fashion, the group makes a collective decision. When the pronoun "I" is overused, other members of the group may feel pushed about or railroaded.

Another characteristic of the cohesive group involves the gains the members perceive that they can get through membership in the group (25). If the group members believe that they can get more rewards from one group than another, he or she is likely to remain in the more rewarding group. Members should be sensitive to demonstrating the kinds of rewards the group has to offer to its members. In fact, if the group provides valuable benefit to its members, these benefits should be made known to the membership. We know of one university, for example, where graduate students in speech communication form a highly cohesive group. They quickly recognize that students belonging to the same group over the years successfully completed their degrees and without exception were able to find jobs in the area of their interest. Even though the demands of the graduate program are high, few students dropped out of the program. They realized that the gains to be received at this university as a member of the graduate student group were higher than the possible rewards to be derived at any other university.

The development of positive interpersonal relationships also influences the group's cohesiveness. When asked to name the people with whom they would most prefer to work during various activities, members of cohesive groups more frequently chose other group members than did members of noncohesive groups (21, p. 197). Again, we

see the influence of member satisfaction. The development and maintenance of pleasant interpersonal relationships within the group contributes to the group's cohesiveness.

A final source of group cohesiveness involves the members' need
for structure. In a series of studies conducted at the University of
Minnesota, Bormann (3, p. 161) reports that members of a group vary
in their need for agenda or group structure. Some people require a
specific set of guidelines to accomplish a given task while others are
content with a relatively unstructured discussion experience. Groups
consisting of members who have a high need for structure were found
to become dissatisfied early in the discussion. Groups of people with
a low need for structure were found to be comfortable with the absence of structure early in the discussion. On the other hand, groups
of people with a low need for structure tended to waste their time
discussing matters irrelevant to the group task. You will seldom be a
member of a group in which each member shares a similar view of
the need for group structure. Most often, the desire for structure will
vary among the participants. In these cases, the group must work out
ways of dealing with the desires of people who want structure and the
wishes of those who do not need as much structure. The use of brain-
storming, for example, seems to meet the needs of low-structure
people as well as contribute useful information to the high-structure
people. Bormann (3, p. 162) found that the group structure notion was
most helpful to those groups experiencing dissatisfaction with their
group progress. Often changes in the manner in which a group structured its discussion resulted in more progress, greater member satisfaction, and higher cohesiveness.

In summary, group cohesiveness refers to the attraction the
group has for its members. We suggested that cohesiveness results
from all of the forces acting upon the individual to remain in the group.
As such, the development of member satisfaction operates as a primary source of group cohesiveness. Other sources involve the use
of plural pronouns, the awareness group members have about their
group membership, the development of pleasant interpersonal relationships, and a sensitivity about varying structural or procedural
needs of the members.

DANGERS OF GROUP COHESIVENESS

We suggested above that a cohesive group does not necessarily imply
a productive group. Irving Janis in his book on "groupthink" (15) has
shown that group members sometimes overlook critical elements of
the task because they do not wish to disagree with the apparent con-

sensus of the group. There is a reluctance to express misgivings about the group's decision for fear of upsetting the congenial atmosphere of the group. We encounter a strange paradox here. Cohesive groups should permit a free exchange of ideas including expression of misgivings about the group's decision. On the other hand, a pleasant interpersonal atmosphere is rewarding and members may fear that a minority opinion will upset this atmosphere.

Again we stress a reoccurring theme of this book. Group members must be committed to a norm of productivity. Effective group meetings are based on a pleasant interpersonal atmosphere. However, when the maintenance of this "we feeling" becomes the group's goal, the norm of productivity has been undermined. We suggest that you recognize the possibility of this danger to group productivity and maintain a priority on the free exchange of information among group members.

SUMMARY

People who are attracted to a group through its rewards develop satisfaction that leads to group cohesiveness. Satisfied members of cohesive groups tend to be more productive (providing the group has agreed on a high productivity norm), communicate with other members more frequently, exert more influence over other group members, and accept more responsibility within the group. The satisfied member of the cohesive group adopts the group goals as her or his own, devotes much energy to the group, and seldom misses group meetings.

CONCLUSIONS AND RECOMMENDATIONS

1. A group member's satisfaction with her or his group depends on rewards provided by the group.
2. Group cohesiveness results from the total impact of all features that make a group attractive.
3. The three factors that most often affect member satisfaction are status congruence, perception of progress toward group goals, and perceived freedom to participate.
4. Members who are able to contribute information about the group's task experience higher levels of satisfaction than those who are not able to contribute such information.
5. Members with proficient small group communication skills experience higher levels of satisfaction with their small group work.
6. Members of congenial groups experience higher levels of satisfaction than members in groups that are not congenial.

7. Members ought to make clear and frequent positive comments about the contributions of other group members.
8. Unless a norm of productivity emerges, cohesive groups may be unproductive.
9. Cohesive groups, given a norm of productivity, achieve their goals more efficiently than groups that are not cohesive.
10. Cohesive group members communicate with each other more frequently than members of groups that are noncohesive.
11. Members of cohesive groups exert more influence over each other than members of noncohesive groups.
12. Members of cohesive groups are more likely to accept responsibility for group tasks than members of noncohesive groups.

REFERENCES

1. Leonard Berkowitz, "Group Standards, Cohesiveness, and Productivity," *Human Relations* 7 (1954): 509–519.
2. Leonard Berkowitz and Bernard I. Levy, "Pride in Group Performance and Group-Task Motivation," *Journal of Abnormal and Social Psychology* 53 (1956): 300–306 .
3. Ernest G. Bormann, *Discussion and Group Methods: Theory and Practice*, 2nd ed. (New York: Harper and Row, 1975).
4. Barry E. Collins and Harold Guetzkow, *A Social Psychology of Group Processes for Decision-Making* (New York: John Wiley and Sons, 1964).
5. Barry E. Collins and Bertram H. Raven, "Group Structure: Attractions, Coalitions, Communication, and Power," in Gardner Lindzey and Elliot Aronson (eds.), *The Handbook of Social Psychology*, 2nd ed., vol. 4 (Reading, Mass.: Addison-Wesley, 1969), pp. 102–204.
6. Morton Deutsch, "Some Factors Affecting Membership Motivation and Achievement Motivation in a Group," *Human Relations* 12 (1959): 82–95.
7. Ralph V. Exline, "Group Climate as a Factor in the Relevance and Accuracy of Social Perception," *Journal of Abnormal and Social Psychology* 55 (1957): 382–388.
8. Leon Festinger, "Informal Social Communication," *Psychological Review* 57 (1950): 271–282.
9. Nicholas T. Fouriezos, Max L. Hutt, and Harold Guetzkow, "Measurement of Self-Oriented Needs in Discussion Groups," *Journal of Abnormal and Social Psychology* 45 (1950): 682–690.
10. Harold B. Gerard, "The Effects of Status, Role Clarity, and Group Goal Clarity Upon the Individual's Relations to Group Process," *Journal of Personality* 25 (1957): 475–488.

11. W. A. Haythorn, "The Influence of Individual Members on the Characteristics of Small Groups," *Journal of Abnormal and Social Psychology* 48 (1953): 276–284.

12. W. Clay Hammer and Donald L. Harnett, "Goal Setting, Performance, and Satisfaction in an Interdependent Task," *Organizational Behavior and Human Performance* 12 (1974): 217–230.

13. Richard Heslin and Dexter Dunphy, "Three Dimensions of Member Satisfaction in Small Groups," *Human Relations* 17 (1964): 99–112.

14. L. Richard Hoffman, "Homogeneity of Member Personality and its Effect on Group Problem-Solving," *Journal of Abnormal and Social Psychology* 58 (1959): 27–32.

15. Irving L. Janis, *Victims of Groupthink: A Psychological Study of Foreign Policy Decisions and Fiascoes* (Boston: Houghton Mifflin, 1972).

16. Thomas J. Knutson and William Holdridge, "Orientation Behavior, Leadership and Consensus: A Possible Functional Relationship," *Speech Monographs* 38 (1971): 177–181.

17. Cedric Larson, "Guidance is Central in Sweden's New School Plan," *Personnel and Guidance Journal* 31 (1953): 532–535.

18. Harold J. Leavitt, "Some Effects of Certain Communication Patterns on Group Performance," *Journal of Abnormal and Social Psychology* 46 (1951): 38–50.

19. Albert J. Lott and Bernice Eisman Lott, "Group Cohesiveness, Communication Level, and Conformity," *Journal of Abnormal and Social Psychology* 62 (1961): 408–412.

20. Stanley Schacter, Morris Ellertson, Dorothy McBride, and Doris Gregory, "An Experimental Study of Cohesiveness and Productivity," *Human Relations* 4 (1951): 229–238.

21. Marvin E. Shaw, *Group Dynamics: The Psychology of Small Group Behavior,* 2nd ed. (New York: McGraw-Hill, 1976).

22. Marvin E. Shaw, "Random versus Systematic Distribution of Information in Communication Nets," *Journal of Personality* 25 (1956): 59–69.

23. Marvin E. Shaw and Lilly May Shaw, "Some Effects of Sociometric Grouping in a Second Grade Classroom," *Journal of Social Psychology* 57 (1962): 453–458.

24. Ewart E. Smith, "The Effects of Clear and Unclear Role Expectations on Group Productivity and Defensiveness," *Journal of Abnormal and Social Psychology* 55 (1957): 213–217.

25. John W. Thibaut and Harold H. Kelley, *The Social Psychology of Groups* (New York: John Wiley and Sons, 1959).

26. Robert S. Wyer, Jr., "Effects of Incentive to Perform Well, Group Attraction, and Group Acceptance on Conformity in a Judgmental Task," *Journal of Personality and Social Psychology* 4 (1966): 21–26.

4

DECISION STRUCTURE

Task-oriented groups are expected to develop an acceptable decision proposal. In time, members of these groups prepare a proposal that satisfies their own interests and hopefully the interests of persons external to these groups. We cannot chart with exact detail the course a group will follow in arriving at its decision proposal, but we can make a number of recommendations that will assist a group in formulating an effective decision proposal. One of the first considerations before the group is identification of the type of task and its requirements. Each type of task is characterized by a different set of demands. Knowing the requirements of the task sets the stage for the group's analysis and information search. In formulating a decision proposal, a group will generally set its objectives (context of discovery), acquire information (context of information search), and justify its proposal (context of justification). The effectiveness of this proposal will depend on the decision-making process that emerges in the group.

Disagreements among group members are an inevitable element of small group discussions. Often we back away from these disagreements and fail to use them constructively. When appropriately managed, these conflicts represent opportunities to improve our thinking and decisions. We have devoted a full chapter to ways that the groups can constructively use conflict.

In the following three chapters we discuss central issues related to task analyses, formulation of a decision proposal, and management of conflict. An understanding of this material should help group members to make effective decisions in their information search and processing.

CHAPTER 8

Task Analysis

INTRODUCTION

As we suggested in Chapter 1, the basic purpose for meeting in groups is to discover ways to control our environment. While much of the content of this book pertains to all types of small groups, we chose to emphasize task-oriented groups. Task-oriented groups work on topics that are external to the group. That is, if the recommendations of the group are adopted, they will affect people outside the task-oriented group. Thus, central to task-oriented group discussions is the task your group chooses. Careful attention to the task will enable us to discover more desirable alternatives than those presently available. We also suggested in Chapter 2 that task demands operate as one key determinant of the success of your group experience. Shaw (13) notes that task characteristics may be expected to exert a strong influence upon group process. Hence, in many ways the task is a focal point of small group discussions. We will describe in this chapter some of the characteristics of tasks that affect the success of your group experiences.

CRITICAL TASK DEMANDS

Some tasks are suitable for group attention and others are inappropriate for small group discussion. The importance of selecting appropriate tasks is underscored by the complaint that small group experiences are often a waste of time and effort. Obviously, factors other than the task itself contribute to unsuccessful group discussions. Selection of an inappropriate task, however, will almost certainly impinge on the value, ease, and success of your group effort. How can we decide whether a task is suitable for group attention? We suggest here that consideration of three critical demands will enable you to decide which tasks are amenable to group work (3). First, the task should be open-ended; second, the task should facilitate division of labor among the group members; and third, the task should require a range of member backgrounds.

The first critical demand involves a judgment about the range of issues or alternatives associated with the task. A suitable task should require discussion of several issues or alternatives. If the outcome is predetermined, few persons are likely to apply themselves to working on the task. In other words, the potential content of the group's final product should be open-ended. Your group should be able to consider several possible approaches to the task. Take, for example, the topic of individualized instruction. If the task were to compile a list of 25 references on individualized instruction published since 1970, it would be closed-ended. You would know in advance the exact content of your final product, and group action probably would not be especially beneficial. Members could work independently to arrive at a list of 25 references. However, if your task were to consider the benefits and limitations of individualized instruction, the task would be open-ended. Your group would need to consider and make judgments about several issues in order to determine the value of this method of learning. The content of your group's decision would not be known in advance. Only after several discussions would the content of your decision begin to materialize. Tasks suitable for deliberation in small groups facilitate discussion and the exchange of ideas.

Second, the task should be complex enough to permit division of labor. If each member were performing the same subtask, the unique qualities and abilities of your group members would not be used. In the end, you would waste the resources your members bring to the group. One possible division of labor would be to divide responsibilities for information search. Your group could decide to interview several persons who are knowledgeable about your task's subject matter. You could select three people to interview and then assign two group members to interview one person, two to interview the second person, and so on. Consider the example of individualized instruction again. If your task were to compile the bibliography of 25 references, each member would be doing approximately the same subtask in information search. When the members returned to the group, there would be very little to talk about. There would be no issues to analyze or decisions to make. This analysis is the exciting and useful part of small group discussions. On the other hand, if you were considering the value of individualized instruction, you could make a variety of assignments in information search. Some members could interview professors who use this method of instruction. Others could talk with students who have taken courses using the method. Some members may wish to investigate how such programs are run. Someone else might seek information on what subjects are appropriate for this kind of instruction. The possibilities for division of labor go on and on. This division of labor brings more diverse information before the group. Different issues and perspectives would be brought before the group. Your group's discussion would likely be lively and interesting as well as productive. In effect, the division of labor enables the group to use its time and resources effectively.

Third, the task should require a range of member backgrounds for adequate resolution. A group with varied member backgrounds can bring more insight and perspectives to a task than a group with members having nearly the same background. Research indicates that when other things are equal groups composed of members who have different ability levels perform better than groups having members with similar abilities (8). Remember that the purpose of small group activity is to discover ways to control the environment. The likelihood of making these discoveries increases when your group is composed of members with diverse backgrounds. Once again let us return to the task on individualized instruction. The task to compile a bibliography entails some minimal background on how to use the library. A variety of member backgrounds would have little, if any, effect on the group's outcome. Going to the library would be the same routine for each member. Approaching the task of assessing the value of individualized instruction would be a very different process. In this case, a variety of backgrounds would be very useful. A group composed of members with different majors and with different educational experiences would bring a variety of experiences and perspectives to the task. This diversity in backgrounds would enable the group to discover a variety of issues related to individualized instruction. The group would also be likely to sift through their information and isolate the most important issues. One other consideration relates to diversity of member backgrounds. In Chapter 1, we suggested that each group is bound by a set of constraints. Constraints are personal, social, and organizational beliefs about reality that guide the thinking and action of a group. Some of these constraints are useful; others dampen the group's discovery process. A group composed of heterogeneous members is more likely to identify useful and inhibiting constraints. If the group investigating individualized instruction were composed only of members who had taken a course taught in this way and who also disliked the class, their view would be quite limited. A more diverse group would create a more balanced and insightful analysis of this instructional method (9).

In summary, tasks appropriate for small group effort are open-ended, permit division of labor, and require diversity of member backgrounds. Let us reflect for a moment on what this means for your discussion in small groups. Small groups are useful when they discover desirable means for controlling their environment. Small groups are productive when they mobilize and use their member resources. For many people, working in small groups is more exciting and rewarding than working by themselves. These outcomes, however, can only be obtained when the group is working on an appropriate task. An appropriate task requires give and take on a variety of issues and uses the unique skills, insight, and knowledge of the group members. Figure 8.1 illustrates how various tasks might best be approached when these three critical demands are taken into account.

Task Characteristics	Assignment
• One correct answer (e.g., solution to a mathematical equation)	• Most capable person
• Routine collection of information (e.g., preparation of a bibliography)	• Individuals working separately, coordinated by one person
• Open-ended task (e.g., solution to a social problem)	• Task-oriented group

Figure. 8.1   Appropriate Assignment of Tasks

BASIC TASK TYPES

We find it useful to think about group tasks in terms of whether they are descriptive, discussion, or problem-solving tasks (5). It is useful to think about tasks in this manner because the task demands for each task are different. Hence, when your group identifies the type of task, you will understand what is required for analysis and discussion.

Descriptive Tasks

The first type of task calls for a description of the present situation. We refer to this type of task as a *descriptive* task. There are two primary task demands associated with descriptive tasks. The first demand involves the selection of categories or concepts used to describe the present state of affairs. The second demand requires that the description be factually true. Let us illustrate these two demands. Suppose your group were investigating the impact of domestic pets on our society. The group would first need to categorize domestic pets. Do you include more exotic pets like snakes and monkeys as well as dogs, cats, and birds? Do you investigate food requirements, psychological benefits, and health hazards? Do you consider economic impact of the pet enterprise? Is there a pet population explosion? There are numerous concepts you could use to describe this task. You need to be assured that your categories are useful in describing the task. This choice of concepts will reflect the interests and expertise of your group members.

Once you have selected the concepts to describe your task, the second demand requires an accurate description of the topic. You will want to compile true statements of fact about the topic. Your descriptions will use the concepts your group feels are necessary for describing the topic. Nonetheless, the emphasis here includes the accuracy of the statements. For example, you need accurate data on the food requirements of our pet population. You will want accurate descriptions of the economic impact of the pet enterprise, and so on.

Groups are frequently formed to arrive at an adequate (appropriate choice of concepts) and accurate description of an event or topic. One of the most enduring "descriptive tasks" of recent times centers on the assassination of John F. Kennedy. Were there two assassins or only one? Was he shot from the front or from the back? The list of questions requiring factual answers seems to grow daily. The primary responsibility of a jury is to decide what is the appropriate factual description of an alleged crime or tort. The judge's instructions generally specify the appropriate concepts or categories, and the witnesses provide the factual descriptions of the case. The jury must decide the accuracy of these descriptions. Fact-finding committees, presidential commissions, and task forces are common in our society. One of the responsibilities of these groups is to arrive at an accurate description of the elements of their task. You too, we are confident, will at one time or another serve on a so-called "fact-finding group." Remember that your two primary responsibilities are to agree on appropriate categories to describe the event and to arrive at an accurate description of the event.

Sometimes we are locked into only one way of thinking about or describing events. In reality, events are more complex and rich than our descriptions of them. Of necessity, our descriptions will be incomplete. Once we have agreed to describe an event in a particular way, we can determine whether or not these descriptions are accurate. We are able to assess these statements of fact for their truth or falsity. We cannot prove, however, that any one set of concepts is the only set or the one "right" set for describing that event. Hence, it is imperative for your group to be creative and perceptive in the selection of concepts to describe an event.

Discussion Tasks

A second type of task calls for an agreement about the important beliefs and values associated with a topic. These important beliefs and values are usually referred to as issues. We will refer to these tasks as *discussion* tasks. Two demands are also associated with discussion tasks. First, the group must reach agreement on what set of beliefs and values apply to the topic. A belief statement expresses a relationship between two events. The comment: "Reducing the speed limit to 55 mph will result in a reduction of traffic fatalities" expresses a relationship between the rate of speed and the number of traffic fatalities. Statements of this type cannot be shown to be true or false, but we do accept them as valid with some degree of probability. If someone provided sufficient evidence in support of this belief, we would be likely to accept it as valid. We cannot, however, seek out an observable event to show that each comment is true or false. Truth or falsity of a comment applies only to statements of fact. Belief statements have an if-then quality about them. If we observe one event, we can expect a second event to occur. There is always an inference involved. We make a judgment that connects event "A" with event "B." For example, we make an assumption that speed limit (event A) is connected to traffic fatalities (event B). We cannot actually see this connection, but we assume that it holds with some degree of believability. Statements of value express the opinion that a specific mode of conduct or end state of existence is personally or socially preferable. Value statements express one's opinion that something or some behavior is good or bad, right or wrong, desirable or undesirable. Some people hold the opinion that premarital sex is bad. Others believe that it is desirable. These are both expressions of value. Most people hold the position that every American citizen should have adequate medical care. Some people believe that every citizen should be guaranteed a minimal annual income. Others hold that one should work for his or her income. Again these are value statements. Therefore, the first demand of discussion tasks is to reach agreement on what beliefs and values apply to the topic.

The second demand is to show why these beliefs and values are useful in thinking about the topic. We can use many different beliefs and values to think about a topic. We need to ask questions such as: Are these the central issues related to the topic? Are these issues the most useful way to think about the topic? How much confidence can we have in the statements of belief? How acceptable are the statements of value?

Representative discussion tasks include the pros and cons of capital punishment, abortion, and guaranteed annual income. Suppose your group were discussing capital punishment. A common argument for capital punishment is that it deters crime. This comment is a belief statement connecting capital punishment with detering crime. How much confidence can we have in this belief. What do the experts say? What statements of fact can we find that support this belief? A common argument against capital punishment is that it is wrong to take a person's life. This comment is a value statement expressing the position that taking one's life is wrong. Why would someone take this position? What reasons do people use to support this position? Eventually, your group would decide on the important beliefs and values associated with the topic and show why these issues were important and useful.

Another example may help to clarify these demands. Recently several groups have devoted considerable attention to the characteristics of a good teacher. Several issues commonly come up in these discussions:

1. Instructors should be knowledgeable about their subject matter, including current material.
2. Instructors should be able to effectively interact with students in the classroom.
3. Instructors should present well-organized and clear lectures.
4. Instructors should be fair in their methods of testing and grading.

Obviously, other issues would likely be raised by a group discussing this topic, but for the moment let us assume that your group agreed that these were the four most important criteria for rating an instructor. Some justification for the selection of these criteria is called for. Some interested parties outside your group may not accept your analysis. An explanation why these issues are more pertinent than others is called for. Your justification of the four criteria might be as follows. We believe that students should obtain meaningful and valid material in the classroom. Instructors who are knowledgeable in their field and also are familiar with the current material are more likely to provide this knowledge than those who are not as well informed. You might argue that students will find their classroom experience more enjoyable and motivating if the instructor can interact effectively with them in classroom discussions. Your group might suggest that clear and organized presentation of information would result in more effective learning by students. Finally, your group might argue that the testing and grading system should be a valid representation of students' achievement in the course. Hence, instructors who are fair in their methods of evaluation are more likely to approach this goal.

We are sure you could continue to elaborate on the desirability of using these criteria for assessing teaching effectiveness. You might turn to published studies that relate these qualities of an instructor to learning effectiveness. Using these results would lend additional support to your agreement about the importance of these criteria. You might turn to the comments of experts in the field to support these criteria. Thus, you could justify your choice of issues by their usefulness, by the support they receive from related statements of fact, and by the support of recognized experts.

Undoubtedly, you have been in groups with discussion tasks. They are often used in classes in which issues are an important part of the class material. Questions about desirable features of a park and recreation program, alternative life-styles, environmental protection, and population control are often discussed in small groups. As you participate in groups with discussion tasks, keep in mind that your purpose is to decide what central issues are related to your task and to justify your selection of a specific set of issues.

Problem-Solving Tasks

Perhaps the most popular type of group task is the *problem-solution* task. In this case your group would be asked to agree on a solution to a particular problem. The task demands associated with problem-solving tasks include a careful description of the problem, selection of an acceptable solution, analysis of the workability of the solution, and recommendations about how to implement the solution. Some common problems that have demanded our attention include means for conserving energy, alternative forms of energy, disposal of nuclear wastes, gang warfare, and other forms of crime. Problem-solution tasks occur when an undesirable condition exists. Someone or some group feels strongly about a problem and seeks solutions to this problem in order to create a more desirable environment.

The requirements for a problem-solution task are more comprehensive than for the descriptive and discussion tasks. To adequately understand the problem, your group must arrive at a thorough factual description of the problem. Hence, the task demands associated with *descriptive* tasks are also a part of the problem-solving task. Obviously, all potential solutions are not equally acceptable. Given the values and interests of your group some solutions will be more desirable than others. The selection of a solution will entail discussion of relevant beliefs and values. Consequently, the task demands associated with *discussion* tasks are also a part of problem-solving tasks. Finally, the group will have to make predictions about the effectiveness of the solution and how to best implement the solution. All of these considerations suggest that problem-solving tasks are generally the most complex of the three types of tasks.

Groups working on problem-solving tasks often presume that a problem exists without thoroughly investigating the situation. Too frequently, it seems, a group advances to the discussion of solutions prematurely. The problem or need is assumed to exist and work is directed toward solving this assumed need. If the problem cannot be clearly identified and described, the work directed toward a solution is meaningless. A group in one of our discussion classes, for example, decided to correct the "disastrous and dangerous conditions" allegedly characterizing the campus security force. Their description of the problem was based on rumors and several bad experiences. The group proceeded almost immediately to discussion of solutions. After spending much effort to develop and analyze solutions, the group discovered that campus security had received several awards for excellence from such diverse organizations as the National Association of Chiefs of Police and the American Civil Liberties Union. As you might expect, the group was embarrassed. They could have saved considerable time by checking the nature of the "problem" before moving to creation of a solution. To improve the quality of the campus security force was a worthwhile goal, but successful achievement of the goal depended on clearly describing and demonstrating the existence of true and bothersome conditions.

The following example illustrates how a group might approach a problem-solution task. Suppose the company where you are employed is experiencing difficulties between supervisors and their subordinates. Also assume that you are assigned to a group to study this problem and make recommendations for change. One of the first things you would need to do is to obtain an accurate description of the difficulty. You might interview a sample of supervisors and subordinates to obtain their perceptions of the problem. You might also want to interview middle management to get their impressions of the problem. You could even go so far as to distribute a questionnaire designed to assess the nature of the problem. You might also be in a position to observe interaction between supervisors and subordinates. Your group could also examine memos and other means of communication between these two groups of people. Perhaps you could examine similar organizations to discover norms and the extent to which your company deviates from these norms. During the process of investigation, you would be trying to figure out the best way to define the problem as well as arriving at an accurate description of the difficulties.

In coming up with an accurate and valid description of the problem, your group would likely have considered several possible courses of action for solving the difficulties between supervisors and subordinates. Your group will find some of these alternatives more attractive than others. Obviously, your group will want to prepare a proposal that will address the factual descriptions of the problem. However, there are many possible solutions that will address the critical factual elements of the problem. The most acceptable solution from your group's perspective will reflect the group members' beliefs and values. Thus, your group should spend some time discussing those beliefs and values and their implications for selecting a decision proposal.

Perhaps in your investigation your group may have discovered that the duties of subordinates were not clearly understood. One possible solution might be to teach supervisors to be more directive and assertive. Another possibility would be to change the working situation so that supervisors and subordinates would meet regularly to discuss job responsibilities openly. If your group members were more task-oriented, they might find the directive solution more attractive. On the other hand, if your group were oriented to human relations, they might find the participatory solution more desirable. Finally, your group must decide how to implement their recommendations for change. Again several options will be open to your group. You may decide that a training course for supervisors held at a nearby resort might be the best means for making change. Perhaps a series of Monday morning staff meetings would be the best vehicle for implementing change. Your group would likely consider other alternatives for implementation of your solution. Your group would also need to determine if the solution is workable. Perhaps the retreat to a nearby resort would be impossible because the company does not have a budget for this kind of training. Maybe the supervisiors would be reluctant to cooperate. On the other hand, there may be available money to support the solution and the supervisors may be eager to cooperate. In any case, your group would need to analyze the situation to determine whether your solution could be implemented. Your group will find it necessary to determine the means most likely to succeed for solution of the problem. Both the description of the problem and the proposal of a solution require accurate analysis. You must be able to prove the existence of a problem as well as prove that your solution solves the problem.

In specifying descriptive, discussion, and problem-solving tasks, we have tried to alert you to the fact that each type of task has its own set of requirements. Knowing the requirements should help your group create a more effective product. We have also tried to emphasize that there is no single right way to approach a task. There are many different ways of conceptualizing each task. Your group can choose from many different perspectives for discussing the elements of your task. Finally, the focus in this chapter is on the internal analysis of your task, that is, how the members of your group think and talk about the task. Remember that a part of task analysis also includes recognition of issues persons outside your group will raise. The final product of a task-oriented group, the decision proposal, is actually prepared for persons outside your group. Consequently, you will need to consider reactions of these persons to your analysis and decisions. A summary of task types and their requirements is provided in Figure 8.2.

Task Type	Task Demands
Descriptive	Selection of an appropriate set of concepts to describe the task Development of a factual information base
Discussion	Selection of an appropriate set of issues to analyze the task Justification of the usefulness of these beliefs and values
Problem Solving	Development of a factual information base to describe the problem Analysis of potential solutions to the problem Selection of a solution to alleviate or correct the problem Assessment of the workability of the solution Prescriptions for implementing the solution

Fig. 8.2   Summary of Task Types and Their Requirements

GENERAL TASK DIMENSIONS

In the previous section we described the requirements associated with descriptive, discussion, and problem-solving tasks. In this section we want to specify the dimensions that characterize tasks in general, whether they be descriptive tasks, discussion tasks, or problem-solving tasks. The purpose of introducing these task dimensions is to help you analyze your group's discussion when your group encounters problems. It is possible that the source of your group's problems resides in the characteristics of the task.

Shaw (13) selected 104 tasks and asked a sizeable number of people to react to these tasks on several dimensions. Then through a variety of statistical techniques he identified six independent dimensions that characterized these tasks. Of the six dimensions the four dimensions of difficulty, solution multiplicity, intrinsic interest, and cooperation requirements seem especially relevant to the task types we described earlier.

Difficulty refers to the "... amount of effort required to complete the task" (13, p. 311). Level of difficulty is a function of the breadth of knowledge required to complete the group's task, the number of issues related to the task, and the clarity of the procedures needed to complete the group's task. A less difficult task would require information from a very limited area and would involve only one or two issues. In conjunction with these characteristics, the group members would know exactly what steps were required to analyze the task and complete their task. A more difficult task would require information from several areas and would involve a number of issues. In addition, the group members would be initially uncertain about what steps were required to complete their task. Tasks of high difficulty require considerable discussion about both the informational and procedural dimensions of group interaction. Let us return to the group working on individualized instruction. The task of compiling a bibliography would be easy. Not much information is required to complete the task, and the steps for completing it are clear. A considerable range of information, however, is required to evaluate the usefulness of individualized instruction. It will take considerable time and discussion to figure out the steps required to complete this task. It would be much more difficult therefore.

Solution multiplicity denotes the degree to which there is more than one correct or acceptable solution to the task (13, p. 311). The level of solution multiplicity involves the number of alternatives a group may consider for task completion and the degree to which acceptable alternatives can be shown to be effective. Low solution multiplicity would entail one or two alternatives, one of which could easily be shown to be effective. High solution multiplicity would involve the consideration of many alternatives, none of which could be easily demonstrated to be effective. The problem of how to stimulate the economy is of high solution multiplicity. Will a tax rebate to individual citizens be effective? Will lowering taxes for business and industry be effective? Should the supply of money be expanded or reduced? Will changing interest rates for loans have a desirable effect on the economy? There are many alternatives, and experts are not sure whether one or all of the alternatives would be effective.

Intrinsic interest is defined as "... the degree to which the task in and of itself is interesting, motivating, or attractive to the group members" (13, p. 311). Intrinsic interest does not necessarily mean that group members find the task to be of great value, although this may be true. Instead, it refers to the challenge and enjoyment of working on a task such as solving a puzzle. The members relate to the task in terms of whether it is exciting or dull.

Cooperation requirements refers to the degree to which members must coordinate their activities to complete their task (13, p. 311). Tasks with high cooperation requirements imply that each member must perform her or his duties at exactly the right time and in exactly the right way. On the other hand, tasks low in cooperation requirements imply that group members can more or less loosely perform their duties in time and exactness. Landing a Boeing 747 at Chicago's O'Hare airport involves high cooperation requirements. The captain, first officer, flight engineer, and traffic controller must precisely per-form their duties at exactly the right moment. The level of cooperation requirements may also be a function of necessary coordination with people outside the group. Sometimes a series of activities must be coordinated with several outside groups. Suppose you were a member of a group working on a campaign to persuade people to conserve water. You would likely find yourself working with radio and TV sta-tions, newspapers, and other interested groups in the community.

TASK DIMENSIONS AND GROUP PROCESS

The dimensions of your task affect both the process of interaction in your group and the productivity of your group. We will now present some of the effects of these dimensions on group process and productivity.

Difficulty

One of the consistent and intuitively obvious research findings shows that the quality of group performance decreases with increasing task difficulty (5, 7). There is also evidence that performance drops if the task is too easy (11). Figure 8.3 illustrates this pattern. The diagram shows that when the task is low in difficulty group performance will also be low. As the task increases in difficulty, group performance also increases. When the task becomes higher in difficulty, group perfor-mance begins to drop off. As problems become extremely difficult, group performance is again low. The plausibility of this pattern seems evident. Difficulty was described in terms of required breadth of knowledge, number of related issues, and clarity of the steps required to complete the task. The higher levels of difficulty place greater de-mands on the group. At some point, these demands become too great, and the performance of the group begins to decrease. If the task were extremely difficult, the group would not be able to make any progress. The group might disband because members could not attain rewards associated with goal achievement. Frustration sets in and members become dissatisfied, saying, "We can't do anything about it." On the other hand, if the task is too easy, it will not capture the attention of group members. Members will fail to apply themselves and hence group performance will be low.

    The pattern of interaction within the group has a moderating effect on the level of difficulty a group can handle. Shaw (12) found that a pattern of interaction that encourages maximum participation by all members enables the group to solve complex tasks more efficiently

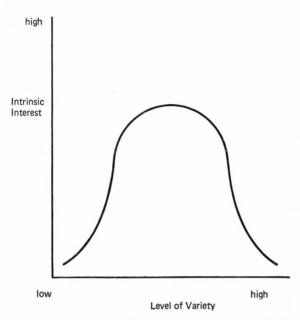

Intrinsic
Interest

low   high
Level of Variety

Fig. 8.3   Relationship of Task Difficulty and Group Performance

than a pattern of interaction that restricted the participation of members. Shaw and Blum (14, 15) found that when members are able to express their feelings of satisfaction with the group process if the task is difficult, it enhances group effectiveness. Open patterns of communication within the group enable the group to handle more difficult tasks. Figure 8.4 illustrates this relationship. A comparison of Part A and Part B of the figure shows that groups with maximum opportunity for participation perform better on more difficult tasks than groups with restricted opportunity for participation.

Hackman (5) studied the relationship between task difficulty and various qualities of the group product. He found that products from more difficult tasks tend to be more original and more involved with issues. Products from easier tasks tend to be better presented and to meet the task objectives more adequately. These findings present a dilemma for persons interested in effective group decision making. One would want a group's product to be characterized by originality, orientation to issues, clear presentation, and fulfilling group objectives. Apparently, as one moves in either direction of difficulty, some aspect of the group's product is sacrificed.

Perhaps the resolution of this dilemma is found in the procedural dimension of group interaction. If the group can establish effective

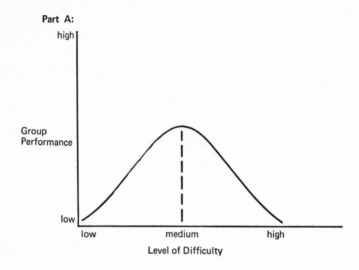

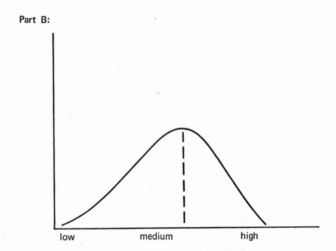

Fig. 8.4 Relationship of Open and Restricted Participation to Task Difficulty and Group Performance

leadership and develop an effective strategy, some of the losses associated with more difficult tasks can be avoided. This suggestion finds support in the research literature. Raven and Rietsema (10) found that goal clarity and goal path clarity are positively associated with group efficiency. A group's productivity increases when needed steps to achieve the group's goals are relatively clear (2). In other words, the impact of informational difficulty of a task can be lessened considerably by emphasizing the procedural dimension of small group discussion.

Solution Multiplicity

The research about solution multiplicity supports our emphasis on the procedural dimension. Shaw (12) suggests that the most appropriate leadership behavior for a task-oriented group depends partially on solution multiplicity. If a task is low in solution multiplicity, directive leadership would be more effective. This finding assumes a pleasant interpersonal atmosphere and an established group leader. On the other hand, if a task is high in solution multiplicity, nondirective leadership would be more effective (15). This finding suggests that when the range of possible alternatives is limited, little time is necessary for exploration. The task is to achieve adoption of one of the known alternatives, and thus the need for directive leadership is obvious. However, when the range of alternatives is large and uncertain, the group needs time and encouragement to explore issues, and thus the need for a permissive, nondirective style of leadership is clear. Suppose you are playing football. During the huddle you are trying to decide on the next play. You expect the quarterback to take charge and to be directive in deciding the next play. If everyone contributed his or her advice and then voted on the next play, your team probably would not win many ball games. However, if you were a member of a group discussing a more complex topic such as energy needs, you would want time to explore various issues. Nondirective leadership would be more suitable for this situation.

Intrinsic Interest

Task characteristics influence the level of intrinsic interest, and intrinsic interest affects group process and productivity. The key factor that affects member interest in a topic is variety (4). Informational variety is the diversity of information required to successfully complete the group's task. Skill variety is the number of functions required to achieve the group's goal.

Informational variety pertains to the content of statements of fact, opinion, and advice. If the number of relevant concepts and sources of information are limited, a task is characterized by low informational variety. To the degree that the number of relevant concepts and sources of information increases, the task is characterized by increasing levels of informational variety. A task to find the location of libraries in a large urban area would involve low informational variety. The number of relevant concepts and sources of information would be limited and well defined. On the other hand, a task that attempts to develop a system for evaluating new methods of mass transportation in a large urban area would involve high informational variety. In this case, the number of relevant concepts and issues would be extensive and would take considerable expertise and skill to define. Nothing "new" would come before the group in the library case after the group's initial meeting, whereas in the task defining mass transit, new issues and developments would regularly come before the group. The important issue here is the contrast between repetitive and similar discussions and changing and dissimilar discussions. As a group considers a task high in informational variety, new issues and information will come before the group as they deliberate over time. The group members would not be able to predict exactly what will be discussed at the next meeting. Berlyne (1) has consistently found a strong positive relationship between informational variety and intrinsic motivation. Schroder, Driver, and Streufert (11) have shown that informational variety is related to intrinsic interest in a task. That is when the variety is manageable, variety of information results in more intrinsic interest among the group members.

Skill variety describes the range of responses group members may utilize to complete their task. A task that requires a variety of responses has higher intrinsic interest qualities than a task in which only a limited set of routine responses is required. Again, when response variety is manageable, the greater the skill variety the more intrinsic interest among the group members.

Skill variety may be considered in terms of the informational and procedural dimensions of group interaction. A group that does library research and interviews experts to obtain needed information uses a greater variety of skills than a group that reads only *Time* or *Newsweek* to obtain information. Group discussions that simply entail the listing of statements of fact requires fewer skills than discussions that include the need to relate different types of information and integrate this material in a way that is suitable to the group. Skill variety related to the procedural dimension includes behaviors such as organizing and coordinating group activity, resolving conflicts, and delegating and directing action. An optimal level of informational and skill variety exists for a task-oriented group. We have argued that low variety is associated with low intrinsic interest and high variety with higher levels of interest. However, the level of informational and skill variety can exceed the capabilities of the group to achieve its goal. We propose that a similar relationship exists between level of variety and intrinsic interest as exists between task difficulty and group perfor-

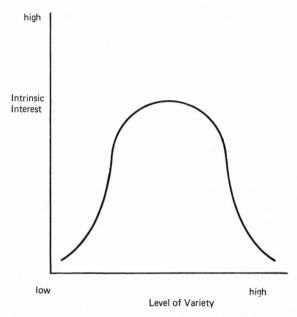

Fig. 8.5 Relationship Between Level of Variety and Intrinsic Interest of Task

mance. If the task requires very low levels of variety, the interest in the task will be low. Interest will also drop if the level of variety becomes very high. Intermediate levels of variety tend to result in higher levels of intrinsic interest. Figure 8.5 illustrates this relationship.

The secret for the effective functioning of the group is to find the optimal level of informational and skill variety. Obviously, the optimal level will vary with the composition of the group. We can only indicate the gross nature of the relationship. There is considerable support, however, for the belief that higher levels of variety result in higher levels of group performance (6, 8).

Cooperation Requirements

The quality of group products is apparently inversely related to co-operation requirements. The greater the required level of coordination in achieving the group's goal, the lower the quality of the group's product (12). Again, we suggest that appropriate leadership behavior (see Chapter 5) and an adequate strategy (see Chapter 9) will tend to reduce the inhibiting effects of high cooperation requirements. Leadership behaviors that seem important here are delegating and directing action and integrating and summarizing group activity. An appropriate strategy will assist your group in coordinating your group's search for information. A well-developed strategy will tell the group what information is needed as well as the means for acquiring this information.

SUMMARY

We have presented three aspects of task analysis in this chapter. We suggested that not all tasks are appropriate for small group work. In trying to decide which tasks are suitable for small group effort, you should consider the three critical demands of open-endedness, division of labor, and backgrounds required of group members.

We described three basic types of tasks: descriptive tasks, discussion tasks, and problem-solving tasks. Each type of task has its own set of primary requirements. We proposed that the most complex tasks were problem-solving tasks since they included the requirements of descriptive and discussion tasks as well as additional requirements unique to problem-solving tasks.

Finally, we described four general dimensions that apply to all three types of tasks. We suggested that levels of difficulty, solution multiplicity, cooperation requirements, and intrinsic interest affect both group process and performance. Sometimes a group experiences difficulties in making progress toward its goals because of the nature of the task. These general task dimensions can be used to pinpoint these difficulties and to suggest ways of overcoming them.

CONCLUSIONS AND RECOMMENDATIONS

1. Tasks appropriate for group effort should be open-ended, permit division of labor, and require a variety of member backgrounds.
2. Tasks can be classified by types—descriptive, discussion, or problem solving.
3. Descriptive tasks require the selection of an appropriate set of concepts and a development of a factual information base using these concepts.
4. Discussion tasks require the selection of central beliefs and values as well as the justification for their usefulness.
5. Problem solving tasks require the development of a factual information base, selection of a suitable solution, and prescriptions for implementing the solution.
6. All three types of tasks can be described by their difficulty, solution multiplicity, cooperation requirements, and intrinsic interest.
7. Tasks of intermediate difficulty result in higher levels of group

performance than tasks that are either very easy or very difficult.

8. Open channels of communication permit groups to handle more difficult tasks, whereas restricted channels of communication limit the group's ability to handle difficult tasks.

9. Directive leadership is more appropriate for tasks low in solution multiplicity, and nondirective leadership is more appropriate for tasks high in solution multiplicity.

10. Tasks requiring intermediate levels of information and skill variety result in higher levels of intrinsic interest than tasks requiring either low or very high variety.

REFERENCES

1. D. E. Berlyne, *Conflict, Arousal and Curiousity* (New York: McGraw-Hill, 1960).

2. Arthur R. Cohen, "Situational Structure, Self-Esteem, and Threat-Oriented Reactions to Power," in Dorwin Cartwright (ed.), *Studies in Social Power* (Ann Arbor, Michigan: Institute for Social Research, 1959).

3. Barry E. Collins and Harold Guetzkow, *A Social Psychology of Group Process for Decision-Making* (New York: John Wiley and Sons, 1964).

4. Robert Cooper, "Task Characteristics and Intrinsic Motivation," *Human Relations* 26 (1973): 387–413.

5. J. Richard Hackman, "Effects of Task Characteristics on Group Products," *Journal of Experimental Social Psychology* 4 (1968): 162–187.

6. Douglas T. Hall and Edward E. Lawler, "Job Characteristics and Pressures and the Organizational Integration of Professionals," *Administrative Science Quarterly* 15 (1970): 271–281.

7. John T. Lanzetta and Thornton B. Roby, "Group Learning Structure and Communication as a Function of Task and Structure 'Demands'," *Journal of Abnormal and Social Psychology* 55 (1957): 121–131.

8. Patrick R. Laughlin, Laurence G. Branch, and Homer H. Johnson, "Individual Versus Triadic Performance on a Unidimensional Complementary Task as a Function of Initial Ability Level," *Journal of Personality and Social Psychology* 12 (1969): 144–150.

9. Edward E. Lawler, "Job Design and Employee Motivation," *Personnel Psychology* 22 (1969): 426–435.

10. Bertrum H. Raven and Jan Rietsema, "The Effects of Varied Clarity of Group Goal and Group Path upon the Individual and His Relation to the Group," *Human Relations* 10 (1957): 29–44.

11. Harold M. Schroder, Michael J. Driver, and Siegfried Streufert, *Human Information Processing* (New York: Holt, Rinehart and Winston, 1969).

12. Marvin E. Shaw, "Some Effects on Problem Complexity upon Problem

Solution Efficiency in Different Communication Nets," *Journal of Experimental Psychology* 48 (1954): 211–217.

13. Marvin E. Shaw, *Group Dynamics,* 2nd ed. (New York: McGraw-Hill, 1976).

14. Marvin E. Shaw and J. Michael Blum, "Group Performance as a Function of Task Difficulty and the Group's Awareness of Member Satisfaction," *Journal of Applied Psychology* 49 (1965): 151–154.

15. Marvin E. Shaw and J. Michael Blum, "Effects of Leadership Styles upon Group Performance as a Function of Task Structure," *Journal of Personality and Social Psychology* 3 (1966): 238–242.

CHAPTER 9

Information Processing:
Three Steps in the Formation
of a Decision Proposal

INTRODUCTION

To a large degree, the effectiveness of your group's product depends on the ability of your group to seek out, discuss, and summarize information. You can expect better outcomes when your group obtains and discusses a broad range of information related to your task. The major responsibility confronting any task-oriented group, therefore, is to find an adequate body of information. This "information base" guides the group in its preparation and selection of a decision proposal. The composition of the information base includes statements of fact, opinion, and advice. The adequacy of your decision proposal will reflect the strengths and weaknesses of your information base. If your group fails to obtain and discuss essential information related to your task, your final product will probably be less effective than it might have been. Therefore, your group needs to develop a plan that will assure the development of an adequate information base. This chapter presents guidelines your group can use to direct your information search and processing in order to build an effective information base and prepare an effective decision proposal.

We find it useful to make a distinction between the multitude of agreements reached during your group's discussions and the final product of your group. The final product of a group has frequently been called the "group's decision." This view tends to overlook the fact that numerous decisions are made by a group as it moves toward completion of its task. To avoid any confusion on this point, we will refer to the final product of a group as its "decision proposal." We refer to the final product as your group's decision proposal because your group's recommendation affects people outside of your group. In one sense, the real test of your group's decision proposal involves acceptance of your final product by people outside your group.

Let us imagine for a moment that you are a member of a group discussing energy sources. Your group immediately faces a number of decisions. Investigating all possible energy sources would be too large a project for any group. Your group would not have the time or resources to discuss solar energy, coal, oil, nuclear power, wind currents, ocean currents, and so on. Your group needs to focus on some smaller part of the total energy problem. This limiting of your task requires that your group make several decisions. Will your group focus on one source or on a small group of sources? Suppose for the moment that your group chose to focus on solar energy. Your group is still faced with a number of decisions. Will you investigate the use of solar energy for homes? For industry? Public buildings? Let us narrow your group's task to investigating the use of solar energy for homes. Again your

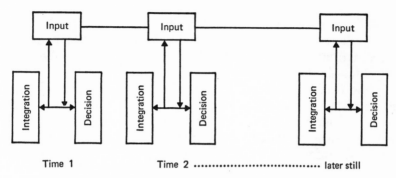

Fig. 9.1 Diagram of the Decision Process in Small Groups

group has several decisions to make. What sources of information will your group use? Will you interview experts? Read technical journals? Look at popular magazines such as *Popular Science*? What information will your group be looking for? Perhaps you would want to investigate what geographical locations are especially suited for using solar energy. You would probably need to investigate the costs and savings of using solar energy devices. What means should be employed to encourage home owners to install solar devices? Hopefully, your group will reach agreement on these issues and develop a useful decision proposal. Your effectiveness as a group would partly rest on the implementation of your proposal by people outside of your group.

How are these decisions made in small groups? We find it useful to think of this decision-making process in terms of input, integration, and decision (3). Input is any statement of fact, opinion, or advice introduced by group members. Integration involves showing relationships among statements and drawing conclusions. A decision occurs when your group members find a conclusion acceptable and express their approval of this conclusion. Figure 9.1 illustrates this process.

For example, take a small group working on a task to make recommendations for adequate protection for women from rape or assault on a university campus. Joan comments that no telephones are located in the parking lots (input). Judy relates the possible situation of not being able to start her car while a man nearby is behaving suspiciously (input). Carol suggests that a telephone in the vicinity would be useful in calling for help (integration). (Carol has shown a relationship between possible danger in the parking lot and access to a telephone.) Joan recommends that they should investigate the possibility of having telephones installed in the parking lots (input; a statement of advice). The other members agree with her recommendation (decision). At this point in their discussion the group has decided to investigate the possibility of installing telephones in the parking lots. Whether this recommendation will be a part of their decision proposal will depend on what information they find about the usefulness and feasibility of this alternative.

Some decisions are better than others. In part, the quality of a decision rests on the quality of information found by a group. There are a few general rules you can use to assess the quality of your information. Most of these rules relate to the characteristics of the source of the information.

1.   Primary sources are more likely to relate accurate and useful information than secondary sources. A primary source is a source who actually observed the event, that is, an eyewitness. Secondary sources report the accounts of primary sources. They have not witnessed the event. They are not eyewitnesses. For example, take your interest in finding out whether the Bergman movie "Scenes from a Marriage" was good or not. You would have more confidence in the impressions of someone who had seen the movie. You are not likely to be impressed by comments from a person who had not seen the movie.

2.   Expert sources are more likely to relate accurate and useful information than untrained sources. A nuclear physicist is more likely to give an accurate judgment about the controversies surrounding the use of nuclear power to generate electricity than a pediatrician. Competent sources do not necessarily have specialized training, however. An individual who has specialized experience may also be a competent source. If your group were investigating the problems of the elderly in our society, it might be a mistake to rely only on medical doctors and social workers who specialize in this field. You might also profit by talking to elderly individuals. Competence refers to the ability of the source to accurately report observations about an event or issue. A common mistake is to assume that a well-known expert is qualified to speak on all issues.

3.   Sources without a vested interest in the topic are more likely to report accurate and useful information than those with a vested interest. The conflict of interest issue assumes that those with a vested interest will make biased judgments. A person with a vested interest in agribusiness is not likely to be a good source of information about the plight of the small farmer in our society. Someone committed to our welfare system is not likely to be a good source for the issue of a guaranteed annual income. A source's vested interest may be difficult to determine. One way to overcome this difficulty is to seek out several different sources of information.

You want to have confidence in the information your group finds and accepts. Using these rules will help you assess the quality of information before your group. In summary, you want to know if the source of the information was both able (an eyewitness and competent) and willing (without a vested interest) to tell the truth.

We mentioned above that the purpose of your group is to create an effective decision proposal. We suggested that the quality of your decision proposal rests on the adequacy of your information base. There are three general issues facing your group in the preparation of its decision proposal. These are the development of a plan or strategy for information search, the development of your information base, and the justification of your decision proposal. We refer to these three issues as the context of discovery, the context of information search, and the context of justification (1). The remainder of this chapter discusses these three contexts.

CONTEXT OF DISCOVERY

The development of a strategy involves a definition of the nature of the task and the approach the group will take to achieve its goal. During the orientation phase (see Chapter 2) your group redefined the task in terms of the thinking and experience of your group members. The essential characteristic of the redefining process is agreement upon the boundaries of the task. The central issue involves a determination of what the task includes and what is excluded. For example, suppose that your group task were to study the operation of the career development center on your campus. Your group could study the administrative structure of the center, the adequacy of the center's channels of communication with potential employers, its effectiveness in reaching students on campus, and so on. Nearly all tasks of this kind are multidimensional and cannot be examined at every level by a single group. Consequently, your group must decide what facet or facets of the assigned task are necessary for your group's decision making. These decisions about what to include and exclude emerge during the orientation phase as the group discusses the topic. The range of dimensions your group sees in a task will depend on the interests and experiences of the group members and on the purposes for the existence of your group.

The success of your group will partly depend on how well your fellow members resolve the issue of definition. If your group includes too many dimensions of the task, time will preclude adequate resolution of these dimensions. If your group chooses inappropriate dimensions, the effectivenesss of its decision proposal will be limited. If the limits of the task are left unspecified, your group will not know what information to include and what to exclude when developing the information base. If your group chooses too few dimensions, essential information relevant to your task will be overlooked. The absence of boundaries will result in a wasteful and inefficient use of your group's time and energy.

The resolution of this first step in the development of your group's strategy distinguishes between successful and unsuccessful task-oriented groups. We have seen many groups produce inferior decision proposals because the group failed to agree on the boundaries of the task. A group in one of our group discussion classes wanted to suggest ways to improve the quality of education for primary school children. Volumes have been written on this topic. Some of the issues involve teaching methods, instructional materials, physical environment of the classroom, disposition of teachers, and parental involvement. The group failed to limit the boundaries of the task and consequently ended up talking in broad generalities about primary education. We should also note that the boundaries may shift as the group moves toward achieving its goal. Sometimes new, unforeseen dimensions of the task will appear that are important for the success of the group. On other occasions, dimensions that were earlier considered important will diminish in significance and be dropped from the group's deliberations. Of course, the emergence of these decisions follows the decision-making process we described above.

After your group has defined its task in terms of limiting boundaries, your group must decide on the specific direction it will take in arriving at a satisfactory decision proposal. In contrast to the process of redefinition, in which decisions about boundaries were general in nature, the decisions at this point are specific. Your group must consider what specific objectives and procedures it will follow to achieve its goal. Your group must now turn the dimensions of the task into specific objectives that you can achieve. These specific objectives refer to the specific content areas your group wants to explore and the procedures your group uses to obtain this information. Suppose your group's task were to study the most efficient construction of dwelling in an urban area for the conservation of energy. This task suggests that a number of content areas such as climate, building materials, and local sources of energy should be explored. Your group must also decide about information sources. Perhaps they will decide to search for articles in professional journals and to interview local architects, engineers, and urban planners. It is also possible that the group would decide to survey a representative sample of local citizens to obtain their reactions to various types of dwellings.

The agreement about a set of specific objectives and procedures helps to channel the group's time and effort efficiently. During its information search phase, your group can periodically review its information base and determine whether your search is complete. If the information search is not complete, you know what additional content is required to fulfill your objectives. In terms of procedures, your group also knows where to look for information. If your group has decided to consider several sources of information, you can efficiently divide the responsibilities among your fellow members.

The effective use of your group's resources partly rests on the adequacy of the group's objectives. These objectives emerge during the formative phase of your group (see Chapter 2). If your group chooses poorly at this time, it will encounter difficulty when searching for information. If specific objectives are absent, the group will repeatedly go over the same issues trying to achieve a sense of direction. This recycling dilemma is a very frustrating experience for group members, and they will soon feel that the group is simply spinning its wheels. Members of unsuccessful groups almost always describe their group experience in this manner: "We never got anyplace. We never agreed on what to do."

In addition to channeling the group's resources efficiently, agreement about a set of specific objects and procedures also affects the level of satisfaction of the group members. When these objectives are clear, the group members can see progress toward achieving their goal. One of the main determinants of member satisfaction is an awareness of goal path clarity and visible progress toward goal achievement (6, 9). (See Chapter 7 on member satisfaction.) The development of a strategy can be illustrated by a group in one of our classes. They undertook the task of examining library hours at the university. The project was chosen because of student complaints that the library was not open for a sufficient number of hours during the week. Administrators at the library had stated the library hours were limited because of fiscal constraints. They did not have enough money to keep the library open for additional hours. In discussing this problem, the group agreed on the following set of objectives:

1. To determine what hours were preferred by students.
2. To compare the hours at other state universities with this university.
3. To obtain the opinions of library personnel about the hours.
4. To determine the fiscal impact of keeping the library open for more hours.

They conducted a survey of a representative group of students to obtain their preference about library hours. They called the other libraries to get a record of hours for the other state universities. They conducted informational interviews with library personnel to obtain their ideas about library hours. Finally, they interviewed the Librarian to obtain budget information and costs for running the library. The group members knew the information they wanted to obtain and the methods they were going to use to obtain their information. This project was enthusiastically supported by the library administration, and the final project was also well received by them. This support was forthcoming partly because the group had developed a clear and well-defined strategy.

Let us now discuss objectives. We have stated that the development of a strategy includes specification of the information your group needs to complete its task and the means for obtaining this information. Obviously a strategy may be sloppily or carefully developed. The keys to keep in mind when developing a strategy are: (a) can your group agree on what information to include and what to exclude when searching for information? and (b) can your group agree on when you have achieved your objectives of information search? In other words, your group should be able to describe specific outcomes that, if achieved, would result in agreement that the objectives were achieved (5).

The first step in preparing your objectives is simply to write down all suggestions. Do not be concerned at this point with grammatical form or with precision. Simply write down the ideas. In addition, focus on what information you want to obtain and not on how you plan to obtain the information. Next arrange the objectives into general categories and eliminate duplicates. Now you are ready to refine these recommendations until they are clearly understood by each member. When an objective is clearly stated, your group members should be able to agree on what information is needed to meet that objective. In other words, your fellow members will know when each objective has been achieved. The final step involves specifying the means your group will use to obtain the information. The search for information may entail library research, interviewing experts, or conducting a survey to obtain opinions and attitudes. Usually a group will use more than one method to obtain its information.

As your group develops its information base, it may decide that some of the objectives are inadequate or that new objectives need to be added. Your group may also choose to modify its procedures for obtaining information. Nonetheless, successful development of an information base depends on the creation of a set of specific objectives and group agreement on procedures for obtaining its information.

Our description of the context of discovery is now complete. We have shown that strategy includes agreement on the relevant dimensions of the task (boundaries) and agreement on a set of specific objectives and procedures. The development of an adequate strategy often distinguishes successful groups from unsuccessful ones.

CONTEXT OF INFORMATION SEARCH

A group's information base includes the factual information, the opinions, and the recommendations or alternatives developed by your group. A coherent information base includes a systematic organization of the information showing relationships among facts, opinions, and recommendations. An adequate information base accurately reflects the dimensions of the task environment organized in a coherent form. We propose that more effective decision proposals emerge from well-developed information bases. We will show in this section the ways in which your group can develop an adequate information base.

The adoption of two general patterns, one cognitive and the other procedural, by a group can assist in developing an adequate information base. We described in the preceding section the decision-making process of input, integration, and decision that is part of the group's deliberations. Remember that integration involves showing relationships among statements and drawing conclusions. The level of integration is associated with the quality of the group's information processing. Higher levels of integration tend to result in more effective decision making, and lower levels of integration result in less effective decisions (7).

Schroder, Karlins, and Phares (8) illustrate these levels of integration with the behavior of a teacher in evaluating the progress of a student. Teacher A engages in categorical thinking when making judgments about students. Students are considered good if they obtain A or B grades and bad if they have lower grades. At this level of integration, the teacher is using only one perspective in making judgments about students. In addition, this perspective uses either/or thinking. Students are either good or bad without intervening shades of degree. Teacher B uses three perspectives in thinking about students. Teacher B also uses degrees within perspectives. Figure 9.2 illustrates these two levels of thinking.

The thinking of teachers A and B illustrates two important concepts in information processing: number of categories and differentiation. The first concept is the number of categories a person uses in thinking about events. One can think about higher education simply in terms of whether it is useful in obtaining a job. A number of other

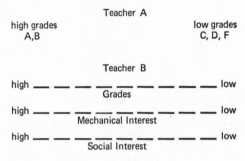

Fig. 9.2   Two Levels of Integration

concepts, however, can also be used in thinking about higher education. One might think of higher education in terms of personal development, intrinsic interest in learning, the creation of new knowledge, solving societal problems, and having a good time. The inclusion of these additional categories is probably a more useful way of thinking about higher education as well as a more accurate portrayal of the realities of higher education. The second concept refers to the level of differentiation within categories. Differentiation is often thought of in terms of shades of gray. Life is not simply black and white. There are many shades between these two colors. Obtaining a higher education does not guarantee a job after graduation. Higher education contributes in varying degrees to obtaining a job. The ability to think in degrees, that is, to differentiate shades of gray, helps us to create a more accurate and useful picture of the events and issues we discuss and seek to resolve in small groups.

The second pattern that assists the group in achieving an adequate information base is maintaining those conditions that facilitate the free expression of ideas in the group (4). The free expression of ideas refers to a group's psychological atmosphere that enables each member to introduce information and to respond positively or negatively to information introduced by other members. This psychological atmosphere rests in part on the ability of the group to maintain higher levels of integration. That is, the free expression of ideas allows the group to discover more relationships among the various statements of information. Free expression of ideas also rests on the acceptance of the procedural norm that each member has some contribution to make toward the group's deliberations. Sometimes personal characteristics of the members and the power structure of the group counteract this procedural norm. Nonetheless, the norm of an open atmosphere facilitates free expression of ideas. An open atmosphere requires group members to make responsible contributions. A responsible contribution implies that a member's comment is relevant to the group's discussion and is important in terms of content. An open atmosphere also implies that one can make positive and negative comments about the input of others without fear of harassment from other members.

There are several general sources available to your group for obtaining information. Obviously, your group members themselves will hold varying levels of information regarding the task. In some cases, group members will be chosen because of their expertise and little outside information search will be required. However, this situation is largely the exception. In most instances, your group will want to go outside its membership to obtain needed information.

This outside information search includes library research and examination of reports and other specialized documents. In Appendix A we give some guidelines to assist you in conducting library research. Usually task-oriented groups will find it necessary to interview experts to obtain needed information. Successful informational interviews are the result of careful preparation. In Appendix B we describe four basic steps for conducting informational interviews.

Upon completion of the information search phase your group should have a substantial and coherent information base. The primary purpose of the information base is to guide your group in preparing an effective decision proposal.

CONTEXT OF JUSTIFICATION

We assume at this point in your group's life span that you have agreed on your information search objectives and that your information search is complete. We also presume that your group has agreed on its decision proposal. Normally, such proposals are prepared for a larger audience than for just members of your group. Although you may be satisfied that your decision proposal is the best alternative, persons outside your group have not had the benefit of your discussions. Thus, you need to provide justification for the selection of your specific decision proposal. Another purpose of justification is to assure the group members themselves that their decision proposal is the best alternative. As you systematically analyze and justify your proposal, you may find weaknesses or gaps that were not previously evident to the group. This finding may entail further discussion and alteration of the decision proposal. Perhaps one of the most well-known models for organizing your justification is John Dewey's reflective thinking process (2).

Dewey recognized five states of thinking. He suggested that these states are not necessarily sequential. One state may be elaborated and others may be ignored at times. New states not included in the five may be included from time to time. The states he described included:

1. Some stimulus in the environment that creates a sense of difficulty or perplexity.
2. Intellectualization of the felt difficulty or perplexity. This state of thinking may include specification of dimensions, specific facts, and other conditions related to the stimulus.
3. The generation of hypotheses to initiate and guide observations.
4. Reasoning about these hypotheses resulting in assessing their probability value.
5. Implementing a hypothesis by overt or imaginative action. This act of testing hypotheses may result in failure and thus create a need to rethink the situation.

Your justification of a decision proposal can easily reflect these states of thinking.

The first segment of your justification might usefully reflect the first stage of thinking described by Dewey. The group's task reflects something in the environment that needs attention. One can reasonably ask why the task is important. Why should others direct their attention to this particular stimulus or issue? Hence, your group should be able to specify why the task is important or significant as well as a general description of the problem or issue.

The second part of your justification should be a careful description of your information search objectives. These objectives reflect dimensions of the environmental condition that resulted in the selection of the group's task. Some explanation of why these objectives were agreed on should also be included in this section. There are numerous ways of approaching any task. It is important to understand why your group took one approach to the task rather than another approach. This segment reflects the second and third stages of Dewey's reflective thinking process.

The third segment should include a summary of the results of the group's information search. This part can most readily be organized around the group's information search objectives. This part would reflect the fourth stage of thinking proposed by Dewey.

The approach to the final section will depend on the type of task considered by your group. If your group chose a descriptive or discussion task, the final section will include the conclusions reached by the group. If your group is working on a problem-solving task, you will need to show why your decision proposal is better than other alternatives considered by your group. You should also show how your solution can be implemented. This point will be of special interest to those outside your group.

Your presentation of how your solution can be implemented might include a force field analysis. A force field analysis assumes that some conditions in the environment will oppose the implementation of your solution and that other conditions will support its implementation. A force field analysis entails listing the conditions that will block the implementation of your solution and those that will support the implementation of your solution. Once these two lists are prepared, your group would rate each condition as to whether it was a major factor, of moderate importance, or of relatively little importance in preventing or supporting the implementation of your solution. Your group then shows how the obstacles can be overcome and how the supporting conditions can be used to make the changes specified by your group's solution to the problem. This method of analysis is one means to visualize implementation of your solution.

Remember that the final test of your group's productivity is the acceptability of your decision proposal to interested parties outside of your group. If you have done your homework in developing a strategy and if you have developed a useful information base, you will have the means at hand for preparing a useful decision proposal. The purpose of the context of justification is to make this sense of accomplishment evident to others as well as, to uncover potential loopholes in your group's thinking.

SUMMARY

The purpose of this chapter was to give some practical guidelines about information search and processing. We suggested that your group recognize the need to create an atmosphere in which members sense a freedom to exchange ideas, to test information, and to explore a range of alternatives related to your task.

During the context of discovery, your group should develop a strategy for achieving your task. The development of an effective strategy demands that all of the creative abilities of your group be used. It is essential that your group develop objectives that reflect the essential dimensions of your task. The creation of these objectives requires a sensitivity to the nuances of the environment as well as an awareness of the values and ideas held by your group members. During the context of information search your group should obtain the best information available to fulfill the objectives specified in your strategy. Library research, informational interviewing, surveys, and personal knowledge are major sources or means for acquiring this information. Your task during the context of justification is to persuade those outside of your group that your analysis should be accepted by them. This final step of acceptance not only tests the effectiveness of your group, but also provides one of the strongest rewards available to your group.

CONCLUSIONS AND RECOMMENDATIONS

1. The final product of your group is called your group's decision proposal because it is directed toward people outside your group.
2. A group's decision proposal is the culmination of numerous decisions reached during the group's discussions.
3. Decision making involves input, integration, and group acceptance of conclusions.
4. Primary sources are more likely to relate accurate and useful information than secondary sources.
5. Expert sources are more likely to relate accurate and useful information than untrained sources.
6. Sources without a vested interest in the topic are more likely to report accurate and useful information than sources with a vested interest.
7. The quality of your group's decision proposal rests on the adequacy of your group's information base.
8. The development of your group's decision proposal involves the preparation of a strategy and preparation of a useful information base.
9. The success of a task-oriented group depends on the ability to identify the most important dimensions of the task and agreement on a set of specific objectives and procedures.
10. Groups that achieve higher levels of information integration will perform better than groups that function at lower levels of integration.
11. Groups that achieve a psychological freedom to express positive and negative comments regarding statements of fact, opinion, and advice will perform better than groups that do not permit this free exchange of ideas.
12. A thorough justification of the decision proposal assures the group that they have created an effective proposal and helps those outside the group to see the merits of the proposal.

REFERENCES

1. Ernest G. Bormann, *Discussion and Group Methods: Theory and Practice,* 2nd ed. (New York: Harper and Row, 1975).
2. John Dewey, *How We Think* (Boston: D. C. Heath, 1933).
3. Joy Paul Guilford, *The Nature of Human Intelligence* (New York: McGraw-Hill, 1967).
4. L. Richard Hoffman, "Group Problem Solving," in Leonard Berkowitz (ed.), *Advances in Experimental Social Psychology,* vol. 2 (New York: Academic Press, 1965), pp. 99–132.
5. Robert F. Mager, *Goal Analysis* (Belmont, Calif.: Fearon Publishers, 1972).
6. Bertram H. Raven and Jan Rietsema, "The Effects of Varied Clarity of Group Goal and Group Path upon the Individual and His Relation to the Group," *Human Relations* 10 (1957): 29–44.
7. Harold M. Schroder, Michael J. Driver, and Siegfried Streufert, *Human Information Processing* (New York: Holt, Rinehart and Winston, 1969).
8. Harold M. Schroder, Marvin Karlins, and Jacqueline O. Phares, *Education For Freedom* (New York: John Wiley and Sons, 1973).
9. Marvin E. Shaw and J. Michael Blum, "Group Performance as a Function of Task Difficulty and the Group's Awareness of Member Satisfaction," *Journal of Applied Psychology* 49 (1965): 151–154.

CHAPTER 10

Management of Conflict in Decision-Making Groups

INTRODUCTION

The word "conflict" evokes a variety of responses from people—most of them negative. What do you think of when you hear someone talk about a conflict they have experienced: embarrassment, hostility, tension, or anxiety? In some cases, we would prefer to avoid hearing about another person's conflict. Ask a friend what conflict means. Almost always, your friend will describe the phenomenon as bad or unpleasant. Neither you nor your friend is unusual. Classroom teachers, for example, seldom endorse expressions of conflict about controversial topics (19). Most people view conflict as something to be avoided (1, 12). We take the position in this book, however, that conflict is not necessarily a bad behavior that should be avoided. Instead, we will suggest that conflict in small group communication can serve useful functions.

Georg Simmel (24), the German sociologist, considered conflict as something that operates as a form of socialization. In other words, conflict can be viewed as a normal and constantly occurring behavior with some positive effects. Conflict exists; it is to be expected. The problem involves what to do with a conflict when it occurs. Most people are unaware of the procedures of conflict management, and this lack of awareness explains why most people tend to view conflict as something to be avoided. We do not like to place ourselves in situations in which we feel unable to cope. Before we suggest strategies for dealing with conflict, let us look at what researchers mean when they use the term conflict.

DEFINITION OF CONFLICT

Thousands of studies have investigated various forms of conflict: intrapersonal, small group, racial, labor-management, sports, war and peace, and politics. In short, virtually nothing has been neglected. Conflict has been viewed as synonymous with battle, struggle, clash, controversy, antagonism, argument, disagreement, combat, competition, discord, strife, and dissension. The point we are making here is simply that even though thousands of conflict studies exist, no one general definition accurately describes a central, common set of conflict behaviors. If anything definite can be drawn from these studies, it is simply that conflict is inevitable.

Since conflict is inevitable, we should develop abilities to predict, experience, and understand conflict in an atmosphere free from dysfunctional anxiety. Perhaps the Indians of Santa Mata in Colombia can provide us with an example of what we mean. The Santa Mata Indians are characteristically peaceful and they carry no weapons.

> When there is a serious grievance between the two of them, they go to a rock or a large tree—each carrying a stick. Thereupon they strike at the tree or rock while uttering a multitude of insulting words until one of them breaks a stick—this person is given the victory. Then they return home and renew their friendship through social drinking (25).

While it is not necessarily our purpose to advocate social drinking, we can learn an important lesson from the Santa Mata Indians. That is, when conflict occurs, it can be dealt with in a constructive fashion. Said another way, there is some value in the old cliché that admonishes us to learn to disagree without being disagreeable.

Conflict in the task-oriented group operates as an inevitable necessity as well as an occasional source of problems. When conflict theorists use the term conflict they refer to a condition when incompatible activities or goals occur (2, 8). From your own experience, you can recall situations in which another person has engaged in behavior that prevented you from reaching your goal. Say you were a member of a group formed to decide how to spend your club's money. You try to convince the group that the money should be spent for a party. Your goal is to get the members together to have a good time. Another person in the group has a goal somewhat different from yours. He or she states that a party would be a wasteful expense and urges the group to spend the money on cleaning the club rooms. At this point, you and the other group member would be entertaining incompatible goals. To the extent a decision must be made in which one goal, *either* a party or a cleanup, must be chosen, your group would experience conflict. An important consideration to remember, however, is that your group could in fact agree on the goal of having your party, but still experience conflict over planning the party. In other words, the group does not experience incompatible goals but incompatible activities that lead to group conflict. An incompatible activity results when another person interferes or obstructs you in achieving your goal. Most small group theorists are content to view the obstruction or interference as a simple message expressing disagreement (10).

However, simple disagreement in and of itself does not constitute a sufficient condition for conflict to occur. Someone might disagree with us, but often we do not care about the issue. We must have some commitment to our position on the issue therefore. Usually this commitment is described as an emotional attachment to our position on the issue. Another way of looking at this component of conflict is to gauge the discomfort that disagreement causes. Thus, when we talk about conflict in task-oriented groups, we refer to communication patterns characterized by disagreement and discomfort (9).

TYPES OF CONFLICT IN TASK-ORIENTED GROUPS

You may recall that our task-oriented group had three distinct communication dimensions: informational, procedural, and interpersonal. The types of conflict potentially occurring in groups correspond to these three dimensions. There may be other forms of conflict, but these three occur most frequently in the task-oriented small group.

Informational Conflict

Informational conflict occurs when members of a group disagree about the substance of the group discussion. The substance or deliberations involve facts, figures, opinions of qualified authorities, and interpretation of evidence. For example, if someone asserted that this book consisted of less than 200 pages, you could cause conflict by pointing out that the book is actually more than 200 pages long. Not only would you be correct, but this example also demonstrates the need for disagreement in discussion. Failure to disagree with the inaccurate statement would have resulted in the group acceptance of an erroneous comment. Conflict may also result from differing interpretations of substantive material. We know that our beliefs, attitudes, and values affect the manner in which we interpret events. Upon reseaching the oil industry, Jerry (politically conservative) concluded that competitive

> The dam is needed to supply agriculture, according to one of the hearing's witnesses. Don White, director of the Department of Food and Agriculture, said that 90 per cent of California's farmlands depend on irrigation water. The two- to six-billion dollar loss in agriculture this year is an example of what can happen due to a lack of water, he said.

"Example of Informational Conflict"

> Tom Pope of the Environmental Defense Fund said that the dam really is not needed for irrigation. Present methods of irrigation can supply agriculture with all its needed water. Furthermore, according to Pope, "There have been substantial questions raised about the possibilities of an earthquake." If the dam breaks, countless thousands would be homeless.

pricing would result from a completely open market, whereas John (politically liberal) believes that federal controls are necessary. The expression of these two differing points of view would lead to informational conflict.

Procedural Conflict

Procedural conflict occurs when a group cannot reach agreement on the steps to follow in reaching a decision. The establishment of a group's agenda, a procedure normally occurring early in the discussion, usually results in some controversy over when to consider various topics or whether to talk about them at all. If you feel strongly about a particular topic, you may want the group to handle it early. If others want to postpone consideration, procedural conflict could occur. Agenda setting, then, is a primary cause of procedural conflict. Another reason for procedural conflict involves the methods employed to get information. Some group members may wish to do library research in order to confirm their ideas; others may argue that library research is not essential when qualified sources are available for interviews. Procedural conflict may also occur during the discussion when some group members are ready to move to another point and others are reluctant to proceed. You no doubt have experienced groups in which you thought people were trying to "railroad" a decision. The likelihood of procedural conflict in those circumstances is quite high. Procedural conflict differs from informational conflict in that information is not the focus of the conflict. Procedural conflict occurs when there are differences over agenda setting, methods of obtaining information, and the progress of the discussion.

Interpersonal Conflict

Interpersonal conflict involves what most people refer to as a personality clash. Members of the group resort to name-calling and expressions of personal dislike or distaste for other participants in the discussion. Interpersonal conflict involves affective comments that relate to the personal characteristics of group members. The major causes of this type of conflict involve the attribution of derogatory motives in explaining another's comment, statements about inadequate intellectual or scholarly ability, accusations of undesirable personal traits, and offensive interpersonal behavior in the group. For example, consider the following hypothetical example of interpersonal conflict:

Jimmy: We simply can't afford these great expenditures for defense.
Jerry: That's a comment I'd expect a peanut farmer to make.
Jimmy: So? How did you get to be President?

Jimmy has advanced a position about a substantive issue. Jerry initiates the interpersonal conflict by attacking Jimmy on a personal basis instead of responding in a substantive or factual manner. Jimmy also responds to Jerry in an affective fashion typical of this form of encounter; once interpersonal conflict begins, it tends to grow and feed resulting in a group's inability to consider factual or procedural matters.

FUNCTIONS OF CONFLICT

By now you should realize that the expression of conflict in task groups has important benefits to the group. These positive consequences, however, will not automatically occur. A group's perception of the value of conflict will depend largely on the manner which the group communicates about conflict. For now, we will view the functions of conflict as potential benefits to the group. Later, we will discuss effective methods of managing conflict.

Probably the most important function of conflict in the task-oriented group involves the quality of the group's decisions. Groups who learn to handle their conflicts invariably produce higher quality decisions than groups who avoid conflict. Irving Janis (17, 18) illustrates this notion in a book he has written about group decision making. Janis points out several unfortunate occurrences that have resulted from a condition he calls "groupthink," a premature group consensus caused by an intentional avoidance of conflict. Among other things, Janis attributes the prolonged duration of the Vietnam War to ineffective group decisions in the executive branch of the federal government. In other words, various low-quality decisions were made because groups did not use conflict as a positive force to generate and test alternative policies and solutions. Hall and Watson (15) found that groups who were instructed in ways of dealing with conflict produced better decisions than uninstructed groups. Thirty-two groups worked on deciding which items would be most critical to the survival of a space crew lost on the moon. The groups instructed in dealing with conflict produced better decisions, exercised more creativity, and arrived at better solutions than groups expected to make decisions on the basis of either the sum of the individual group member's efforts or the efforts of the group's most proficient member. Therefore, conflict can be channeled in a fashion designed to increase the quality of the group's decisions. In fact, based on the research investigating quality of decisions, it might be wise to suggest that groups intentionally generate conflict to test the group's decision. You have heard people respond to another's comment by prefacing their remarks with the phrase, "let me play devil's advocate for a moment." In a very real sense, the devil's advocate creates conflict to test the quality of the ideas being discussed. When a group develops an ability to manage this conflict, the quality of their decisions should increase.

One of the reasons for the higher quality of decisions in groups that experience conflict involves an important consequence of conflict: information generation. When group conflict occurs on the substantive or informational level, often members of the group will look for more information to resolve the problem (13). This generation of new or additional information results in a closer consideration of the issues involved. Hoffman, Harburg, and Maier (16) found that expressions of conflict resulted in groups generating more alternatives to their group's decision. In other words, under these circumstances, conflict acts as a check against a group's premature consensus or "groupthink." For example, we know of a group organized to analyze the student health center at a major eastern university. The majority of the group initially felt that the staff at the health center was incompetent and insensitive to student needs. The primary communication during the initial phases of the group discussion served to justify the belief that the health service was a substandard medical facility. The group was prepared to label the health service as bad and list recommendations for improving the service when one of the members suggested that the group was moving too quickly and that the indictment of the health service was premature and largely inaccurate. The participant generated considerable conflict by refusing to consider recommendations for improvement until the disagreements surrounding the health service adequacy were resolved. The group decided to adjourn for the day, and members agreed to find more information on the topic. When the group reconvened two days later, the discussion addressed the new information that had been generated. Among other things, the group discovered that the health service had received numerous awards for excellence in providing service to its patients. The group was able to continue and, with the cooperation of the health service administration, secure several improvements in an already good operation. The point here is that the group avoided the embarrassment of a premature conclusion because one of the members generated conflict.

Conflict can also help to increase the cohesiveness of a group. A cohesive group consists of members who work well together, feel that the group has an identity, and encourage achievement of group objectives (4). A group that consistently avoids conflict normally contains members who may be apathetic or reluctant to participate fully in the group's activities. When managed properly, expressions of conflict often serve to increase interest in the group's work and generate a feeling of excitement among members. We have all been in groups where the norm has been to avoid conflict. This more or less conscious effort to avoid conflict is frequently associated with tension, anxiety, and restrained participation. These experiences are often unpleasant, if not boring. The groups that generate considerable excitement, however, are likely to have experienced the appropriate management of conflict. To the extent conflict in these groups was managed, the individual group members developed stronger ties to the group. In other words, regardless of whether the conflict was resolved, the group begins to recognize that the group reacted to his or her remark. Eddie Foy, the great vaudevillian, once said, "I don't mind being looked over, but I can't stand being overlooked." The same principle operates here. The individual member begins to see his or her remarks as valuable to the group deliberations because the conflict generates considerable interaction. In short, conflict can be viewed by the group member as an indication that what he or she has said is important to the other group members.

The relationship between conflict and cohesiveness can best be described as reciprocal. That is, conflict does not only contribute to cohesiveness, but also the relationship operates in the reverse. Once a level of group attraction and well-being has been achieved, members of the group recognize that norms are typically established with greater ease to deal with group conflict. Consequently, members can engage in conflict with relatively little fear of being rejected. The group has learned to confront its problems openly and work as a group to solve them.

Probably the most important function of conflict in the task-oriented group is clarifying and resolving issues about the group's informational and procedural dimensions. As we have seen, conflict can act as a test of the group's facts and ideas resulting in the generation of more information and, generally, a higher quality decision. Thus, on the informational dimension, conflict clarifies and provides the group with a test of the information available for solving its problem. The same basic procedure operates for the group's procedural dimension as well. Conflict over agenda matters often results in the generation of several alternate methods for solving a problem, a variety of sources of information, and a clarification of the role structure within the group. These functions give the group a direction in dealing with the problem. For example, a group can experience considerable conflict over the method employed to solve a problem. Some members of the group may be content with a superficial analysis of issues and information; others may view the problem as sufficiently important to require the application of more stringent tests of information. This form of conflict can lead the group to pursue sources of information not previously considered. You may have been in a group in which members have said that a given problem should not be taken lightly and more rigorous tests of information should be used. If handled properly, this type of conflict can result in the group's consideration of more information. A typical conversation under these circumstances may sound like this:

Mary: Well, that's one way of going about it. How about trying some other means of solving the problem? I mean, we know what our Dean said, but is she correct?

Jack: Yeah, but we don't need any more information. The Dean sets the policy and we can't do anything about that.

Mary: Oh c'mon, she (the Dean) is open to our input.

Linda: Well, let's take a look at some other schools. How do they handle this problem? Maybe we ought to go over to the library and check out some catalogs from other schools.

Mary: Good idea, we can also interview the deans at the other schools around the town and see how their colleges handle the problem.

Jack: I still don't think it's as important as you say, but I can see your point about getting more information. If you want me to, I'll be glad to check out the publications of the American Association of University of Professors. Maybe I can find something there that will help us out.

This hypothetical example illustrates what can happen in a group experiencing procedural conflict. The conflict acts as a catalyst to obtain additional information. Jack was content to make his decision solely on the information received from the dean. The other group members, however, saw a need to check the dean's information by doing more research. Although Jack was not completely satisfied with this point of view, nonetheless he recognized the needs of his fellow discussants and agreed to search out more information. In this fashion, the group can not only generate new sources of information, but also have a better basis for testing the dean's position.

The procedural dimension of a group also involves the establishment of individual roles. The manner in which we come to recognize the roles people play in groups involves conflict. Take the leadership position for example. Often the emergence of the role of the leader is associated with much struggle. Several people within the group may try to exert power and influence, but by definition, only a few people can lead. In most groups, Bormann (1) suggests, one person finally emerges as the group's leader. This situation can produce a condition known as role conflict on the procedural dimension. Bormann developed a method of residues that explains how the leadership role emerges through conflict. Again, conflict acts as a test to determine the best possible leader for the group. People are eliminated from consideration for a certain role through conflict. The group literally tests the ability of its members to engage in certain roles through conflict. In addition, as we have seen on the informational dimension, people who occupy roles achieved in the absence of conflict are often not the best person for that particular role.

The functions of interpersonal conflict are not quite as easy to determine. In fact, of the three types of conflict, interpersonal conflict is probably the least useful to a group. Two main functions, however, seem important enough to label. Interpersonal conflict can be used in a humorous fashion to build interpersonal solidarity providing the group perceives the conflict as humorous rather than threatening (11). If a group member becomes arrogant or pedantic, for example, interpersonal conflict may serve to refocus the discussion on more substantive issues. The second important function of interpersonal conflict involves a demonstration of trust and unity. The group members engaging in lighthearted interpersonal conflict often demonstrate their willingness to take risks because of the trust shared by the group members. The consequence of both of these functions raises the cohesiveness of the group (5, 6).

Thus, conflict can be considered functional if it results in higher quality solutions to problems, the generation of information, an increase in cohesiveness, and an overall clarification of informational, procedural, and interpersonal issues before the group. It is important to emphasize that these functions do not occur automatically. In order to achieve the beneficial functions of conflict, the various disputes must be managed properly. Before we turn to conflict management, however, we should look at the potential negative effects of conflict.

DYSFUNCTIONAL FORMS OF CONFLICT

We have tried to stress thus far that conflict can have a useful function. You may have some doubts about our emphasis in light of your past experiences with conflict. These doubts may reflect your experience of dysfunctional conflict.

When conflict is not managed, the group experiences significant frustration and hostility. The group's goal becomes unobtainable because members of the group have polarized and reached an impasse. Under these circumstances, the group's existence is threatened and members may elect a decision that avoids the conflict. This decision, as we have seen, often lacks the quality of decisions arrived at through negotiation and analysis. In addition to the substantive problems surrounding the quality of the decision, group members may also develop hostility toward one another on an interpersonal dimension. Occasionally, members blame other participants for the group's failure to deal with the conflict. On the procedural dimension, conflict becomes dysfunctional when it obscures the goal of the group. When members argue exclusively over how to accomplish a given task rather than what the solution should be, the participants often feel the frustration of "spinning wheels." You no doubt have been in groups in which you had little satisfaction with the group's progress. Part of the feeling can be attributed to dysfunctional procedural conflict.

Conflict most frequently becomes dysfunctional when the interpersonal dimension interacts with either the informational or procedural dimension. When factual disagreements become emotional or when agenda arguments become personal, almost invariably the resulting conflict will be dysfunctional. The members focus on the interpersonal dimension rather than on handling the conflict along informational and procedural dimensions designed to assist the group's progress toward its goal. The interpersonal aspects of the group support but do not relate directly to the task-oriented group's reason for existence. Consequently, the group experiences the frustration of personality conflict and failure to make progress on informational and procedural matters.

METHODS OF MANAGING CONFLICT

Undoubtedly, you have inferred from this chapter that we do not believe that conflict is necessarily bad. In fact, in order to develop an effective means for dealing with conflict, we should probably begin with a positive attitude about conflict. In order to achieve the benefits of conflict in a functional fashion, we should anticipate that conflict will occur without developing corresponding negative attitudes or anxieties about its occurrence. These negative attitudes and anxieties operate to avoid conflict and to preclude the beneficial effects of conflict. In other words, conflict should not alarm us if we recognize the positive functions of conflict and avoid its dysfunctional aspects. The successful management of conflict should be the group's goal.

We have chosen the term conflict management in favor of "conflict resolution," which is more popular, for a variety of reasons. If you agree that conflict provides some useful functions for small group deliberation, you probably would not want to resolve conflict. If resolution of conflict causes a cessation of conflict, the beneficial consequences of conflict would also cease. Consequently, in situations where conflict is functional, we choose to manage the situation in order to achieve the best possible consequences. On the other hand, where conflict has become dysfunctional, we need to discover means whereby we can channel conflict into more appropriate and useful consequences. The *resolution* of conflict seems to imply that conflict is bad; the *management* of conflict seems more compatible with our notion that conflict has its good points.

Successful management of conflict depends on the group's commitment to solving the problem. Campbell (3) coined the term "entitativity" to refer to the degree a group has a real existence or views itself as an entity. One of the basic means of developing entitativity among group members involves a recognition of common fate or the extent to which all members of the group experience similar outcomes as a consequence of the group discussion. The notion of common fate has interesting implications for cohesiveness. Deutsch (7) and Grossack (14) both found that members in groups who perceive that they share a common fate with the other members develop a higher degree of cohesiveness than groups who fail to see a common fate. As we have seen, the cohesive group tends to tolerate a wide variety of conflict in an atmosphere free of the dysfunctional aspects of conflict. In other words, a fundamental means of dealing with conflict involves the establishment of entitativity and cohesiveness.

The procedural dimension of the group discussion affords group members another means for managing conflict. Knutson and Kowitz (22) found that under conditions of informational and interpersonal conflict, procedural communication is most effective in assisting a group to manage its conflict. When group members disagreed over facts, the researchers had a confederate raise procedural points of view. For example, when the group disagreed over the number of college students directly affected by a certain rule change in the university catalog, the confederate make comments such as:

> "Okay, where can we get some more information?"
>
> "Let's summarize and see how we got where we are."
>
> "We seem to have some disagreement here between Ralph and Joan. Tom, what do you have to say about that?"

Notice that the content of the confederate's message is completely free of factual material, and no explicit attempt is made to engage in any interpersonal communication. These procedural appeals enable the group members to manage their conflict by addressing the reasons for disagreement rather than the disagreement itself (20, 21). In addition to the effectiveness of the procedural comments in managing informational conflict, the generation of additional facts about the informational dimension appears to assist groups in informational conflict. Often informational conflict is managed by discovering more factual information. In other words, continued discussion of the factual conflict often results in management of the conflict.

The impact of the procedural messages is even greater in groups experiencing interpersonal conflict. For many years, communication theorists recommended that group members avoid personality conflicts. If that rather obvious strategy failed and the group did engage in personality conflict, members were urged to "stick to the facts." Recent research, however, has cast doubt on the value of the recommendation (22). The investigators found that procedural appeals were more effective than factual appeals in managing interpersonal conflict. The reason for this effectiveness of procedural messages under conditions of interpersonal conflict seems quite simple. If you were involved in a personality clash with another group member, the interpersonal dimension of the discussion fails to provide the communication necessary for managing the conflict. On the informational dimension, your perception of the other person's "facts" would be influenced by your momentary affective dislike for the individual. On the other hand, the procedural messages contain certain indicators that the situation can be redeemed and the group can be open to negotiation and continued discussion. The procedural appeals seem to defuse the conflict and enable the group to continue toward its goal.

Perhaps the best example of procedural messages useful in managing conflict involves Sherif and Sherif's (23) concept of superordinate goals. When group members are in conflict, an attempt is made to determine issues on which the group members agree. The simple question, "What can we agree on?" acts as a procedure to indicate certain important substantive issues on which the group has reached consensus. In comparison to the issue over which the group is experiencing conflict, these areas of agreement often seem more important to the group. For example, imagine that you are on your club's entertainment committee and you are experiencing conflict over the type of weekend party you should plan. Marty and Mike both express great enthusiasm over a beer party, but Buddy and Joan prefer a more sedate tea party. One line of dealing with this conflict would be to appeal to superordinate goals. You might point out that the group agrees that the party should be fun, that everyone agrees that some sort of party will definitely be held, and that the club is important enough so that members would have a good time regardless of the party's format. A series of agreements on these more important, overriding goals will often be the catalyst for reaching agreement on the party's activity. Mike and Marty may see the value of a tea party and Buddy and Joan could possibly agree that a beer party would be fun. We are not saying here that superordinate goals act to resolve or eliminate conflict. Rather, the group's understanding that they agree on several important issues acts to build the group's cohesiveness and, consequently, makes the conflictual problem easier to handle.

So far we have discussed informational and interpersonal conflict. You may be wondering what to do in a group that experiences procedural conflict. Basically, the same advice is valid as for informational and interpersonal conflict conditions. That is, continue procedural comments in an effort to generate a greater number of alternative procedures. With the group's purpose or goal in mind, these procedural appeals reinforce the group's importance while maintaining an atmosphere of open discussion. Appeals to the interpersonal goodwill of the group are also helpful. An attempt to build more interpersonal attraction and trust on the interpersonal dimension can also help to manage procedural conflict. In addition, if information can be found attesting to the value, efficiency, or worth of a specific procedure, these substantive considerations should be voiced.

Managing conflict is a difficult task requiring tact, insight, ability, and knowledge about the workings of small group problem solving. We hope that you will be able to recognize the types of conflict and engage in the most suitable management techniques. We further hope that you will recognize that conflict has some good points and should not be avoided. Try to direct your efforts to the group's goal, build cohesiveness, and try to find common ground. Also remember that any given issue can have several points of view. When necessary and useful, you can still agree to disagree.

SUMMARY

Conflict has been defined to include events ranging from war to classroom discussion of controversial events. For small group deliberations, we have narrowed the definition of conflict to communication patterns characterized by disagreement and discomfort among two or more group members. Disagreement may emerge over the substance of the group's discussion, procedures, or attacks on the personal characteristics of group members.

Conflict has several important benefits for task-oriented groups. Appropriate management of disagreement over the substance of the task tends to improve the quality of the group's decision proposal. Management of conflict may increase the cohesiveness of the group. The proper management of conflict clarifies the direction of the group and resolves leadership issues. Lighthearted interpersonal conflict may help to create trust and unity.

The appropriate management of conflict begins with a positive attitude about the usefulness of conflict in group deliberations. Successful management of conflict depends on member commitment to the group and its task. Procedural comments tend to be useful in the management of conflict as well as introduction of additional informative statements of fact, statistics, and comments of qualified sources. Sometimes a group experiencing conflict may need to step back and attempt to determine issues on which the members agree. In any case, considerable objectivity and tact are required in the exchange of messages necessary for the management of conflict.

CONCLUSIONS AND RECOMMENDATIONS

1. Conflict is an inevitable event in task-oriented groups.
2. Conflict may occur over informational, procedural, or interpersonal issues.
3. Appropriate management of conflict helps the group to attain a higher quality decision proposal.
4. Conflict is the means by which the leadership role is resolved in task-oriented groups.
5. The proper management of interpersonal conflict may result in higher levels of trust and unity among group members.
6. A positive attitude toward the usefulness of conflict in group deliberations is the first step in appropriate management of conflict.
7. Informational and procedural conflict may be resolved by the exchange of informative or procedural statements or by appeal to the goodwill of the group members.
8. Interpersonal conflict may be best resolved by appeal to procedural matters.
9. Awareness of a common base of agreement or appeal to a superordinate goal may be useful in managing conflict when a deadlock is reached.

REFERENCES

1. Ernest G. Bormann, *Discussion and Group Methods* (New York: Harper and Row, 1975).

2. Kenneth E. Boulding, *Conflict and Defense: A General Theory* (New York: Harper and Row, 1962).

3. Donald T. Campbell, "Common Fate, Similarity, and Other Indices of the Status of Aggregates of Persons as Social Entities," *Behavioral Science* 3 (1958): 14–25.

4. Dorwin Cartwright, "The Nature of Group Cohesiveness," in *Group Dynamics*, Dorwin Cartwright and Alvin Zander (eds.) (New York: Harper and Row, 1968), pp. 91–109.

5. Lewis A. Coser, *The Functions of Social Conflict* (Glencoe, Ill.: Free Press, 1956).

6. Lewis A. Coser, *Continuities in the Study of Social Conflict* (New York: Free Press, 1967).

7. Morton Deutsch, "An Experimental Study of the Effects of Cooperation and Competition upon Group Process," *Human Relations* 2 (1949): 199–232.

8. Morton Deutsch, "Socially Relevant Science: Reflections on Some Studies of Interpersonal Conflict," *American Psychologist* 24 (1969): 1076–1092.

9. Michael Dues, "A Manager's Guide to Conflict Resolution," unpublished manuscript.

10. Donald G. Ellis and B. Aubrey Fisher, "Phases of Conflict in Small Group Development: A Markov Analysis," *Human Communication Research* 1 (1975): 195–212.

11. Jacqueline D. Goodchilds and Ewart D. Smith, "The Wit and His Group," *Human Relations* 17 (1964): 23–32.

12. Dennis S. Gouran and Jone E. Baird, "An Analysis of Distributional and Sequential Structure in Problem-Solving and Informal Group Discussions," *Speech Monographs* 39 (1972): 16–22.

13. Harold Guetzkow and John Gyr, "An Analysis of Conflict in Decision-Making Groups," *Human Relations* 7 (1954): 367–382.

14. Martin M. Grossack, "Some Effects of Cooperation and Competition upon Small Group Behavior," *Journal of Abnormal and Social Psychology* 49 (1954): 341–348.

15. Jay Hall and W. H. Watson, "The Effects of Normative Intervention on Group Decision-Making Performance," *Human Relations* 23 (1970): 299–317.

16. L. Richard Hoffman, Ernest Harburg, and Norman R. F. Maier, "Differences and Disagreement as Factors in Group Problem-Solving," *Journal of Abnormal and Social Psychology* 64 (1962): 206–214.

17. Irving L. Janis, *Victims of Groupthink: A Psychological Study of Foreign Policy Decisions and Fiascoes* (Boston: Houghton Mifflin, 1972).

18. Irving L. Janis, "Groupthink," *Psychology Today* 5 (1971): 43–46 and 74–76.

19. M. K. Jennings and L. H. Ziegler, "Political Expression Among High School Teachers: The Intersection of Community and Occupational Values," unpublished manuscript cited in *The Handbook of Social Psychology*, 2nd ed., vol. 4, Gardner Lindzey and Elliott Aronson (eds.) (Reading, Mass.: Addison-Wesley, 1969), p. 440.

20. Thomas J. Knutson, "An Experimental Study of the Effects of Orientation Behavior on Small Group Consensus," *Speech Monographs* 39 (1972): 159–165.

21. Thomas J. Knutson and William E. Holdridge, "Consensus, Orientation Behavior, and Leadership: A Possible Functional Relationship," *Speech Monographs* 42 (1975): 107–114.

22. Thomas J. Knutson and Albert C. Kowitz, "Effects of Information Type and Level of Orientation on Substantive and Affective Small-Group Conflict," *The Central States Speech Journal* 28 (1977): 54–63.

23. Muzifer Sherif and Carolyn W. Sherif, *Groups in Harmony and Tension* (New York: Harper and Row, 1953).

24. Georg Simmel, *Soziologie* (Berlin: Duncker and Humboot, 1958).

25. William G. Sumner, Albert G. Keller, and Maurice R. Davie, *The Science of Society*, vol. 4 (New Haven: Yale University Press, 1927).

5

ANALYZING GROUP PROCESS PROBLEMS

Chapter 11: Analyzing Small-Group Decision Making
Chapter 12: Process Evaluation

We have described the three basic structures of task-oriented groups, and we expect that you now have a clear understanding of the interaction, group, and decision-making components of group process. The purpose of Part 5 is to give you some specific guidance in diagnosing your group when it seems to be making little or no progress toward achieving its goals. Chapter 11 focuses specifically on diagnosing decision-making practices. Chapter 12 is more comprehensive and focuses on problems in the informational, procedural, and interpersonal dimensions. In Chapter 12, we make reference to the specific sections in Parts 2, 3, and 4 that will assist you in diagnosing and solving these process problems.

CHAPTER 11

Analyzing Small-Group Decision Making

INTRODUCTION

We presented some guidelines in Chapter 9 that are designed to help a task-oriented group create an effective decision proposal. We suggested that a group consider the achievement of its goals in terms of three task-oriented steps. The purpose of this chapter is to describe the underlying dynamics of information search, information processing, and decision making in a small group. Although this chapter is more theoretical, an understanding of the concepts and processes explained here can be of considerable practical importance for your behavior in a small group. The approach is designed to help you understand how groups reach decisions and to help you identify and correct shortcomings in your group's decision-making process. The chapter will also help you identify and reinforce behaviors that are helpful in reaching an effective decision proposal.

GOAL OF A TASK-ORIENTED GROUP

The ultimate purpose of a task-oriented group is to create a decision proposal that most effectively resolves the task chosen by the group or assigned to the group. We noted earlier that a decision proposal can be evaluated by three criteria. These criteria are: (1) to what extent does the decision proposal reflect the values and ideals of the group members; (2) to what extent does the decision proposal reflect the empirical realities of the particular situation; and (3) to what extent do the group members find the decision proposal acceptable? Hence, for the group to arrive at an effective decision proposal, group members must exchange messages about what they find desirable, exchange information related to the situation, and express their level of acceptance or rejection of the alternatives considered by the group. To the degree that any of these exchanges are short-circuited, the final decision proposal will be less effective than might otherwise be true. Suppose, for example, your group was discussing which movie to attend this weekend. You would need to know what kind of movie the group members wanted to see. At least for this weekend, you need to know if a mystery, comedy, or dramatic movie was of special interest to the group members. Knowing what kind of movie the members find desirable relates to the values and interests of the group members. You will also need to know various details about the movies that are showing this particular weekend. You could simply write down the title of each movie and then draw one at random from a hat. This method of selecting a movie might not, however, reflect the values and interests of the group members. Your group may not find a haphazard choice very satisfactory. You need information about the movies to make a wise choice. Knowing various details about the movies is what we mean by the empirical realities of the particular situation. Finally, the group members will need to reach agreement on which movie to see. If some members choose one movie and others a second movie, the idea of going to the movies as a group falls apart. If no expression of acceptance about a specific movie is forthcoming, the group can go on for a long time much to the frustration of the members. The group would not be able to take concerted action about which movie to see. Agreement on a particular choice is what we mean by the notion that group members must find the decision proposal acceptable. This acceptance permits the group to take action regarding its decision proposal.

A COMMON PROBLEM IN SELECTING A DECISION PROPOSAL

The solution finally selected by small groups usually reflects the group's emotional attachment to that alternative (8). For one reason or another, an alternative comes before the group that the members find desirable and hence they collectively support that proposal. Hoffman and Maier (8) found that a large percentage of the groups they studied became emotionally attached to an alternative early in the group's life span. The attachment to this alternative resulted in a neglect of other alternatives that were subsequently introduced in the group's discussions. Alternatives that obtained collective support early in the group's life span were often inferior to those introduced later.

Another group of researchers found that groups exhibited a need to agree rapidly on an alternative (6). The sense of the group seemed to be to quickly reach a decision and discharge their responsibility. We often see and hear what we want to see and hear early in the discussion. Hall and Watson referred to this need to reach a decision quickly as a "strain toward convergence" (5). The closer these groups came to reaching agreement, the harder they pressed for group consensus. Again, as the group coalesced around an alternative, the group members would neglect other alternatives and become intolerant of opinion differences.

The outcomes of these studies suggest that group members search for an acceptable alternative early in the life span of their group. As the members become attached to an alternative, the analysis of other alternatives is neglected. Usually, these decision proposals are inferior when compared to those subsequently introduced.

Finally, it was observed that once group members became emotionally attached to an alternative, the possibility of eroding that support was minimal. The crux of the problem seems to be that group members try to reach quickly a decision that is inferior when compared to other possibilities. We often want to finish our discussions early, but "instant" decisions without effort frequently result in embarrassing results. You probably remember negative consequences associated with snap judgments.

Consequently, we need to consider ways that will prevent a small group from reaching a decision before the group has considered several possible decision proposals. The approach described on the following pages explains why groups reach an early decision and also explains courses of action you can take in your group to overcome the strain toward convergence. The approach specifies relationships among three elements. These elements include a list of alternatives, member search for information, and processing information during group deliberations. The relationships specify how the list of alternatives affects information search and information processing.

LIST OF ALTERNATIVES

When we make a decision regarding some course of action, such as ways to conserve energy, we usually choose among several alternatives. We look to see what means for conserving energy are available to us. We may consider more efficient modes of transportation, different types of housing, efficient means of preparing and conserving food, and so on. There are several alternatives and courses of action available to the group, and the group members must decide what they consider to be the best course of action to take regarding a particular situation.

Central to the decision-making process is the list of alternatives available to the group. As alternatives are discussed by group members each alternative acquires some degree of acceptability to the group as a whole.

The list of alternatives can be analyzed in terms of two important characteristics. The first feature relates to the number of alternatives. It is possible, of course, that there would be only one alternative before the group. Usually, however, there is more than one alternative available to the group for solving its task. We refer to the number of alternatives considered by the group as the range of alternatives. The list of alternatives may include only one or two or range up to seven or eight alternatives.

The second feature of the list of alternatives is the degree to which the individual alternatives are acceptable to the group. We may find one alternative preferable to another. On the other hand, we might find that all are about equally acceptable. We need a term to denote the variation in the acceptability of the alternatives. If all the alternatives are equally acceptable, one might say that the list is neutral or unbiased. When one alternative is particularly favored over the others, the list would be highly biased. Thus, we can also describe the list of alternatives in terms of the degree of bias.

When these two features of range and bias of the list of alternatives are combined, we have an indication of how much uncertainty the group faces in reaching a decision. If your group has reached agreement on an alternative, no uncertainty faces the group. However, if the group is trying to decide among three or four equally acceptable alternatives, your group would experience considerable uncertainty. Uncertainty refers to the predictability of the group in selecting one alternative over another. Uncertainty relates to the number of alternatives before the group and their degree of acceptability to the group. Suppose two movies are showing on a particular night. There would be more uncertainty if the movies were equally acceptable than if one was acceptable and the other was considered a waste. In other words, it would be more difficult to predict which movie you would go to see when both were equally good. Suppose that four movies are showing one night and all four were equally acceptable. Prediction of which movie you would go to see would be even more difficult than when there were only two acceptable movies in town. The uncertainty in the list of alternatives, however, is not simply a function of the number of alternatives. If there were four movies in town and only one were good, it would be relatively easy to predict one's choice. Hence, the degree of uncertainty faced by a group is linked to both the number of available alternatives and the nearness of their acceptability. The degree of uncertainty in the group's list of alternatives has important implications for the group's information search and processing. These implications will become apparent as we describe the other elements in the decision-making process.

MEMBER SEARCH FOR INFORMATION

We have stated that the goal of a task-oriented group is to create an acceptable and effective decision proposal. Therefore, the set of alternatives considered by the group is a focal point throughout the group's deliberations. A number of behaviors are required for the group to achieve its goal. The majority of these behaviors relate to information search and information processing. Central to these behaviors is member search for and introduction of information. Member information search refers to the behavior of trying to find information from various sources and then introducing that information during the group's discussions. Searching for information might entail reading a newspaper, talking to people outside the group, or going to the library. Once information is introduced, the group must discuss the information with the goal in mind of selecting the best alternative.

We define information as statements of fact, opinion, and advice (1). Statements of fact make reference to observable events and can be shown to be true or false. If one member of the group states that both a Hitchcock movie and *King Kong* are showing this evening, the group members can then check the truth or falsity of that statement. If both movies are showing, it is an accurate reference to those events. If *King Kong* is showing but not the Hitchcock movie, the statement does not accurately describe those events and is false. Statements of opinion refer to beliefs and values made by the group members or those made by others and reported by group members. A group member might relate his or her opinion that the new *King Kong* movie is inferior to the original *King Kong* and give reasons for this opinion. The group member might also introduce the opinions of the movie critic writing for *Newsweek* stating that the new *King Kong* movie does not match the quality of the original. Statements of advice refer to courses of action the group should take with respect to its task. A group member might suggest that the group see both the new and original *King Kong* movies and then compare the qualities of each. This suggestion proposes a course of action that the group could undertake.

If the group wished to develop an effective decision proposal, the members must be willing to search for all three types of information and be prepared to introduce the results of their search into the group's discussion. We want to introduce a technical term here that will make the following discussion somewhat easier. We wish to refer to the outward search for information and relating that information to the group during its discussion as member threshold. The one defining characteristic of member thresholds is openness.

Openness refers to the search for information and willingness to introduce information that relates to various facets of the task and different points of view toward the task. Obviously, one would not search for all information, whether it was related to the task or not. Nor would members introduce everything they read or experienced.

There is a purpose in the search for and the introduction of information. Your group needs sufficient information to make a wise choice. Your group will waste time if your discussions are cluttered with information that does not relate to your group's objectives. On the other hand, your group will have difficulty making a wise decision if needed information is not made available to the group.

The openness of member thresholds may result in both beneficial and detrimental outcomes for the group. The thresholds result in screening information for the group's discussion. If the state of the threshold is such that it causes a member to ignore needed information in his or her search, the group's decision proposal may not be as effective as it otherwise might be. If the state of the threshold is so open that trivial or irrelevant information is sought and introduced, the group will experience process loss and not use its time and resources as effectively as it might. Hence, the state of the thresholds may result in beneficial outcomes when irrelevant information is screened out and needed information is sought and introduced. This may result in detrimental outcomes when relevant information is prevented from entering the group's discussion and superfluous information is introduced.

For example, consider the problem of library hours. Suppose a number of students voiced complaints that the current library hours were unsatisfactory. If your group were working on this problem, you would need to know what hours were most satisfactory to students. Information regarding the library budget, staffing requirements, and other operating costs would be needed by your group. Information about the role of security officers on campus, parking problems, and funding of intercollegiate athletics would probably not be needed by your group. Thus, your group can create a more effective decision proposal when needed information is made available to your group and irrelevant information is screened out by member thresholds.

INFORMATION PROCESSING

Once information is introduced, it is processed by the group members. Processing information may entail a variety of behaviors (3, 10). At one extreme, the group members may simply ignore the comment. On the other hand, they may agree with the statement and press onward. Usually, however, more attention than a simple expression of approval or disapproval is awarded to member comments. Group members may attempt to clarify the comment. A member may relate additional information to substantiate the original statement. Or a member may point to flaws in the stated information. A member may interpret the statement in terms of its implications for one or more alternatives. Another member may relate the comment to issues considered earlier in its discussion. Finally, members may express their approval or disapproval of the statement. The major thrust of processing information is to refine initial comments until group members find them acceptable (10).

The determination of whether the group finds a statement acceptable involves three considerations. Acceptance implies that the group members agree on *what* meaning can be derived from the statement in terms of its content per se and its implications in terms of an alternative. Second, acceptance entails agreement *with* the content of the statement. Whereas the first consideration involves assessment of the meaning of a statement, the second consideration involves whether the members find the meaning of a statement to be true (in the case of statements of fact) or useful (in terms of statements of opinion or advice). The final consideration involves whether the group is favorably or unfavorably disposed toward the content of the statement. In essence, this judgment simply refers to whether the group members think the content is good or bad. Obviously, the consideration of statements by group members ordinarily does not follow the sequence of understanding, agreement, and favorableness. These judgments are intertwined as the group processes information. Suppose your group was discussing the application of solar devices for heating water and homes. One member might comment that solar heating units are now available to consumers. If this observation is true, it means that interested parties could purchase these units and have them installed. Another member might ask where a person could purchase a unit and how much the solar heating units cost. This member seeks to determine both the veracity of the comment and the usefulness of the information. Eventually the group will agree that the units are available from Companies A, B, and C for X number of dollars. At this point, the information would be anchored in the group's thinking. They have refined the original comment until the members find it acceptable.

If the thrust of information processing is the determination of the acceptability of statements, the focal point of processing is the list of alternatives. The group processes information pertinent to specific alternatives with the eventual purpose of rejecting or accepting these proposals. As we mentioned earlier, the list of alternatives stands out in the foreground against the backdrop of the group's discussion. The ultimate goal of the group is to select one alternative, or combination of alternatives, from the set of alternatives available to the group.

The function of information processing is to transform information until the group finds it acceptable. The group then uses this information to select an alternative from the set of alternatives before the group. Certainly the dynamics of this process are complex. The major constraints impinging on this process include the informational, procedural, and interpersonal sources of influence. We have discussed these dimensions in earlier chapters. For now, we will briefly summarize each dimension and relate how these dimensions may constrain the processing of information.

The informational dimension relates to the content pertinent to the task. Comments comparing the original and new *King Kong* movies are informational in nature. Some characteristics of information include its clarity, its usefulness, its level of opinionatedness, and its degree of differentiation (4, 11). The characteristics of clarity and usefulness seem self-explanatory, but the other two characteristics call for elaboration. Opinionated statements refer to those that are high in certainty and leave little or no room for modification. The statement, "The original *King Kong* is a better film than the new *King Kong,* and that's all there is to it," does not allow the opportunity for different opinions or for modification of this opinion. Unopinionated statements are lower in certainty and encourage reactions from other members.

Differentiation refers to the number of concepts one uses to describe an event and to the shades of a single concept used to describe an event. One could describe the new *King Kong* movie simply in terms of whether it was entertaining or not. This description involves only one concept and only two levels of that concept. Messages higher in differentiation might consider the technical quality of the film, its entertainment level, its commentary on American culture, and so on.

The procedural dimension refers to the roles, norms, and procedures that emerge in a small group. Roles refer to the behaviors we come to expect specific members in the group to perform. We may come to rely on some members to consistently give information. We may come to expect others to consistently coordinate the group's activity such as delegating and directing action, integrating and summarizing the group's discussions, and so on. We yet may expect others to release tension by being witty or to smooth ruffled feathers during discussions.

Norms denote shared expectations of right actions or beliefs that result in guiding and regulating the group member's behavior. Norms develop in terms of the content of the group's task, in terms of the group's work habits, and in terms of the social relations within the group. Content-oriented norms refer to shared attitudes, beliefs, and values that emerge during the group's discussions. Work-oriented norms denote expectations regarding procedures for achieving the group's goals. Socially-oriented norms include those expectations regarding how members should relate to one another during their discussions.

Roles, norms, and procedures are critical in guiding and regulating the group's exchange of messages. Some comments will be looked on favorably because of the norms that have developed during the group's life span. Others will be looked on unfavorably for the same reason. Some items of information will be thoroughly discussed whereas other items will pass with little comment because of these norms. The comments of one member may receive a good deal of attention whereas the comments of another member will receive little attention. Hence, the roles and norms that emerge in a small group are very prominent in constraining the group in its information processing. In other words, because of these roles and norms, some outcomes are much more likely than others.

The interpersonal dimension of information processing reflects the attitudes and perceptions group members hold toward one another. The most prominent perceptions and attitudes include those related to member friendliness, cooperativeness, and status. *Who* says what to *whom* does make a difference in the outcomes of information processing. Members who are perceived as friendly, cooperative, and with higher status will have more influence over the group's deliberations than members perceived as unfriendly, uncooperative, and with lower status.

We are suggesting that these three dimensions constrain or guide the group's information processing. Another way of looking at information processing and constraints is to identify sources of influence. The three dimensions we have described here encompass all possible sources of influence guiding and regulating the group's discussions. One source of influence is the informational content of the messages. Statements of fact that specify the decrease in number of deaths per million miles on our highways since the 55 miles per hour speed limit is another example of informational influence. For example, if the group shares a belief that preventing highway deaths is a desirable outcome, that norm will also influence the group's decision making about the speed limit. Finally, if the comments regarding the effects of the speed limit on highway deaths is made by a member that others perceive as highly competent, the message will have more influence than if it were made by a member who was not considered competent on this topic.

The critical feature of member thresholds, we noted earlier, is the degree of openness. We suggested that this characteristic faced two directions: openness to information outside the group and willingness to give information during the group's deliberations. The critical outcome with respect to the information processing is the diversity of information that the group discusses and finds acceptable. High diversity implies that the acceptable information relates to several alternatives. Low diversity implies that the information considered by the group relates to few or possibly only one alternative. We assume that the greater the diversity of information considered by the group, the greater the likelihood of selecting an effective decision proposal. For example, take the decision regarding which movie to attend on a Friday evening. If there are four movies showing and you only consider information regarding one of them, your choice might not be as satisfactory as making a choice after considering information related to all four movies.

Once information has crossed a member's threshold it becomes available to the group. The group will discuss the information until it is in a form the group finds acceptable. The influences over this process come from the information itself, the roles and norms of the group, and characteristics of the group members themselves. The purpose of processing this information is to assist the group in selecting an alternative from the set of alternatives available to the group. This choice should be an effective resolution of the group's task.

CRITICAL RELATIONSHIPS IN THE DECISION-MAKING PROCESS

We have described the three basic elements of small group decision making. The list of alternatives, member thresholds, and information processing comprise the parts of a system that moves the group toward achievement of its goals. We have emphasized the centrality of the list of alternatives and have suggested that reaching an effective decision proposal is the focal point of the group's interaction. We want to specify how relationships among the three components affect information processing and decision making. Once these relationships are specified and explained, we will show how to avoid the common problem found in many task-oriented groups.

Member thresholds act as a screening device for the selection and introduction of information. The characteristic change in member thresholds is the degree of openness. When the thresholds are characterized by considerable breadth, a relatively broad range of information will pass through. When the thresholds are characterized by little breadth, a narrow range of information will pass through. The first basic relationship we want to specify is between member thresholds and the list of alternatives. *The openness of the group members' thresholds taken as a whole is a function of the degree of uncertainty reflected in the list of alternatives.* When the list of alternatives is characterized by higher levels of uncertainty, the member thresholds will be characterized by relatively high levels of openness. As the list of alternatives reflects increasingly less uncertainty, the degree of openness will become increasingly more narrow.

This relationship finds dramatic support from Irving Janis's study of decision making in the executive branch of the federal government (9). The Cuban uprising occurred during the Kennedy Administration. The Cuban revolution led to the Bay of Pigs incident. During the planning stages, one of the cabinet members wanted to express reservations regarding the planned invasion. When he mentioned his doubts to Robert Kennedy, the Attorney General at that time, Kennedy suggested that he not voice these thoughts. The decision to invade was a highly acceptable alternative; thus, there was very little uncertainty in the list of alternatives. This low level of uncertainty effectively precluded the introduction of information unfavorable to that alternative. The member threshold was low in openness. If the decision-making group had been considering several alternatives with approximately equal acceptability, the threshold would have been relatively open and such information would likely have been introduced. Perhaps the unfavorable consequences of the Bay of Pigs invasion could have been avoided if the group had not been so set on a single alternative. Janis reports that President Kennedy changed his group discussion strategy during the Cuban missile crisis. Many people view that incident as a highlight of the Kennedy Administration.

The function of information processing is to create acceptable information that assists the group in selecting one alternative from a range of alternatives. We mentioned earlier that the characteristic change in the information processing is the diversity of acceptable information that is created through the group's deliberations. This observation brings us to the second important relationship among the components of the decision-making process. *The diversity of information created by the group through its discussion is a function of the uncertainty characteristic of the list of alternatives.* As the list of alternatives changes from high to low uncertainty, the creation of acceptable information changes from high to low diversity. If you and some friends decided to go to a movie tonight and four approximately equal choices were open, your group would discuss the merits of each movie, consider the type of movie, the mood you were in, and whether your favorite actor or actress was in the movie. Your group would use a diverse range of information to help make a choice. If the group thought that only one of the movies was worthwhile, little time would be spent in discussing which movie to attend.

Obviously a task-oriented group must narrow the range of acceptable alternatives until one becomes the group's choice. This goal of arriving at an acceptable alternative brings us to the third important relationship. We described in an earlier chapter that a small group passes through four phases during its life span. The purpose of the first phase is to orient the group members to each other and to the task. During the second phase, the role structure of the group stabilizes and the group develops a strategy for achieving its task. The third phase is characterized by information search and processing in an effort to select the most appropriate alternative from the range of alternatives available to the group. Finally, the group makes a choice and completes its decision proposal. If the group has already decided on its decision proposal during the second phase, the third phase of information search and processing is largely perfunctory. For the most part, it becomes a time of justification for an alternative chosen earlier. When this happens, the decision proposal will probably not be as effective as it might be.

We suggested earlier in this chapter that a common problem of many groups is that a decision proposal is agreed on early in the group's life span. Frequently, this early choice results in an ineffective decision proposal. In terms of the dynamics of decision making, we propose that these groups quickly created a list of alternatives characterized by low uncertainty. Consequently, their information search and processing were restricted. The third critical relationship in the decision-making process relates to the time during the group's life span that the list of alternatives is characterized by little uncertainty. *We suggest that the time in the group's life span that the list of alternatives becomes low in uncertainty is related to the productivity of the group.* If the list becomes low in uncertainty later in the life span of the group, the productivity of the group will likely be considerably higher than when the list of alternatives becomes low in uncertainty early in the life span of the group. Alternative lists high in uncertainty result in a broader information search, creation of more diverse information, and consideration of a broader range of alternatives than lists low in uncertainty (2, 7, 12). We propose that this broader consideration of information usually results in more effective decision proposals.

IMPLICATIONS FOR GROUP DISCUSSIONS

In Chapter 9 we described the three steps in reaching a decision proposal. During the context of discovery a strategy is developed for achieving the group's goals. The context of information search is the period when the group considers alternatives in an attempt to select the most appropriate decision proposal. During the context of justification, an appropriate rationale is prepared for the selection of that alternative. The process of decision making presented in this chapter implies that the group should create a list of alternatives with high uncertainty during the context of discovery. Often new alternatives will be added to the list during the context of information search. It is critical for the success of your group, however, that a list of alternatives characterized by low uncertainty not be created during the context of discovery.

We have proposed that more effective information processing and decision making reflect treatment of diverse information. The implications of this judgment may be summed up with four questions.

1. When will groups search for diverse information?

The argument we have made in this chapter is that we generally do not search for information unless we have a good reason to do so. The so-called good reason we have suggested here is uncertainty. Uncertainty involves the need to select one alternative from a range of somewhat acceptable alternatives. We will search under these conditions until we have sufficient information to make a decision.

2. What types of information will group members search for?

When a group has selected an alternative or has nearly agreed on an acceptable alternative, group members will search for information that supports the selection of that alternative and information that shows the weaknesses or undesirability of other alternatives. When the group discussions are characterized by uncertainty, group members will search for information that shows the strengths and weaknesses of more than one or sometimes several alternatives.

3. How would a group member prevent the rapid acceptance of an alternative?

Expressing doubts or reservations may assist the group from selecting a final decision proposal too soon. By asking questions and expressing doubts you will keep your own threshold open and will help other members to maintain a more open mind regarding your task. The expression of these doubts should not reflect a totally negative attitude toward the alternatives before the group. Categorically suggesting that a recommendation is not good or will not work is rejection and not an expression of doubt or concern. Expressions of doubt should be accompanied by what you find useful or good about the recommendation. You will want to look at both the positive and negative aspects of the proposal.

In addition, you might find it useful to introduce other alternatives. Making these suggestions and providing supporting information highlights other possibilities. As others attend to these recommendations, a sense of uncertainty emerges. We are now back to our original position. The presence of uncertainty results in the search and processing of more diverse information.

4. At what time during the four phase sequence should the group reach agreement on the decision proposal?

We suggest that the most useful time to reach this agreement is at the conclusion of the coordination phase. Thus, the purposes of information are most readily realized and the purposes of justification are appropriately applied.

SUMMARY

We suggested that the ultimate purpose of a task-oriented group is to agree on a decision proposal that most effectively resolves the task taken on by your group. Frequently, however, a group will fail to consider a broad range of alternatives. Instead, the group will focus on a single approach to the task. This narrow approach to the task frequently results in an inferior decision proposal.

In the remainder of this chapter we made an attempt to explain why certain groups are motivated to take a narrow or comprehensive approach to their task. We proposed that the process of decision making in small groups involved three basic elements. These are the list of alternatives, member threshold, and information processing. Central to this process is the list of alternatives.

We hypothesized that information search and information processing would reflect a more comprehensive approach to the task when the list of alternatives was characterized by higher levels of uncertainty. As a group becomes increasingly certain of its approach to the task, members will restrict or narrow their search for information and their processing of information. Obviously, a group must eventually agree on a final decision proposal. A group will need to narrow its focus to a single approach to the task. However, if the group restricts its approach to the task too early in its life span, the final decision proposal is not as likely to be as good as it might otherwise have been. We recommend, therefore, that the group maintain an open stance toward its task until the later phases of its life span. The primary mechanism available to the group for maintaining this open posture is the list of alternatives.

CONCLUSIONS AND RECOMMENDATIONS

1. The ultimate purpose of a task-oriented group is to create an effective decision proposal.
2. Groups frequently adopt a narrow approach to their task that restricts their ability to create an effective decision proposal.
3. The decision making process in small groups includes a list of alternatives, member thresholds, and information processing.
4. The essential feature of the list of alternatives is its level of uncertainty.
5. The central feature of member thresholds is their openness.
6. The critical outcome with respect to information processing is the diversity of information created.
7. The purpose of finding acceptable information is to assist the group in choosing an alternative from the range of alternatives before the group.
8. When the list of alternatives is characterized by higher levels of uncertainty, member thresholds will reflect higher levels of openness.
9. When the list of alternatives is characterized by higher levels of uncertainty, a greater diversity of information will be created and found acceptable by the group.
10. Groups will perform more effectively if the list of alternatives is characterized by higher levels of uncertainty during the early phases of their life span.
11. Groups can maintain a more open approach to their task by encouraging members to express both their positive reactions and doubts regarding alternatives before the group.

REFERENCES

1. Ernest G. Bormann, *Discussion and Group Methods: Theory and Practice,* 2nd ed. (New York: Harper and Row, 1975).
2. James M. Driscoll and John T. Lanzetta, "Effects of Two Sources of Uncertainty in Decision-Making," *Psychological Reports* 17 (1965): 635–648.
3. B. Aubrey Fisher, "Decision Emergence: Phases in Group Decision-Making," *Speech Monographs* 37 (1970): 53–66.
4. Dennis S. Gouran, "Variables Related to Consensus in Group Discussions on Questions of Policy," *Speech Monographs* 36 (1969): 387–391.
5. Jay Hall and W. H. Watson, "The Effects of Normative Intervention on Group Decision-Making Performance," *Human Relations* 23 (1970): 299–317.

6. Jay Hall and Martha S. Williams, "Group Dynamics Training and Improved Decision-Making," *The Journal of Applied Behavioral Science* 6 (1970): 39–68.
7. C. K. Hawkins and John T. Lanzetta, "Uncertainty, Importance and Arousal as Determinants of Pre-Decisional Information Search," *Psychological Reports* 17 (1965): 791–800.
8. L. Richard Hoffman and Norman R. F. Maier, "Valence in the Adoption of Solutions by Problem-Solving Groups: Concept, Method and Results," *Journal of Abnormal and Social Psychology* 69 (1964): 264–271.
9. Irving L. Janis, *Victims of Groupthink: A Psychological Study of Foreign Policy Decisions and Fiascoes* (Boston: Houghton Mifflin, 1972).
10. Thomas Scheidel and Laura Crowell, "Idea Development in Small Discussion Groups," *Quarterly Journal of Speech* 50 (1964): 140–145.
11. Harold M. Schroder and Peter Suedfeld, *Personality Theory and Information Processing* (New York: Ronald Press, 1971).
12. Joan R. Sieber and John T. Lanzetta, "Conflict and Conceptual Structure as Determinants of Decision-Making Behavior," *Journal of Personality* 32 (1964): 622–639.

CHAPTER 12

Process Evaluation

INTRODUCTION

We have presented information in the previous chapters about group process and performance. We suggested that a group must provide essential informational needs, procedural needs, and interpersonal needs to develop an effective and acceptable decision proposal. We also commented on external constraints that affect a group's decision-making process. If a group uses its resources effectively and external constraints are not prohibitive, it should make satisfactory progress toward reaching its goals. Nonetheless, task-oriented groups do encounter difficulties. Interaction among members and progress toward goals are often not as satisfactory as we would like. We may become disenchanted, discouraged, and disappointed with our group's activity. Our group experiences process loss, that is, our group does not utilize the potential of its membership.

If you have read carefully so far, you will undoubtedly experience fewer problems in your small group discussions. You now have appropriate information to assist you as your group makes progress toward its goals. In this chapter we focus on common problems experienced by those involved in small group communication. We suggest possible solutions to those problems and refer you to sections in this book where information about these problems is presented in more detail. In other words, this chapter helps you to identify and correct problems of small group communication. You will find it useful as a practical guide to which you can refer in your future small group experiences.

DIAGNOSING PROBLEMS OF SMALL-GROUP COMMUNICATION

We have emphasized that small group processes can be broken down into three dimensions: informational, procedural, and interpersonal. We have organized the remainder of this chapter in terms of these dimensions to further assist you in your analysis of process-oriented problems. The major problems encountered by task-oriented groups include poor information, attempting solutions before defining problems, inadequate progress toward achievement of goals, unsatisfactory coordination of member activity, and failure to maintain member interest. All of these problems may be the result of more specific problems. In the following sections we have presented specific problems and have tried to identify the general problem. In almost all instances, the general problem will be one of the five we mentioned above. Next, we examine the problem from different points of view.

Is it a problem associated with the informational dimension? Is it a problem associated with the procedural dimension? Is it a problem associated with the interpersonal dimension? Possibly, the problem reflects issues associated with more than one dimension. Try to be as specific as you can in describing your group's difficulty. Once the problem has been identified, apply the recommendations we give below that seem most appropriate.

DIAGNOSING PROBLEMS RELATED TO THE INFORMATIONAL DIMENSION

Remember that the informational dimension pertains to the content of the task itself. Issues related to this dimension include task analysis, selection and presentation of information, and constraints.

Problem 1: Is the task suitable for group effort? Some common symptoms of this problem include one member doing most of the work, all members performing essentially the same subtasks, and very little discussion of issues.

Recommendation: Examine whether the task is open-ended, permits division of labor, or requires diversity of member backgrounds (see Chapter 8, pp. 130–133. If your present task does not entail these critical task demands, you should consider choosing a different topic. If this task was assigned to your group (e.g., your department head asked your group to solve a departmental problem), you should discuss with the person who made the assignment the possibility that the task might not be suitable for group effort. Finally, if your group decides to keep the topic, you should expand the scope of the task so that issues open to discussion are included.

Problem 2: Has your group correctly identified the primary requirements of its task? We discussed the primary requirements of descriptive, discussion, and problem-solving tasks (see Chapter 8, pp. 133–140). Often problem-solving groups discuss the merits of solutions before they have carefully described the problem. This behavior reflects a basic misunderstanding of primary requirements for problem-solving tasks.

Recommendation: Identify the type of task your group is working on (descriptive, discussion, or problem solving). Then list the primary requirements associated with your type of task. Focus on the group's problem before discussing actual solutions. Without a clearly understood problem, group efforts at solution result in little more than wasted time.

Problem 3: Is the task easy or too difficult for group assignment?

The elements related to difficulty include range of required information, number of issues, and number of alternatives (see Chapter 8, pp. 140–144).

Recommendation: If your task entails discussion of too little information, too few issues, and too few alternatives, you should consider expanding the scope of the task, select a new task, or suggest that members can better complete the task by working independently. If your task entails discussion of too much information, too many issues, and too many alternatives, you should narrow the scope of your topic.

Problem 4: Are group members losing interest in the task because required informational and skill variety is too low or too high? Informational variety refers to diversity in methods of information search and diversity in sources of information. Skill variety includes such behaviors as organizing and coordinating group activity, resolving conflicts, and delegating and directing action (see Chapter 8, pp. 145–147).

Recommendation: If your task entails too little variety, you will want to expand the scope of your task to create a need for greater informational and skill variety. If you cannot expand the problem, you probably do not need a group to solve it. If your task requires too much variety, you will want to reduce the scope of your task in order to create an appropriate interest level. Groups cannot do everything; frustration and disinterest result from trying to do too much and, in the process, accomplish very little.

Problem 5: Is the group failing to make progress toward its goal because too little information is available? Successful completion of the group's task requires an adequate information base. If you find group members consistently report "I don't know" or "We ought to look into that," your group is not conducting sufficient informational research to complete its task.

Recommendations: Examine your group's strategy in terms of information search. List your information search objectives and determine which segments of your information needs are completed and which segments are incomplete. Once your informational needs are clear, make specific assignments to group members regarding information search (see Chapter 9, pp. 155–159).

Problem 6: Have your group members failed to agree on priorities and values regarding their task? The most common symptom of this problem is a sense of going in circles. Your group will meet, make superficial agreements, and then discuss the same issues again at the next meeting.

Recommendation: Have each member write a list of priorities and value statements. Members can then present their positions as lucidly and logically as possible. Treat differences of opinion as a sign of incomplete information sharing. Assign one member the task of writing the list of priorities as they are discussed and agreed upon (see Chapter 9, pp. 155–159).

Problem 7:   Is the range of alternatives considered by your group too conventional or ordinary? Is the group discussing worn-out options and solutions? Your cue to this problem is a sense that this option has been tried before or that the particular option is usually recommended for this task or problem.

Recommendation: Your group might profitably examine assumptions or constraints associated with your discussions. Have members list their personal, social, and organizational assumptions (constraints) regarding the task and alternatives associated with the task. Discuss these constraints and try to identify the constraints that are preventing your group from creatively analyzing your task (see Chapter 1, pp. 10–12 and Chapter 9, pp. 155–159).

Problem 8:   Has your group reached premature agreement on an alternative or solution? Often groups will agree on an alternative or solution very early in their discussion. You will notice that when the group has agreed on an alternative, that expression of differences of opinion will be discouraged, and that information search will be directed toward support of that alternative or solution.

Recommendation: At least two options are open to you and your fellow group members. One possibility is to obtain permission to play "devil's advocate." You might suggest to your group that a decision was reached very quickly and that it would be helpful to discuss the alternative or solution in more detail. When your group agrees to this action, you can begin to argue against the decision to test its strengths and weaknesses. A second option is to introduce other alternatives or solutions. If your group members are willing to listen to your suggestions, the introduction of new proposals will create uncertainty. This uncertainty will lead to a broader range of information search and a more comprehensive discussion of alternatives (see Chapter 11, pp. 198–199).

DIAGNOSING PROBLEMS RELATED TO THE PROCEDURAL DIMENSION

The procedural dimension of small group communication relates to the coordination of group member activities. The leader of a group typically engages in considerable behavior on the procedural dimension, but all members should have the capability of performing procedural behaviors. Remember the analogy between the procedural comments and the guidance system on a space capsule headed for the moon. Just as the guidance system makes adjustments in the capsule's course, each group member should be able to summarize group activity, delegate and direct action, introduce and formulate goals, assist with role and norm development, and, in general, keep the group moving toward its goal.

Problem 1:   Do members in your group express frustration by complaining, "We're not making progress," "We're just spinning our wheels," "We'll never finish this job"?

Recommendation: This problem frequently occurs in groups where the emphasis is placed on either the informational dimension or the interpersonal dimension. Attention to procedural details can manage this frustrating experience. If you are in a group in which members express this type of dissatisfaction, go to the procedural dimension in an effort to point out what the group has already accomplished. Summarize the group's progress and demonstrate the group's success in approaching its goal (see Chapter 4, pp. 60–62).

If the group in fact has not made sufficient headway, obviously a summary will not be very helpful. In this case, guide the discussion to deliberation over what needs to be done in order to complete the task. Many times group members have the necessary information but lack the ability to organize their information. In this case, provide the group with orientation statements that keep the group headed toward its goal (see Chapter 4, pp. 61–62).

Problem 2:   Do members in your group continually return to discuss the same issues over and over again?

Recommendation: We suggested earlier that a task-oriented group develop a concrete strategy for accomplishing its task. A group has agreed on an inappropriate strategy when it goes in circles by returning to discuss the same issues. Probably the most appropriate action to take is to stop and agree on your group's goals and how your group hopes to achieve these goals. We recommend that a member of your group write down the strategy so the group may refer to it from time to time while working on its task (see Chapter 9, pp. 155–159).

Problem 3:   Do members of your group express uncertainty regarding what information is relevant to your group's task? Sometimes a member will report the results of her or his information search only to find that other members think the information is irrelevant.

Recommendation: These symptoms suggest that your group has not sufficiently narrowed its task. Your group needs to discuss what issues are to be included in the task and what are to be excluded (see Chapter 9, pp. 155–159).

Problem 4:   Do group members talk too much and waste time accomplishing simple tasks?

Recommendation: This problem typically occurs as a function of leadership and problems low in solution multiplicity. Someone in the group should provide more directive leadership. Someone should take the initiative and guide the group in quickly solving its task or simply point out that the group has solved its problem and recommend adjournment (see Chapter 8, p. 145).

Problem 5:   Do group members seem reluctant to participate and, consequently, make little headway in solving complex problems?

Recommendation: This problem frequently is caused by inappropriate leadership. In a situation where a group's problem is high in solution multiplicity, the leader should avoid directive leadership. When a group faces a complex problem, members providing leadership functions should encourage toleration for a variety of points of view. The leader should operate on the procedural dimension to invite participation, which in turn allows the group to benefit from more information. The leader who facilitates this information distribution will find a greater willingness to participate as well as a higher quality decision. Chapter 8 describes this process in more detail (see also Chapters 3 and 4).

Problem 6:   Does the group spend considerable time joking around and engaging in social conversation when they should be processing information suitable for solving problems?

Recommendation: This problem could be caused by a failure to handle primary tension, a topic discussed in Chapter 5. This tension results from an inability to stabilize the roles performed by individual members. Members should be made to understand their respective responsibilities. Once the members understand what is expected of them, primary tension decreases and the group can make progress on the task. Follow the strategies described in Chapter 5 to assist your group in stabilizing roles.

Problem 7:   Does the group direct the majority of its remarks to one member or do some members fail to participate sufficiently?

Recommendation: The manner in which the group arranges itself can cause this problem. Chapter 3 provides information relating to the group's seating arrangement. Members should arrange themselves so that each participant has an equal opportunity to communicate with every other participant. When seating arrangement facilitates equal participation, but unequal communication still occurs, try to encourage others to talk and then reinforce them for doing so. Group size also has an effect on participation. Large groups inhibit participation. Following the guidelines in Chapter 3, you may wish to reduce the size of the group.

Problem 8:   Do members continually express dissatisfaction with the quality of the group's decision-making practices?

Recommendation: Many times the roots of this problem rest in the group's norms. Your group may wish to list and examine your group's work-oriented norms (see Chapter 6). Perhaps your group's information search and presentation are too restricted. Perhaps your group spends too much of its time socializing. Perhaps your decision-making practices are inappropriate. Two common decision-making rules that usually result in inferior decisions are permitting one group member to make the decision and the majority vote. In most instances, the best decision-making rule in consensus. Consensus is a decision rule whereby all members must agree to a decision before it is accepted by the group.

DIAGNOSING PROBLEMS RELATED TO THE INTERPERSONAL DIMENSION

The interpersonal dimension reflects the attitudes members hold toward one another and the perception of capabilities and personality traits of group members. A pleasant interpersonal atmosphere provides a base that facilitates member participation in the group's activities. Groups have considerable difficulty achieving their goals when experiencing an unpleasant interpersonal atmosphere. To complicate matters even further, interpersonal problems are usually the most difficult to solve.

Problem 1:   Do group members experience considerable interpersonal conflict that threatens the continuance of the discussion?

Recommendation: When groups experience severe "personality" conflict, the value of group membership decreases. Members become dissatisfied and cohesiveness suffers. Of course, no magic formula can be applied to solve personality conflicts. If they can be managed, however, your best strategy involves discussion on the procedural dimension. Some communication experts recommend "sticking to the facts" under conditions of interpersonal conflict. We have not found this to be a useful strategy. If you experience interpersonal conflict, presenting additional information has little effect. On the other hand, a sincere acknowledgement of the difficulty and subsequent discussion about how to handle the conflict allows the group to continue achieving its goal. If your group is unable to solve its interpersonal conflicts, you may find it useful to ask a knowledgeable person outside the group to mediate the conflict (see Chapter 10, pp. 176–179).

Problem 2: Do members express dissatisfaction about their participation in the group's activities?

Recommendation: Our society does encourage us to comment on positive aspects of one's performance. Usually we are quick to notice shortcomings and faults. Often our comments about the work of others reflect these negative features. Our behavior in task-oriented groups is often in keeping with this societal norm. Hence, we comment on the shortcomings of one's performance and fail to express our positive reactions to one's work for the group. We recommend that you make positive comments regarding the performance of your fellow group members. Obviously you must be discriminating regarding these comments. You do not want to commend someone for poor work. Nonetheless, when members adequately perform their responsibilities, you should feel free to commend them (see Chapter 4, pp. 62–70).

Problem 3: Do one or more of your group members express unwillingness to cooperate with the group?

Recommendation: The success of your group will depend on the willingness of its members to cooperate, accept responsibility, and freely participate. Of course, many other elements enter into the equation for success, but without member cooperation your group will not be able to begin work. We suggest that you confront this problem directly. Ask the uncooperative members why they are unwilling to engage in group activities. Perhaps you will find there are issues for uncooperativeness that can be addressed by the group. If you find that the member(s) are not willing to cooperate under any circumstances, we recommend that the member(s) withdraw from the group and that you seek new member(s) (see Chapter 4, pp. 62–70).

Problem 4: Do you find that the interpersonal atmosphere seems negative and unpleasant?

Recommendation: An unpleasant group atmosphere usually results from a sequence of negative comments. These comments may reflect the nature of the task, progress toward goals, or the performance of group members. Sometimes individual members are blamed for group failures. Sometimes derogatory comments are made about the motives or personality of group members. We suggest that your group list the negative comments that are creating the unpleasant atmosphere. Then examine the basis for these statements. Finally look for ways to express positive comments about the task and member performance. If the situation has deteriorated too far, you may wish to disband the group and recommend that a new group be formed for the task (see Chapter 4, pp. 176–179).

Problem 5: Do you find that one member dominates the group and intimidates other members?

Recommendation: This problem usually results when a person with high status is a member of the group. Some professionals such as medical doctors, supervisors, vice-presidents, or parents may dominate the group and inadvertently create an atmosphere in which other members do not feel at ease in voicing their ideas or opinions. This situation should be addressed by the group. Why do members feel reluctant to participate? The successful resolution of this problem depends on the attitude of the high-status member. This member must be willing to listen to the other members, must be willing to modify her or his behavior, and must be willing to accept recommendations made by the other members. If this participatory attitude is not forthcoming, there is little reason for continuance of the group (see Chapter 4, pp. 63–66).

FORMS FOR ASSESSING GROUP PROCESS

We have listed throughout the book essential informational, procedural, and interpersonal functions required for effective group performance. From time to time, you may wish to check the performance of your group against the recommendations in this book. To assist you, we have developed a Group Function Form. On a separate sheet of paper, have each group member respond to each item on the Group Function Form. Then, on another sheet, compile a tally for each of the sixteen items. For example, the results for item 1, Creative Analysis of Task, might turn out as follows for a group of seven members:

1. Creative Analysis of Task
   a = 3
   b = 3
   c = 1
   d = 0

If most of the tallys are in the adequate side, your group is likely to be performing that function satisfactorily. When the tallys fall on the inadequate side, your group should discuss the issue and plan how to correct the deficiency. To help you with your diagnosis and treatment, we have indicated the location in the book where you can find material on the respective group functions.

Form For Assessing Performance of Group Functions

	Very adequate	Fairly adequate	Fairly inadequate	Very inadequate
Informational Functions (Chapter 3)				
1. Creative Analysis of Task (Chapter 8)	a	b	c	d
2. Information Giving (Chapter 9, Chapter 3)	a	b	c	d
3. Opinion Giving (Chapter 3)	a	b	c	d
4. Evaluation and Criticism (Chapter 9)	a	b	c	d
5. Elaboration (Chapters 8 and 9)	a	b	c	d
6. Integration (Chapters 8 and 9)	a	b	c	d
Procedural Functions (Chapter 4)				
7. Eliciting Communication (Chapter 4)	a	b	c	d
8. Delegating and Directing Action (Chapters 4 and 5)	a	b	c	d
9. Summarizing Group Activity (Chapter 4)	a	b	c	d
10. Conflict Management (Chapter 10)	a	b	c	d
11. Process Evaluation (Chapters 11 and 12)	a	b	c	d
12. Tension Release (Chapter 5)	a	b	c	d
Interpersonal Functions (Chapter 4)				
13. Positive Reinforcement (Chapter 7)	a	b	c	d
14. Solidarity (Chapter 7)	a	b	c	d
15. Cooperativeness (Chapter 4)	a	b	c	d
16. Respect toward Others (Chapter 4)	a	b	c	d

Task Orientation Checklist

The task orientation checklist is an inventory of how effectively your group analyzes and discusses your task. The first issue is whether the task is appropriate for group effort (see Chapter 8, pp. 130–133 for more detail). If your group can answer "yes" on task appropriateness, it is useful to proceed to step 2. If not, your group will find it useful to select a different task or redefine your present task. The second step pertains to the appropriateness of your group's strategy (see Chapter 9, pp. 155–159). When your group is satisfied with its strategy, you will be searching for information and presenting information to your group. At this point you will want to examine how effectively your group is processing information. Chapter 9, pp. 159–161, and Chapter 10 present material on this issue. Finally, you will want to examine the appropriateness of your decision proposal. Chapter 2, pp. 23–25, and Chapter 9, pp. 161–163, include material on this issue. Your group can use this checklist to evaluate the effectiveness of your group effort. It is set up in a sequential manner. Your group may wish to use the form at various times as you work toward completion of your task.

Task Orientation Checklist

1. Appropriateness of Task
   a. Open-ended   yes   no   undecided
   b. Permits division of labor   yes   no   undecided
   c. Calls for varied member backgrounds   yes   no   undecided
2. Appropriateness of Strategy
   a. Task properly limited   yes   no   undecided
   b. Goals are clear and concrete   yes   no   undecided
   c. Means for achieving goals are clear   yes   no   undecided
3. Appropriateness of Information Processing
   a. An adequate range of information is
      available to the group   yes   no   undecided
   b. Group members discuss issues from
      different points of view   yes   no   undecided
   c. Decisions are made by consensus   yes   no   undecided
4. Appropriateness of Decision Proposal
   a. Decision proposal is logically sound   yes   no   undecided
   b. Decision proposal is empirically sound   yes   no   undecided
   c. Means for implementing decision proposal
      is clear   yes   no   undecided

SUMMARY

We have tried to give you a systematic means for diagnosing group process problems and for finding solutions to these problems. We do, however, want to leave you with a disclaimer: do not feel that all of the problems associated with small group communication will be identified and cured based only on your reading and understanding of this book. Chapter 12 exists only to give you advice where we know it applies. The tremendous complexity of small group communication defies universal, simple answers to detailed problems. We are confident, however, that your future experiences in small group communication will be more effective and more exciting as you put your new ideas to the test. Even though we will probably never know as much as we should about small group communication, you now know more than most small group participants. Your job is to help them get the most out of every group to which you belong.

APPENDIX A

Library Research

A proper attitude toward libraries will help you in your research on any question. First, a library is there for your benefit. Sometimes people avoid library research because the library seems like an impossible maze to master. We suggest that you don't have to figure out the maze for yourself. Obviously, the more you know about its resources and how to obtain access to them, the more efficiently you can use your time there. Regardless of your ability to use the library, however, a sense that librarians are there to assist you will go a long way toward a successful information search. Librarians are members of the helping professions. Sometimes we as users forget that and sometimes librarians forget it. Nonetheless, we strongly urge you to ask librarians for assistance in order to make your library search more complete and efficient. You will be surprised to learn that many easy-to-use resources are available. Libraries consist of more than the card catalog and the *Reader's Guide to Periodical Literature*.

Librarians need some guidance from you, however, to meet your requests for information sources. Your requests for assistance can most effectively be answered if you have a clear idea of your information needs. If your group has carefully prepared its strategy, then you should be able to make specific requests of librarians. This advance preparation enables them to assist you more effectively. A general question on solar energy does not give a librarian enough information to help you. A more specific question on the methods of using solar energy to heat water gives a librarian more guidance in assisting you to find needed information.

Books, reference works, and periodicals are obvious sources of information. Most libraries have several indexes that help you locate information in such sources. Some of the major indexes are *Public Affairs Information Service*, *Reader's Guide to Periodical Literature*, the *Social Science Index*, the *Humanities Index*, and the *New York*

Times Index. Some of the more specialized indexes include *Statistical Abstract of the United States, Monthly Labor Review, Business Periodicals Index,* and *The Education Index.* Another source of information you may find useful includes encyclopedias such as *Britannica, World Book, Americana,* or *International Encyclopedia of the Social Sciences.*

There are numerous local, state, and federal government publications available at most libraries. These documents often contain pertinent information not found in other sources.

Suppose your group was investigating teaching writing skills in the primary school. If you went to *The Education Index,* you would find listed numerous articles providing information on this topic. The *Statistical Abstract of the United States* contains a variety of information on population, business, industry, and so on. The sources of information are almost endless. Just remember that efficient use of the library can make your life easier.

Once useful information has been located, you will probably want to write some notes based on the article or report. Such notes should also include a record of the source of information. If the notation is to a book, include author or editor, title, publisher, place and date of publication, and page numbers. If reference is to an article, include not only author and title, but the periodical title, issue date, volume, and page numbers. This information will be useful if you need to go back to the source for more information. It will also be useful when the time comes to justify your decision proposal. Think of an occasion where you were in an argument with someone. Remember how suspicious you were of comments such as: "I don't remember where I read it, but I know it's true." If you make a precise record of the location of your information, not only will you have a greater impact on your group's discussion, but you can also show other group members where to go to analyze your interpretation of the information. When other members are able to check the information and discuss its interpretation, you are likely to prepare a more useful decision proposal.

APPENDIX B

Informational Interviewing

Task-oriented groups frequently find it necessary to interview various individuals in order to obtain information regarding their task. If a group were working on a task related to public transportation in a urban area, it would be useful to interview various officials associated with public transportation. Often people assume that a group member can run downtown, conduct the interview, and return with the necessary information. Actually, interviews are complex endeavors and require careful preparation. Proper planning greatly increases the probability of obtaining relevant and complete information from an outside expert. We recommend that a group follow four basic steps in conducting these interviews.

Step 1: Determination of Specific Objectives

The specific objectives for any interview will likely emerge from the objectives the group has developed as a part of its strategy. However, any one interview usually does not relate to all of these objectives. Therefore the group members need to specify what information they hope to acquire from any single interview. For example, it is improbable that an effective interview would result if a group member just listened to a monologue on general transportation by our urban transit official. The group member ought to decide what he or she wants to know and then ask the appropriate questions. Such things as gas consumption, number of passengers, wages paid to employees, etc., will be more useful to the group's discussion than a general interview.

Step 2: Selection of the Target Person

There are a series of questions the group members should consider when selecting the person they want to interview. First, determine whether the person has access to the information required by the objectives. Second, find out if the person is readily available. If the target person does not reside nearby, for example, then the group will have to consider the costs of transportation. Also, some individuals have demanding schedules, and it may be difficult to obtain an appointment. Third, the group needs to consider whether the target person is willing to give them the information they want. Some issues are sensitive, and the target person may not be willing to openly discuss matters with the interviewers.

Step 3:   Preparation of an Interview Schedule

There are various types of questions the group can prepare to ask the target person. One distinction is between open-ended and closed-ended questions. Open-ended questions permit the target person considerable freedom in determining the amount of information to give. Frequently, information is volunteered for which the interviewers had not thought to ask. Open-ended questions are identified by the use of these words: *who, what, where, why, how,* and *when.* Questions using these words are difficult to answer with a simple yes or no response. They require information. Closed-ended questions include the possible answers in the questions themselves. Asking the target person to specify the number of persons that use public transportation in that city each week limits the response to that specific information. Asking the same person to describe the problems associated with public transportation in that city is open-ended and gives the person considerable latitude in answering. Closed-ended questions are useful in checking an interviewee's responses. For example, "Did you tell the mayor that gas to run the transit system costs 60 cents per gallon?" can allow you to determine whether or not the person being interviewed is consistent in her or his answers. Lawyers often use these questions in cross-examination to determine whether a witness has committed perjury. Closed-end questions also enable you to determine whether you have understood accurately. For example, "Let me see if I understand you. Did you say that unless more funds are forthcoming the transit system will be forced to cease operations?" For most interviews, therefore, your schedule should include a majority of open-ended questions interwoven with some closed-ended ones.

Another distinction is between neutral and directed questions. A neutral question allows the target person to respond without direction or pressure from the interviewer. A directed question suggests the answer the interviewer expects or wants from the target person. For example, "Do you oppose the purchase of more buses, like most officials we have talked with?" places some pressure on the respondent to agree with the comments of the other officials. A neutral phrasing of the question would be "What are your attitudes toward buying more buses?" Sometimes the pressure to respond in a certain way is very subtle. For example, "Don't you think tax increases are unfair for those who don't use the transit system?" pressures the target person to agree. On the other hand, "How do you feel about the argument that tax increases for those who don't use the transit system would be unfair?" is neutrally phrased. The group should avoid the use of directed questions in the development of its interview schedule.

Your group's interview schedule should include the major questions the group wants answered with a few follow-up questions for each of these. These questions are then placed in a sequence that seems to make logical sense to the group. There may be times, of course, when the schedule will include only a list of possible topics and other times when a tight sequence of specific questions are asked. The schedule should be sufficiently flexible so as to allow for examination of unexpected answers that may occur during the interview.

Step 4: Conducting the Interview

At the beginning of the interview, the interviewers will want to establish rapport with the target person and to make the person ready to communicate freely and to the point. There are several ways the interviewers can open the interview to accomplish these purposes. One pattern is to briefly state the problem the group is working on and then make reference to the target person's position. Demonstrate that you believe that the person is in a position to convey information that relates to the group's task. Another opening would be to make reference to a person that suggested you see the target expert, then briefly summarize the group's task. In all cases, the interviewers should clearly identify themselves, and the target person should know what is expected of her or him.

Interviewers may want to take notes during the interview with the target person. Always ask if the person being interviewed minds if you take notes. The interviewers should maintain eye contact with the person and take abbreviated notes. The interviewers should maintain a constant flow of note-taking. A sudden flurry of note-taking may influence the responses of the target person. The interviewers should review their notes as soon as possible after the interview and expand selected portions when necessary. In the case where note-taking is impossible, write down your recollections immediately following the interview.

Tape-recording the interview assures more accurate and complete reception of the target person's information. Of course the interviewers must obtain the permission of the target person. When an interview is recorded, the interviewers should be very familiar with the recorder before they conduct the interview. This familiarization will avoid wasting time and will also help to assure that the interview is actually being recorded. A blank tape is of no use to the group.

During the interview, the interviewers should be alert to unclear or incomplete information. They will want to ask additional questions to clarify the information or to fill in gaps. The interviewers will need to use considerable judgment in moving through their interview schedule to make sure they are getting the desired information. Considerable control should be exercised by the interviewers during the interview to use their time wisely and at the same time, care should be taken not to antagonize the target person.

At the completion of the interview, the interviewers will want to show their appreciation for the time and effort of the target person. They can close by telling the person when their task will be complete and asking if the person would be interested in obtaining the results of the group's investigation. The interviewers may also want to ask the target person about other persons who would be useful for them to interview.

When the interview is of critical importance to the group's deliberations, a transcript should be made of the target person's comments. This transcript can be mailed to the target person along with a cover letter asking if the transcript accurately describes what happened in the interview. Include a self-addressed, postage-paid envelope for the interviewee to return the transcript with any editing he or she cares to make. We don't recommend that you do this for every interview, but you can protect your group's information on important matters if the interviewee has indicated that you interpreted the remarks accurately.

We recommend that when possible two group members be present during an interview. One member should be in control of the interview, but both can ask questions. Two members will be able to present a more accurate and complete report to the group than a single member. If possible your group should interview more than one expert. Interviewing more than one person will help your group to obtain more accurate and useful information. For additional information on interviewing we suggest you study:

Charles J. Stewart and William B. Cash, *Interviewing Principles and Practices* (Dubuque, Iowa: William C. Brown, 1974).

Index